Teen T

# Teen TV

## Genre, Consumption, Identity

Edited by
Glyn Davis and Kay Dickinson

*bfi* Publishing

First published in 2004 by the
British Film Institute
21 Stephen Street, London W1T 1LN

The British Film Institute promotes greater understanding of,
and access to, film and moving image culture in the UK.

Copyright Introduction and editorial arrangement © Glyn Davis and Kay Dickinson, 2004
Copyright individual chapters © the authors

Cover design: Ketchup
Cover illustration: *Dawson's Creek* (Kevin Williamson, 1998–2003)

Set in the UK by Servis Filmsetting Ltd, Manchester
Printed by St Edmundsbury Press, Bury St Edmunds, UK

British Library Cataloguing-in-Publication Data

A catalogue record for this book is available from the British Library
ISBN 0-85170-998-2 (hbk)
ISBN 0-85170-999-0 (pbk)

# Contents

*Notes on Contributors* — vii

Introduction
*Glyn Davis and Kay Dickinson* — 1

## Part I: Genre

1. A Boy for All Planets: *Roswell*, *Smallville* and the Teen Male Melodrama
   *Miranda J. Banks* — 17

2. Teen Futures: Discourses of Alienation, the Social and Technology in Australian Science-Fiction Television Series
   *Leonie Rutherford* — 29

3. Chosen Ones: Reading the Contemporary Teen Heroine
   *Jenny Bavidge* — 41

4. *Dawson's Creek*: 'Quality Teen TV' and 'Mainstream Cult'?
   *Matt Hills* — 54

## Part II: Consumption

5. 'So Who's Got Time for Adults!': Femininity, Consumption and the Development of Teen TV – from *Gidget* to *Buffy*
   *Bill Osgerby* — 71

6. Selling Teen Culture: How American Multimedia Conglomeration Reshaped Teen Television in the 1990s
   *Valerie Wee* — 87

7. 'My Generation': Popular Music, Age and Influence in Teen Drama of the 1990s
   *Kay Dickinson* — 99

8. *Total Request Live* and the Creation of Virtual Community
   *Richard K. Olsen* — 112

## Part III: Identity

9. 'Saying It Out Loud': Revealing Television's Queer Teens
   *Glyn Davis* — 127

10. Dormant Dormitory Friendships: Race and Gender in *Felicity*
    *Sharon Ross* — 141

11. 'We Don't Need No Education': Adolescents and the School in Contemporary Australian Teen TV
    *Kate Douglas and Kelly McWilliam* — 151

12. *Roswell High*, Alien Chic and the In/Human
    *Neil Badmington* — 166

13. 'Feels Like Home': *Dawson's Creek*, Nostalgia and the Young Adult Viewer
    *Clare Birchall* — 176

*Index* — 191

# Notes on Contributors

**Neil Badmington** is Lecturer in Cultural Criticism and English Literature at the Centre for Critical and Cultural Theory, Cardiff University. He is the editor of *Posthumanism* (Palgrave, 2000), and his next book, a monograph entitled *Alien Chic: Posthumanism and the Other Within*, will be published by Routledge in 2004.

**Miranda J. Banks** is a doctoral candidate in the Department of Film, Television and Digital Media at the University of California, Los Angeles. Her dissertation explores the representation of female action heroes on television.

**Jenny Bavidge** lectures in the Department of English, University of Greenwich. Publications include articles in *London: From Punk to Blair*, eds. Andrew Gibson and Joe Kerr (Reaktion, 2003) and *The Swarming Streets: London in Twentieth Century Literature*, ed. Lawrence Phillips, forthcoming from Rodopi Press. She is also on the Editorial Board of the e-journal *Literary London*, homepages.goldsmiths.ac.uk/literarylondon

**Clare Birchall** is Lecturer in Media and Cultural Studies at Middlesex University. She has published on conspiracy theory and issues of interpretation in various journals including *New Formations* and *Continuum*.

**Glyn Davis** lectures on Screen History and Theory at Edinburgh College of Art. His recent publications include work on British cinema and homosexuality, and the films of Todd Haynes.

**Kay Dickinson** lectures in Film Studies at King's College, University of London. She is the editor of *Movie Music: The Film Reader* (Routledge, 2002) and has published on music in film and pop videos.

**Kate Douglas** researches and teaches in Literary and Cultural Studies at the University of Queensland, Australia. She is one of the editors of *M/C Reviews*.

**Matt Hills** lectures in Media and Cultural Studies at Cardiff University. He is the author of *Fan Cultures* (Routledge, 2002) and *The Pleasures of Horror* (Continuum, forthcoming).

**Kelly McWilliam** researches and teaches in Film and Media Studies at the University of Queensland, Australia. She is the General Editor of *M/C Reviews*.

**Richard K. Olsen** is an Associate Professor in Communication Studies at the University of North Carolina at Wilmington. His research uses traditional rhetorical concepts to critique aspects of contemporary popular culture such as the NBA Draft, sport utility vehicles (SUVs) and Martha Stewart.

**Bill Osgerby** is a Senior Lecturer in Cultural Studies at London Metropolitan University. His key publications include *Youth in Britain Since 1945* (Blackwell, 1998), *Playboys in Paradise: Masculinity, Youth and Leisure-Style in Modern America* (Berg/New York University Press, 2001), *Youth Media: Markets, Representations and Identities* (Routledge, forthcoming) and a co-edited anthology, *Action TV: Tough-Guys, Smooth-Operators and Foxy Chicks* (Routledge, 2001).

**Sharon Ross** recently received her PhD in Radio–TV–Film Studies from the University of Texas at Austin, where she is also currently teaching. Her dissertation examines the female friendships in *Buffy the Vampire Slayer* and *Xena: Warrior Princess*, focusing on audience responses to the shows.

**Leonie Rutherford** lectures in English and Communication Studies at the University of New England (New South Wales). She has published articles on various facets of children's cultural production.

**Valerie Wee** lectures on Film and Media Studies in the Department of English Language and Literature at the National University of Singapore. In addition to her research on teen culture and the American culture industries, she has published papers on American science-fiction films and on issues of gender and representation in the media.

# Introduction

## Glyn Davis and Kay Dickinson

In the penultimate scene of *Dawson's Creek* episode 323 ('True Love'), central protagonist Dawson Leery returns home, distraught at having just been abandoned by his girlfriend Joey for his best male friend, Pacey. To underscore the emotion of the scene, a soft country-rock track with a warbling female vocal[1] plays quietly in the background. Walking into his bedroom, Dawson discovers three of his closest friends – Andie, Jack and Jen – lounging on his furniture. They have invited themselves in, in order to console him.

> DAWSON: Thanks guys, I really appreciate you coming over, but I . . . I really think what I need right now is just –
> ANDIE : Sorry Dawson, no can do.
> JEN: Yeah, I think that the words 'I want to be alone right now' are used far too often around here.
> ANDIE : It kinda rates up there with, 'Er, can we talk?'
> JACK: Yeah. And there's those countless references towards all things Freud and Spielberg.
> JEN: Yeah, I'm pretty sure that we're not in Capeside any more, Toto. This is some alternate reality where our intellects are sharper, our quips are wittier and our hearts are repeatedly broken while faintly in the background some soon to be out-of-date contempo-pop music plays.
> DAWSON: So why does it hurt so much?
> ANDIE: Because our pain makes us real, Dawson. But we can't do it alone. None of us can.

For those readers with even a passing knowledge of this programme, or even merely others like it, this sequence could be seen to clearly encapsulate the workings of the contemporary teen drama series. Witty, knowing and slightly mawkish, such dialogue highlights key elements of the texture of *Dawson's Creek*: a use of language which is too sophisticated for the ages of the characters; frequent intertextual references; recourse to a sense of community based on generation; a blunt, somewhat melodramatic use of emotion and aphoristic psychological reasoning; and a prominent pop music soundtrack. Although this dialogue springs from *Dawson's Creek*, its source could just as easily have been any other recent teen series such as *My So-Called Life*, *Smallville*, *Buffy the Vampire Slayer* or *Roswell High*. It is the intention of this volume to unravel these recurrent characteristics of teen dramas from the last decade or so, to scrutinise them and to speculate upon their wider implications and inspirations.

## The Importance of Television in Teen Life

The 'teenager' is a relatively new phenomenon, coming to prominence in the Western world (mainly in affluent North America) in the 1950s.[2] It is a near-impossible task to fathom the extent to which what we now know as 'teenage' states of consciousness and behavioural trends have always existed, or whether the 'invention of the teenager' erupted at a specific historical moment, one where adulthood became increasingly deferred[3] and new youth consumer markets seemed eminently exploitable. One thing is certain, however: in this period of both economic and baby boom, 'the teenager' developed as a recognised cultural identity in close synchronisation with the rise of television as a widely consumed domestic medium. Whether or not this was a chance occurrence or part of a greater and inextricably linked socio-economic chain of circumstances, it is still vital that any history of culture aimed at, produced for and consumed by adolescents should pay particular critical attention to television. Alongside the production of other mass-cultural artefacts for teenagers to consume – from pop music to make-up – television has proffered, as Rachel Moseley points out, 'a significant history of programming featuring and addressing teenagers and teenageness in the anglophone television landscape, beginning with the introduction of television pop music coverage'[4] (a topic and a history which Bill Osgerby traces in Chapter 5 of this book).

Becoming a teen and acting out some or all of what is expected of that position in life often means assuming certain leisure-time practices, and television features centrally in these. As Karen Lury maintains in *British Youth Television: Cynicism and Enchantment* (which discusses a specific shift in 1980s' and 1990s' TV programming, but which continues to be relevant to contemporary viewing practices):

> the way that media images and sounds were [and, we would argue, still are] used by these young people was not as a substitute for their real surroundings but as a *part* of their actual surroundings. In other words, the relationship between mediated worlds and the self was no longer about an escape from the real world, but an integral part of how the world is made sense of, and how it was consumed.[5]

Significant amounts of teen time are spent in front of the TV. According to Gauntlett and Hill:

> In 1996, young adults (16–24 year olds) spent 14 hours per week watching television, but they also spent 16 hours per week talking, visiting and socialising with friends, and eating and drinking out (*Social Trends*, 1996). As this group of young adults have a total of 40 hours of free time per week, this would suggest that after socialising and watching TV, there is very little time left for other leisure activities.[6]

Their empirical research also suggests that teens often watch TV in order to socialise, to have common frames of reference through which to talk to others and that their desire to view is frequently motivated by peer pressure and a need to 'belong' through a discussion of the media, rather than more conscious personal impetus.[7]

These instances of anxiety about segregation, even otherness, reveal not only the importance of television as a means of sociability, but also just how conformist teenagers can be. Theirs is a life of distinct limitations (of having to go to school, having to be home at certain times) and yet, concurrently, it is a phase when autonomy and a certain (although extremely managed) notion of individuality is expected. In this, the struggle to choose and project a distinct taste is paramount, although there are very few deviations allowed in what this might be, and peer judgments of these tastes are often cruelly executed and potentially ostracising.

In her book, Karen Lury explores how these apprehensions about taste and engagement extend across teen television viewing. She argues that certain youth shows were successful because they elicited an ambivalent response in the teen viewer, one which allowed them to hedge their bets about their involvement with the material, rather than committing wholeheartedly to any particular programme's ethos. For her, British series like *Snub TV*, *The Word* and *Don't Forget Your Toothbrush* encouraged both cynicism and enchantment as plausible and simultaneous responses (or, at least, this is how their audiences often chose to read them). In turn, these responses afforded audiences the opportunity to vacillate while their tastes and identities were being stabilised, and opened up for them a means of interacting with an old/parent technology in a way that was both wary and joyful.

And yet we cannot deny that there is significant input from dominant adult society in these programmes at most points of planning, production, distribution and marketing. These may be 'our' shows to teenagers, but (beyond some of the actual cast and the characters they play) the programmes are created by adults, arguably with a particular adult agenda. In the broadest sense this might be: to educate and inform while entertaining (something central to many strands of television in the Western world); to set certain agendas at this delicate time just prior to the onset of a more prominent citizenship; and/or to raise crucial issues (of *adult* choosing) in a 'responsible manner' that is entirely hegemonically negotiated. Recurrent topics of discussion – even within the most fantastical of shows – are sex and sexuality, drug and alcohol use, family tensions and negotiating one's place among one's peers, all issues encountered by the average teenager. However, the difficulty for these programmes lies in presenting views on such themes without preaching to or alienating teens, without destroying the sense that these are 'their' shows. Certainly many of these programmes are earnest enough (or cynical enough in the face of parental group pressure) in their commitment to building a certain recognised type of future citizen (namely a politically liberal one). Additionally, these series have to deal with the fact that they are mainly commercial ventures, struggling to make money out of the teen market and, in this sense, they have to consider how to pander to the customer. On the one hand many programmes have – and are definitely expected by worried parents and adults at large to follow – an ethical agenda geared towards creating a certain notion of political subjecthood before the freedoms of adulthood are attained. On the other, they are also required to negotiate a further freedom that many a teen in Western society possesses in abundance: the power to buy, the power to choose some consumer items and reject others.

All this has to maintain its composure while situated upon the shaky equilibrium between teenagers' exploratory curiosity and their defensive small-mindedness. These shows' problematic negotiation of how to maintain this aesthetic and political balance, alongside a reliance for survival on teenagers *as consumers* with the capacity to switch channels, is a fascinating topic and, surprisingly, one that has attracted very little academic attention.

## The Academic Treatment of Teen Television

By and large, scholarly consideration of teen culture has circled around topics which have little to do with television. Certainly, there have been publications about single shows like E. Graham McKinley's *Beverly Hills 90210: Television, Gender and Identity*,[8] Roz Kaveney's *Reading the Vampire Slayer: The Unofficial Critical Companion to Buffy and Angel*[9] and Rhonda Wilcox and David Lavery's *Fighting the Forces: What's at Stake in Buffy the Vampire Slayer?*[10] (the latter two being edited collections). However, these have all been fairly tightly focused, examining, mainly, either televisual texts themselves or their audiences without wishing to concentrate on teen TV as a genre or on the place of youth programming in the commodity culture of adolescents. At the other end of the spectrum, there are a multitude of more sociological or cultural studies-style texts on youth subcultures,[11] most of which seek out pleasingly subversive aspects of adolescent behaviour. For a variety of reasons, television viewing has rarely been considered by intellectuals to be counter-cultural[12] and, as such, it seems that many a leftist scholar has found it a more difficult topic to research in a politically rewarding manner.

It is perhaps an endemic trait of scholarly writing that we feel we have to *either* eulogise and champion to the end our objects of study (as some of the essays in Roz Kaveney's collection on *Buffy* do) *or* condemn their ideological dangers (as Marsha Kinder does in *Playing with Power in Movies, Television and Video Games: From Muppet Babies to Teenage Mutant Ninja Turtles*[13]). Perhaps this kind of rhetorical solidity is not particularly appropriate to inquiries into both a set of TV programmes and a viewing demographic which are unpredictable, whose agendas are subject to change and which are, by turns, both infuriatingly disappointing and surprisingly clever and engrossing. Teen TV is precarious: precarious in its appeal (its audience may 'grow out of it' and another one may not assume its place) and in its conviction about its themes (about-turns on major narrative issues in the name of market forces are commonplace). In this, these sets of programmes mirror the unsettled nature of the adolescent state itself. Yet the rapid sell-by date of certain shows – like the quickfire turnover in teen clothing fashions – does not invalidate them as subjects to study; their impermanence and their particular historical emergence and disappearance are enormously telling. Indeed, the very fact of transience is itself as pertinent and complex as the fluctuating knowledges, tastes (and even physical appearances) of the particular demographic to, for and about which these shows purport to speak.

In contradiction to this image of teen TV, however, the delicate foundations upon which such programmes rest are, arguably, being more and more fortified as time goes on. For every show that reaches its final season all too soon or is prematurely axed by the network (such as *My So-Called Life*), there are both long-running series like *Saved by the Bell*,

*Hollyoaks* or *Grange Hill* (whose characters may change as the show's life cycle continues) and programmes which move out of the schoolyard and on to university (like *Buffy the Vampire Slayer* and *Dawson's Creek*). This latter development is discussed by Kate Douglas and Kelly McWilliam in Chapter 11. Episodes of teen shows are also becoming increasingly available on durable formats like DVD and video. This asks all manner of interesting questions about, firstly, the commodification and fetishisation of youth culture, and, secondly, about how a sense of 'worth' is created for such programmes and how this might filter them at a greater speed into the academic canon. Related to this movement is an increasing sense that adults can and do watch these shows (*Buffy* in particular, and it is no surprise that this is where the lion's share of academic attention has been trained). Teen shows are not just for teenagers in contemporary society, and this is something that we intend to discuss later on in this introduction. Often shows like *Buffy the Vampire Slayer* are valorised precisely for their nourishment of our particular adult needs, like the desire for mainstream feminist discourse – and this is no bad thing. However, beyond this, there is still a reluctance amongst academics to entrench themselves in certain aspects of teen TV which lie outside our direct political and aesthetic priorities.[14]

Another reason we might feel insecure about writing about teens is because, not only are we no longer adolescents ourselves, but we would also hate to fall into that 'square' category of trying to 'understand' teens, and getting it hopelessly wrong. Although there have been a whole series of manoeuvres to reclaim similar denigrated popular cultures and their audiences (the feminist writing on the woman's film, for example), these moves have usually been made by members of the 'minority' group in question. What, then, does it mean for a group of academics over the age of nineteen to begin to rummage around in teen culture? What would enable us to do so and what would the barriers be? To what extent are any of us 'inside' or 'outside' the culture we are analysing? Why and *how* would such debates matter in relation to this specific type of television programming and viewing? Here the limits to what we might know, might not know and might seek to know are, *as they are in any academic inquiry*, extremely ideologically opaque and it is vital that we ask ourselves what it is about this particular form of culture which might bring such issues to the fore even more prominently. With these concerns in mind, it now falls upon us to define what is in this book and to ask the reader to think critically about why it is structured in the way it is, and why it deals with its chosen range of topics. First, we have to point out that – in the name of defining a coherent and manageable field of study – we have chosen to concentrate predominantly upon fiction-based, English-language programming (largely from the USA) which has mainly been aired during the last decade.[15]

One blatant dilemma of any such anthology is how to identify teen TV in the first place. Should one think about it primarily in relation to a target audience (and, indeed, one wonders if this viewer group is strictly teenaged anyway), or is it more of a genre with an intricate interrelationship between recurrent thematic concerns, certain types of audience and their modes of engagement with these defined texts? If so, is teen-TV-the-genre dependent upon or related to other, more discussed, stratified or established genres (perhaps ones with fewer semantic tensions in their very titles)? Which ones would these be and why? These are the kinds of questions that the first part of this book seeks to explore.

## The Question of Genre

In his article 'Rethinking the Intersection of Cinema, Genre and Youth: The "Teen Film"', James Hay opens up the concept of the teen genre within cinema. He makes a case for a study of genre which would incorporate an understanding of social practices, *as well as* messages embedded within the text in its narrowest sense, in order to comprehend how these groups of objects matter to people. Hay argues that

> understanding genres in relation to 'overall structures' and socio-historical 'contexts' is not just a matter of extending the nexus of cultural forms (e.g. to include 'non-entertainment' forms), but of focusing more squarely on cinema's mattering and assemblage/articulation to and through historical and spatial mediations and on genres as one of many technical mechanisms of agency, mobility and conduct within/across regions of sociability.[16]

Following this line of thought, genre should be dealt with in terms not only of how it is configured by society, but also how genres themselves shape society, or are, in fact, an inseparable feature of it. With this kind of scope in mind, the essays in *Teen TV* amalgamate analyses of the textual conventions of teen television with an attention to much more wide-ranging practices of consumption and regulation (a tension which such programmes themselves both embody and generate).

One of the most striking and media-incestuous ways in which these connections are made in the earlier stages of production is through these programmes' borrowings from other genres. This provides them with a semantic and meta-textual vitality, which will be anatomised in the first section of this book. The generic hybridity of these programmes, in turn, asks the question: is there a teen genre *per se*, or is what we call teen TV simply a collection of different, previously existing genres, mutated in order to take adolescent sensibilities into account?

Certainly soaps and comedy shows are adolescent favourites – whether or not they are specifically made for or marketed to teens. In relation to soap operas, what does it mean to incorporate adolescents into this kind of ongoing and largely community-based narrative? What implications might this have for the genre at large and its regular audience? Some of these concerns are confronted by Kate Douglas and Kelly McWilliam in Chapter 11. Less overtly, many of the essays in this book (particularly Chapter 10 by Sharon Ross) touch upon the politics of comedy and how it functions in relation to teen tastes.

Miranda J. Banks' essay, the first in the anthology, delves into another well-established genre which teen TV draws upon: melodrama. As she notes, the adoption of the (male) melodramatic mode in shows like *Smallville* and *Roswell High* sustains and also updates a long theatrical and filmic lineage. Despite proffering new models of heroism, such shows also maintain the genre's propensity for tackling greater social problems through individualised struggle (a trend which Clare Birchall also questions in Chapter 13). Although Miranda J. Banks' essay is the only one to explicitly talk about teen series as melodramas, it is apt to consider the extent to which these programmes as a whole express key cultural concerns through this model of personal, psychological plight, rather than proposing the possibility for larger macro-political or societal change. To what extent might the turmoil of teen existence provoke an inclination towards these often myopic responses to problems? What philosophies might these particular encapsulations of selfhood spark, both in teen shows and in their viewers? Such issues are considered and complicated within the last section of this volume, demonstrating the impossibility of untangling genre from social subjecthood – a tension which also informs Chapter 3.

In this essay, Jenny Bavidge examines how *Buffy the Vampire Slayer* draws upon the recurrent trope (and frequent role model) of the 'American Girl' in at least a century's worth of youth literature, comic books and cinema. In dealing with a tradition of adolescent popular culture which revolves around the girl protagonist, Bavidge's chapter, unlike so much writing on *Buffy the Vampire Slayer*, sees its feminist tendencies as a continuity rather than a break from texts which have consciously aimed to delineate and debate appropriate models of girlhood. She examines the extent to which *Buffy*, like its predecessors, strives to create, reinforce and inspire a particular brand of youthful femininity.

Just as influential as a generic reference point is the impact of science fiction upon teen drama. Rachel Moseley, in a discussion of teen sci-fi/fantasy shows, links these popular genres with commonly experienced aspects of the adolescent condition:

> Many of these shows deal with questions of difference, otherness, increased power and the impact of these on personal and community relationships: a significant number of them draw on other cult television forms, using supernatural power as a motif through which to explore these concerns. Many shows give the sense that to be a teenager is to be not quite human.[17]

In other words, the alienation teenagers may experience in their lives becomes metaphorically mapped onto the representation of extraterrestrials and monsters in these series, something which Leonie Rutherford's essay on Australian (teen) sci-fi narratives (Chapter 2) and, later on, Neil Badmington's on alienation (Chapter 12) pore over in greater detail. Indeed, as both essays point out, a lot of teen shows – and especially those of a science-fiction/fantasy format – root for the outsider, celebrating otherness and rarely sympathising with 'the jock' or 'the cheerleader' unless these characters are themselves insecure in these highly fabricated and difficult to maintain social roles.

Such thoughtful and almost counter-cultural perspectives, as well as the string of strategic alliances with certain pre-established genres we have already identified, also allow teen TV, as Rachel Moseley further argues, to assert a strangely paradoxical claim to being a 'quality' product – paradoxical in so far as both television and adolescent culture have not had the greatest of access to critical approval and prestige in the past. This 'quality' could be seen to derive from all sorts of different aspects of the texts and their audiences, including the academic championing of certain teen series. Some shows, after all, have bigger budgets and more exacting production standards (for example, those which have a longer running time, employ star actors or utilise more expensive special effects, as opposed to studio-bound sitcoms like *Malibu* and *Hang Time*). These higher-profile programmes look like the more lauded format of film, and their stars and directors – as both Matt Hills and Valerie Wee explicate in Chapters 4 and 6 – cross between cinema and television with an ease that puts both products on a more equal level. The 'quality' shows also, as Matt Hills asserts, present what is generally held to be a more sophisticated set of references and ideas, an aspiration towards auteurism (albeit a specially modelled and particularly potent strain of genre auteurism), and a preconceived knowingness and questioning of the teen genre itself, all of which, amidst our specific current social priorities, deem texts like *Dawson's Creek* to be of 'quality'.

Further, there are some programmes which seem to have accrued the status of 'quality' due to having been cancelled (a sign to their fans that, perhaps, television executives wouldn't know quality if it stared them in the face). *My So-Called Life*, for instance, is often named by critics as the high point of teen television of the 1990s,[18] and such a sense of value is imbued, in part – as it is in many cult objects – precisely through the assumed discernment of devotees in the face of the undiscriminating corporation that unthinkingly churned out such products. Even beyond such prematurely lost texts (and certainly at the level of fandom at the very least) supporters of these programmes wilfully disregard the fact that television marketed at a youth demographic has usually been seen as 'disposable', ephemeral and, often by implication, as 'low culture'. This is something which the makers of such series – acting regardless of more distanced critical opinion anyway – have consistently financially exploited through extra-textual manifestations such as novelisations, soundtrack CDs, VHS and DVD box sets, to name but a few spin-off items. While these consumer durables allow both cult collection practices and the prolonged intellectual engagement necessary for their elevation to the status of 'quality' TV, they also open up yet more questions about how teen television functions within the larger world of objects, exchanges and buyers. Which TV-related products become available and why? How do teenagers structure their identities around buying and what part do teen shows and their merchandise play in all this? These are the kinds of questions asked in the second part of the book.

## Teen Buying Power, Television and the Marketplace

Any exploration of how the adolescent self and its modes of individualism shape and are shaped by teen TV must take into account an array of economic factors. The teen condition (as a way of life rather than an age) arises out of a specific historical and, in particular, financial state, that owes its existence to relatively recent developments within capitalism. These economic circumstances – alongside other social factors – have encouraged the increased spending power and belated entry into full-time, adult wage-earning and responsibility (often including a prolonged sojourn in education) which mark out the archetypal teenager. Although many adolescents (even many countries) do not have access to all these privileges, this does not mean they can escape the often idealised portrayal of the commodity-hungry and commodified teenager on their TV screens – an influence which should not be taken lightly and which Valerie Wee notes in Chapter 6. Teenage financial clout should not be underestimated; as Henry A. Giroux states with reference to a 1992 Roper Organization, Inc. study, 'the current generation of 18–29-year-olds have an annual buying power of 125 billion'[19] (although he does not specify a currency, or whether this is a global or national – presumably US – statistic). In Chapter 5 of this book, Bill Osgerby fleshes out a forty- or so year history of this teen market with regard to its interaction with television production, and the sorts of teen identities these alliances have encouraged. Later, Valerie Wee analyses the collusion between various segments of the youth market in the creation of intertextual references on teen TV. These instances often facilitate a linkage between different products manufactured by the same large multinational corporations and thus establish and strengthen the predominance of certain horizontally integrated media conglomerates.

In a sense, then, the teen sensibility arises from, and is moulded by, the motivations of consumer capitalist invention and self-preservation. As with so many other social identities, being a successful, popular teen often means engaging in the 'right' types of consumer culture. Adolescent self-construction puts to use a large number of building blocks from the world of commodities, particularly those specifically targeted at a strategic preconception of 'youth'. Whilst a teenage sense of individuality is vehemently striven for (at the very least, as an opposition to parents or parent culture), this sense of autonomy is gained, paradoxically, through a group-mediated sense of belonging that is far from unique (be it peer, corporate or ideologically driven). In many instances, these performances of singularity, being 'cool' and so on are already in circulation and, because of this, can easily be understood by other teens. Moreover, this prior presence is established by the promotional industries and is infused into television through such things as advert breaks, product placements, the uses of certain commodities on drama series and guest appearances of bands promoting their songs on music shows. For critics like Marsha Kinder, the very centrality and familiarity of television inculcates a worrying identification with commodities in younger viewers. Talking about pre-teens, she contends that 'the newly emerging subject comes to perceive himself or herself as a gendered commodity around which a whole commercial nexus is organized . . . the child comes to believe that this nexus is activated and extended whenever he or she consumes a product'.[20] Coming from a similar yet more ambivalent perspective, in Chapter 8 Richard K. Olsen argues that the sense of interactivity so eagerly cultivated in the current climate is clearly channelled towards limited options and specific, commercially motivated outcomes in certain popular teen shows.

Here, Richard K. Olsen is not just pointing out the means by which capitalism embeds itself within the teen lifestyle (an action which was always already taking place and thus comes as no great surprise), but also asks questions about the moral and ethical ramifications of such an allegiance. Scrutinising the clustering together of certain teen commodities, the ways in which they are sold, and the aesthetic and political motivations behind such acts, Kay Dickinson investigates (in Chapter 7) the relationship between several teen drama series and the popular music implanted within them. Just as importantly, she asks what sorts of people we are encouraged to be by these unions and, in this aspect, she and the other contributors to this section edge towards something which is more centrally tackled in the last part of the book: how do teen shows shape subjectivity? What kinds of ideals or normalities do they present? This tension between the unique buying subject and the goods on offer to him or her (including, and especially, television shows), and how they mold each other, is what this book goes on to consider.

## How to Be a Teenager: Identity, Stricture, Licence and Age

For many people in the 'developed' world, then, adolescence is a protracted term of adjustment and self-construction through culture with conditions all its own, rather than a momentary rite of passage which initiates the child into instant adulthood. This often lengthy period of transition between perhaps more controllable, socially comprehended life stages is heavily monitored. There is a great deal at stake in the movement over the chasm between childhood and adulthood and a heavy investment in making sure the journey into responsible maturity is successfully completed. Any traumas that are suffered throughout this period reflect significantly on the wider parameters of the family, particularly the parents who, in turn, invest much time in encouraging certain hegemonically inflected forms of nascent adulthood.

Television plays a pivotal role in the way teenagers are managed: what they are allowed to do, what is forbidden and what they are encouraged to become. Unlike many other youth leisure activities (like cinemagoing, eating out or clubbing), teenage TV viewing mostly takes place in the/a *family home* with all the rules, prohibitions, habits and prejudices that such a space embodies. Viewing might have to take place in a more surveyed communal room, or it may be condoned in the semi-private space of a bedroom – a privilege which, in turn, could raise issues of trust for the parent/child relationship, depending entirely on what is considered 'suitable' programming or scheduling. Moreover, the television hardware itself becomes part of the web of capitalism and family ideology. If part of a parent's role is to provide for the family, then this might easily be played out through (and commercially exploited by) the pressure to buy televisions (and video or DVD players) for teenagers to own exclusively and to position in a space which is more solidly 'their own'. If there is maybe an adult peer pressure all its own on parents to make such provisions, then there is an equally strong emphasis upon making sure offspring aren't 'harmed' or 'misguided' (however these concepts may be socially constituted) by what they are viewing – a responsibility which programme makers are also requested to share.

Consequently, teen TV is obliged to be liable for the shaping of both young adults' burgeoning senses of freedom and the prescribed limitations which are still (and perhaps always will be) thrust upon them within their social positions, both present and future. Within many of our societies, the role of the media is considered vital – if not somewhat accountable – for the handling of teenagers' greater entry into citizenship, responsibility, and wider and more multifaceted forms of social interaction. The subsequent shaping of teen TV in line with this role must necessarily take into consideration what is generally accepted to be 'appropriate' to the exploration and cementing of teenagers' new-found positions within the world. This might also include the treatment of certain so-called minority groups (to which any given teen viewer may not even belong) in order to not only raise debates about the social treatment of others, but also to cater for those who *would* affiliate themselves with these groups and who might have, until that point, felt alienated by popular culture's schemes of representation. Both Glyn Davis and Sharon Ross (Chapters 9 and 10) confront the issue of depiction, tackling, respectively, how images of homosexuals and African-diaspora peoples are framed within teen TV. The reader is also entreated to think through the broader social reasons and ramifications which uphold and spring out of such portrayals.

The more general feelings of otherness and disenfranchisement faced by many adolescents are interrogated in Chapters 11 and 12. These present such emotions as something common to the teen condition itself and argue that they are by-products of various social practices which designate 'the teen' as a marginalised group in its own right. An adolescent life straddles a huge and often incommensurate set of situations – the inability to vote, to access the welfare state independently, to earn little more than the minimum wage (if such things are available) – at the same time as offering increased rights, mobility and, of course, consumerism. Kate Douglas and Kelly McWilliam explore how such often contradictory forces are negotiated through the school and its televisual representations, while Neil Badmington ponders the common media metaphors which describe teenagers as not only aliens, but also extraterrestrials. However, Badmington sees many benefits to these analogies, ones which might have a certain potency for all kinds of audiences of differing ages. This sense of the broader appeal of teen television is a major concern for Clare Birchall in Chapter 13 and also a fitting end to a collection such as this.

While any strict definition of 'the teenager' in terms of age would cover less than a decade, our current cultural understanding of 'youth' (or at least the youth market) could be seen to welcome anyone from pre-teens to people in their forties. As Karen Lury points out, youth programming encourages

> a viewing sensibility which is not necessarily only adopted or understood by this specific generation of young people. It is better understood as a sensibility that is primarily informed by an experience of television, or an accumulation of knowledge about television, which cannot be confined solely to this particular generation of television viewers.[21]

Factors accounting for the broad appeal of youth TV could include: a complicated but generally increased accessibility to higher or further education; the social pressure to grow up quickly[22] and then to stay young for longer (all of which are encircled by enticing and helpful consumer goods); and the current decay of the notion of the 'job-for-life' whose acquisition was so often a marker of adult maturity in the past. As we have already seen, there is money to be made in selling youth, and the reasons why a distinctly 'teen' set of commodities might attract so many different types of consumer are compelling.

Clare Birchall wonders whether teen series manufacture a kind of nostalgia in their older viewers: a desire to revisit, to envisage a more articulate, more successful adolescence. In this, she identifies not only a certain widespread viewer fantasy, but also the very knowing make-up of shows like *Dawson's Creek* which deliberately court such audiences with their intelligence and intertextuality. Through such considerations, her chapter raises our awareness of a characteristic which Matt Hills also describes: a televisual style which openly solicits adult viewers through certain trademarks of 'quality' and 'sophistication', one which significantly diminishes any of the 'guilty pleasures' non-teen fans might have previously experienced when watching these programmes. Thus, not only does another lucrative market open up, but non-teens are allowed an even greater opportunity to revel in a certain performance of adolescence, be it an active denial of ageing, a bitter-sweet nostalgia for things past, or a more complicated aggregation of emotions.

What goes almost without saying is that those with a scholarly interest in teen TV (who are mostly over nineteen, we would imagine) will have an awkward relationship with their object of study. These programmes are both for us, and not for us. Why might we want to consume them? How might we be perceived by any 'real' adolescent audiences for doing so? Although often morally self-righteous, teen shows also define themselves in the crassest of commercial terms, refusing to acknowledge or account for the possible contradictions in such a composition. These shows scream for our attention, then completely alienate us; they are banal, yet profound. And, in all these paradoxes to adult rationality, they reflect aspects which we ubiquitously attribute to the 'teen'.

## Notes

1. 'I Will Be There for You' by Jessica Andrews.
2. Unfortunately, it is beyond the scope of this volume to chart this historical development in any real detail. We recommend that interested readers search out this information in books such as G. Palladino, *Teenagers: An American History* (New York: Basic Books, 1996), B. Osgerby, *Youth in Britain Since 1945* (Oxford: Blackwell, 1998) and J. Austin and M. Willard (eds), *Generations of Youth: Youth Cultures and History in Twentieth-Century America* (New York: New York University Press, 1998).
3. During this period, thanks to a complicated reconfiguration of certain national economies, educational systems, patterns of labour, family ideology, urban and suburban geography and a post-war reshaping of values, this drawing out of the movement from childhood to adulthood became more widespread.
4. R. Moseley, 'The Teen Series' in G. Creeber (ed.), *The Television Genre Book* (London: BFI, 2001), p. 41.
5. K. Lury, *British Youth Television: Cynicism and Enchantment* (Oxford: Oxford University Press, 2001), p. 40.
6. D. Gauntlett and A. Hill, *TV Living: Television, Culture and Everyday Life* (London: BFI, 1999), p. 82.
7. Ibid., pp. 84–6.
8. E. McKinley, *Beverly Hills 90210: Television, Gender and Identity* (Philadelphia: Philadelphia University Press, 1997).
9. R. Kaveney (ed.), *Reading the Vampire Slayer: The Unofficial Critical Companion to Buffy and Angel* (London: I.B. Tauris, 2001).
10. R. Wilcox and D. Lavery (eds), *Fighting the Forces: What's at Stake in Buffy the Vampire Slayer?* (Lanham, MD: Rowman & Littlefield, 2002).
11. Such as S. Cohen, *Folk Devils and Moral Panics: The Creation of the Mods and Rockers* (London: MacGibbon and Kee, 1972), S. Hall and T. Jefferson (eds), *Resistance through Rituals* (London: Hutchison, 1976), D. Hebdige, *Subculture: The Meaning of Style* (London: Methuen, 1979), S. Thornton, *Club Cultures: Music, Media and Subcultural Capital* (London: Routledge, 1996), K. Gelder and S. Thornton (eds), *The Subcultures Reader* (London: Routledge, 1997) and A. McRobbie, *Feminism and Youth Culture*, 2nd edn (Basingstoke: Macmillan, 2000).

12. This may be, for instance, because television is a domestic technology and very few subcultures have sprung up in spaces which are so heavily coded as familial.
13. M. Kinder, *Playing with Power in Movies, Television and Video Games: From Muppet Babies to Teenage Mutant Ninja Turtles* (Berkeley: University of California Press, 1991).
14. A similar criticism could be levelled at this collection where a very specific notion of 'quality' is perhaps guiding our interests in and selection of certain shows. We would openly encourage the reader to question the motives of our contributors for concentrating with greater enthusiasm on such texts as *Dawson's Creek* rather than less critically lauded programmes like *Sabrina the Teenage Witch*. Matt Hills' chapter may provide useful ammunition for any such critique.
15. However, the essays in this anthology by Bill Osgerby and Richard K. Olsen work outside these parameters. Anyone wishing to pursue an interest in more music- and quiz-based shows should read Lury's *British Youth Television*.
16. J. Hay, 'Rethinking the Intersection of Cinema, Genre and Youth: The "Teen Film", Genre Theory and the Moral Universe of Planetariums' *Scope*, June 2002: www.nottingham.ac.uk/film/journal/articles/cinema-genre-youth.htm, pp. 2–3.
17. Moseley, 'The Teen Series', p. 43.
18. As Steven Capsuto notes '*My So-Called Life* won rave reviews, support from such organizations as Viewers for Quality Television, and ratings of eleven million viewers per week' in *Alternate Channels: The Uncensored Story of Gay and Lesbian Images on Radio and Television, 1930s to the Present* (New York: Ballantine Books, 2000), p. 300. The show also won a GLAAD award and four Emmy nominations.
19. H. Giroux, *Breaking in to the Movies* (London: Blackwell, 2001), p. 65.
20. M. Kinder, *Playing with Power in Movies, Television and Video Games*, p. 38.
21. Lury, *British Youth Television*, p. 24.
22. One could easily argue that many of the social and commercial pressures that this Introduction has highlighted are equally borne by younger, pre-teen children who similarly integrate a consumption of teen TV and its related products into all manner of cultural situations.

# Part I

## Genre

# 1

## A Boy for All Planets: *Roswell, Smallville* and the Teen Male Melodrama

Miranda J. Banks

Two recent television series have crash-landed alien boys into the heartland of America. Both Max Evans and Clark Kent are handsome, intelligent young men who purposefully try not to stand out in the communities of Roswell, New Mexico and Smallville, Kansas, respectively. While still boyish and innocent, these orphaned other-worldly teenagers each seem to possess a superlative emotional sensitivity and a deep desire to do good in the world, arguably characteristics as foreign to the typical teenage boy as are their superhuman powers. These extraterrestrial arrivals heralded a transformation in genre television with the construction of a new hero for the teen male melodrama.

Like their protagonists, *Roswell* and *Smallville* have interesting origins. Not only did both originate as popular series within another media form (*Roswell* is based on the young adult book series *Roswell High* by Melinda Metz; *Smallville* is a retelling of the Superman myth first made popular in comic books, and subsequently on radio, television and film), but these television programmes are also generic hybrids. *Roswell* tells the story of three teenage aliens, survivors of the 1947 crash in Roswell, New Mexico: Max Evans, who was adopted along with his alien sister, Isabel, by a 'normal', bourgeois family who are unaware of their extraterrestrial origins, and their friend Michael, who as a foster child has always shown more interest in finding out about their origins. The emotional centre of the television programme's narrative is the romance between Liz Parker, a human teenage girl, and Max. In the pilot episode, Max uses his special powers to heal the fatally wounded Liz, thereby revealing his alien origins, as well as his attraction to her. *Smallville* imagines Clark Kent before he becomes Superman, when he is still a teenager living on a farm with his adoptive parents, Jonathan and Martha Kent. The series begins when Clark, already exceptionally fast and strong, learns the true story of his arrival in Smallville during the meteor shower that had accompanied his spaceship's crash landing. Clark's closest companions include Chloe, who initiates his journalistic interests; Pete, the only friend who learns Clark's secret (in Season Two); Lana Lang, the girl of his dreams, and the precursor to Lois Lane; and the congenial Lex Luthor, who series fans know will one day become Superman's greatest rival.

*Roswell* and *Smallville* are both able to bring in a variety of niche audiences with their blend of science fiction, action-adventure, young romance and melodrama. Though much of the action in these series is based in science fiction, character development and interaction maintain the emotional tone of the melodrama, and in particular the teen male melodrama. Unlike the typical melodramatic male whose struggles emanate from his position within an Oedipal triangle, Max Evans and Clark Kent exemplify a new television hero who is motivated to action by enlightened dreams for an equal partner, emotionally fulfilling relationships and a sense of duty to his community. Though these shows often triangulate relationships it is more useful as a mode of analysis with these two series to read Clark and Max as examples of a new protagonist for the melodrama genre: the beautiful, self-sacrificing, yet resilient hero.

Traditionally, scholarly work has applied psychoanalytic theory to map relationships between characters within the melodrama, particularly melodramas centred on a teen male.[1] Yet these series simultaneously pull from and upset established patterns within two classic modes of family melodrama – the male melodrama and the women's picture – thereby creating a new dynamic within the genre. This generic blending, both within the melodrama and through the addition of science-fictional elements, demands a new method of interpretation, one that still situates these programmes within the history of melodrama, yet presents a new kind of protagonist.

This chapter traces the generic origins of the teen male melodrama in order to uncover the transformation of the genre heralded by the introduction of a new breed of heroic male. I will first situate the teen male melodrama within the larger history of the family melodrama. This will then allow me to distinguish the character traits, as well as the character interactions, that present themselves as significant transformations within this new iteration of the melodrama.

## Not of This Earth, But of the Genre: The Teen Male Melodrama

The teen television melodrama, like most Hollywood melodrama, has its roots in the bourgeois domestic drama, as well as the French-influenced 'romantic melodrama'.[2] Drawing from its base root, the Greek term *melos* (meaning music), the genre employs music as an aural background that underscores the drama unfolding on stage or in front of the camera. Through music, the narrative is given an emotive base that, when tied to thematic tropes of the genre, is designed to provide the audience with a heightened dramatic experience. The story generally centres on a group of individuals whose relationships with the protagonist are contrapuntal to one another. Through a series of interactions, the storylines reveal conflicts about personal and social identity, and the positioning of the family. The teen male melodramas under discussion here still follow many of the tropes of bourgeois family melodrama, while at the same time, through the re-inscription and transformation of these elements, establishing a new subgenre. These tropes include: the blending of drama and music characteristic of the genre as a whole; the representation of a heroic, self-sacrificing character typical of the women's melodrama; and the portrayal of the troubled youth of the male melodrama.

The use of popular music on these programmes, in their title sequences as well as throughout each episode, gives the stories a lush background that enhances the emotion of the drama unfolding on screen, while defining these dramas as distinctly young and trendy.[3] In the ethereal sounds of pop chanteuse Dido's song 'Here With Me' (the title music for *Roswell*), she tells the story of a desperate passion: 'I won't go, I won't sleep, I can't breathe, until you're resting here with me./I won't leave, I can't hide, I cannot be, until you're resting here with me.' If ever a song spoke to the drama of teen love, this might be it, as its swirling vocals lure in the listener and capture the almost overwhelming intensity of Max and Liz's bond. More moody rock, with alternately dark and uplifting lyrics, *Smallville*'s theme song 'Save Me', performed by Remy Zero, cries out for a hero: 'You were all I wanted . . . Somebody save me/I don't care how you do it/Just save me, save/Come on/I've been waiting for you.' Licensing up to ten songs an episode, contemporary teen programmes use introspective, seductive pop anthems to boost the emotional content of the drama, while creating a second level of in-programme commercials by luring viewers at the end of each episode into buying the latest pop music from the programme's website.

Melodrama is typically female-oriented – that is, women are generally the protagonists of the narrative, and virtually always the primary audience for the genre (consider *Mrs Miniver* (Wyler, 1942), *Now, Voyager* (Rapper, 1942), *Letter from an Unknown Woman* (Ophuls, 1948)). Classically, in the family melodrama, the world of the narrative exists within a bourgeois, patriarchal social order, where fathers provide structure, guidance and authority, and mothers are self-sacrificing caregivers. The character of the mother within the melodrama often holds a precarious position in that she lives in the shadow of an idealised image of femininity and motherhood, one she rarely attains. This ideal femininity is constructed around the notion of self-sacrifice: women give of themselves completely for the sake of the preservation of the family. Self-sacrifice is the ultimate heroic act within the women's melodrama, also known as the women's 'weepy'. However, in the teen male melodrama the focus of attention is a young adult, making the parents into characters that, at the most basic level, either support or frustrate the lives of the teens that fall under their care.

Unlike the central character in the tragic male melodrama of 1950s' cinema, often represented as an over-emotional, somewhat effeminate young man who struggles desperately to convey his pent-up emotions (George Eastman in *A Place in the Sun* [Stevens, 1951] or Cal and Aron Trask in *East of Eden* [Kazan, 1955]), Clark and Max are expressive, heroic and comfortable in their own skins. The new protagonist within melodrama that they represent can articulate with great emotion teens' fear of their own coming of age, while remaining an object of desire for audiences. By contrasting his character with a more ruggedly masculine, rebellious male best friend, these shows prime viewers to favour the tragic beauty of the innocent, yet sexualised hero over his more dangerous friend. Though teen rebellion is often accepted in film, on television the text always privileges the more thoughtful, obedient boy.

*Roswell* and *Smallville* are also particularly male-focused melodramas.[4] For both series, the action of the narrative, as well as the fate of all the characters in both programmes, revolves around a central teen male. The major narrative arcs centre on Max and Clark, often in relation to those people they hold most dear, and the choices they must make to discover their origins as well as their destinies. This gendered designation does not necessarily imply that the target viewership is male. Yet, with the inclusion of the science-fiction aspect of each of these programmes, producers are seemingly trying to widen the male audience for what otherwise would be a more female-oriented teen melodrama.

As part of this blending, a transfer of character traits has effectively taken place: the self-sacrificing mother has been erased, as her hip, young teenage son has become the hero and martyr. Max and Clark are emotionally capable, thoughtful young men, aware of their masculine and feminine sides – and comfortable with both. They choose as their friends and lovers smart, self-confident girls, and they look up to their young companions with an affection bordering on reverence. In addition, they are respectful of their gentle, supportive male guardians (Jonathan Kent, Sheriff Valenti). However, the strong female role models who raised this new style of young man – namely their biological mothers – are missing. The erasure of a self-sacrificing mother figure forces a dynamic change and, in this iteration, inscribes the teen male as the suffering martyr within the text. This new hero, who at the same time can be unabashedly emotional and decidedly masculine, offers himself up each week for physical as well as emotional torture. And because of his alien status, which allows him to spontaneously heal himself, this suffering hero can return each episode anew.

## TV Teens: The Generic Roots of Orphaned Boys

In television, genre is not a static system. A single series can make generic transformations from season to season, and sometimes even from episode to episode.[5] Even as multi-generic television programmes though, *Roswell* and *Smallville* are more than anything teen male melodrama. To break down this term into its component parts seems useful here. In both film and television, 'teen' has arguably become its own genre. Timothy Shary in 'The Teen Film and Its Methods' posits that the teen film challenges traditional genre studies, in that 'this genre is defined not so much by its narrative characteristics (although there are considerable generic similarities among teen films) as it is by the population that the films are about and to whom they are directed'.[6] While I might argue with Shary, in that I would label teens as the *intended* audience, teen television follows this same generic trend, in particular with the rise of the new American networks (or netlets, namely Fox, WB and, more recently, UPN) that have used teen programming as a method to draw in a niche teen audience.[7]

Melodrama has translated to television primarily in the form of the daytime soap opera, but increasingly, since the advent of *Dallas* (1978) and *Dynasty* (1981), there has been a substantial rise in the number of evening television melodramas. Because of the nature of the medium, television melodrama differs from its cinematic or theatrical counterparts in two particular ways, namely, its use of interruptions and suspense, and its less tragic nature. Television's melodramas, in their episodic, serial design, are structured by interruptions, creating a constant process of deferment. In 'Crossroads: Notes on Soap Opera', Charlotte Brunsdon argues that television serials are designed to continually defer closure or resolution.[8] It is inherent within the design of the medium – through commercial breaks, weekly instalments and seasons – that the text is structured to keep audiences tuned in for the next instalment. This is achieved through the development of drama, suspense and a longing for resolution – something that is particularly delayed in both the melodrama and the science-fiction genres. And, while secondary characters will often be killed, each instalment of the series must never be too tragic. The nature of television melodrama demands this, both because of a need to keep a returning cast each week, as well as an economic necessity not to depress audiences so much that they are unable to focus on the programme's commercial sponsorship during breaks.

Teen male melodrama has a short history on television, but its origins lie both within film and the television drama. The genesis of the genre is doubtlessly Nicholas Ray's *Rebel without a Cause* (1955); James Dean's portrayal of Jim Stark, a tentative and scarred American teenager, spoke to a generation's pain and, in many ways, defined the genre. Before *Rebel without a Cause* though, Dean had made more than twenty-five live and filmed television dramas, and sometimes melodramas, often playing a young hoodlum or a troubled juvenile.[9] Though they rarely reached a melodramatic pitch, a number of early television series, in particular Westerns, showed moments of tenderness between fathers and sons: for example, on *The Rifleman* or *Bonanza* where moral dilemmas turned into lessons learned. In the 1970s, *The Waltons*, *The White Shadow* and *James at 15* all featured young men who were discovering themselves, and whose stories sometimes veered into the melodramatic.

The teen male melodrama seemed to come into full puberty with the rise of the netlets on American television. In 1990, Fox premiered *Beverly Hills 90210*, a serial dramedy – or arguably, traumedy – that detailed the joys and tribulations of a clique of rich teens at West Beverly Hills High School. *Beverly Hills 90210* introduced two crucial developments into the evolution of the teen melodrama: the first pairing of a beautiful boy with a more rugged, rebellious best friend, and the first steps toward the erasure of the parents (later, just mothers) as central figures within the drama. Though this group of friends did suffer greatly at times, the narrative rarely presented these teens' tales as melodramatic – except for Dylan McKay's. Dylan, played by Luke Perry, was the troubled, brooding, poor little rich boy, who at the age of seventeen was both a recovering alcoholic and a multimillionaire. The first teen idol of the decade, Perry portrayed Dylan as a modern-day Jim Stark: rebellious and emotional, with mood swings that flirted with full-scale melodrama. Strangely, though, the focus of the drama was not on Dylan, but rather on his best friend Brandon, who was privileged by the text (through on-screen time, number of storylines and narrative perspective). Brandon, the safer, more responsible boy was continually re-inscribed as the protagonist and hero of the narrative.

What started with the pairing of Brandon Walsh and Dylan McKay was repeated again between Bailey and Charlie Salinger on *Party of Five*, and later with Dawson Leery and Pacey Witter on *Dawson's Creek*. In all of these cases, the text privileged the pouty-lipped, doe-eyed beautiful boy, even though fans would often state their preferences for the rebellious one. Ironically, while this more family-oriented boy captured the focus of the narrative, the traditional family began to disappear within these series. In the early seasons of *Beverly Hills 90210*, the Walshes were central to the narrative; as the teens grew up, their parents became superfluous to the drama, and conveniently moved overseas. However, it was the Salinger family on *Party of Five* that set the standard for absent parents and for emotional intensity in television's teen melodrama.

After a drunk driver killed their parents, the five Salinger siblings rarely experienced a day of levity in their six seasons on television. The series tackled virtually every controversial issue or major event in the life of a young adult, and never failed to deal with the consequences of its characters' actions. While some viewers lost interest in the show when, season after season, storylines became increasingly depressing, the programme was particularly influential in the development of the teen male melodrama and the creation of a new teen hero for the genre. Though they sometimes struggled with their emotions, the Salinger boys, and in particular the middle son, Bailey, were gushing, thoughtful young men, capable of an ease of self-expression, and possessing a respect for young women.[10] Soft, vulnerable and caring, these orphaned teens had an exceptional ability to emote – perhaps brought on by the dramatic experience of losing their parents in such a violent and sudden manner. Or, one might wonder, did their mother teach them that it is okay for boys to cry? The erasure of freethinking, liberal parents was starting to become a trend.

*Roswell* and *Smallville*, like *Party of Five*, follow the stories of children orphaned after a dramatic crisis. This traumatic, apocalyptic act (whether a car or a spaceship crash) sets the trajectory of the series, and binds these orphans together with the other central characters of their respective dramas through their collective pain. Equally, these initial acts of devastation seem to work within these series, at least in part, as a justification for why the males in these programmes are given licence to be eloquent, emotive beings. Out of the tragic loss of their parents, which serves to redefine the stakes of life and death, these young men justifiably experience life with an emotional intensity and, more importantly here, an eloquence about their situation not typical of the average television teen male. They are not the shy, insecure, neurotic or effeminate teen males of 1950s' cinema melodrama, paralysed by their emotions. Rather it is their willingness – often even eagerness – to be reflective and emote without losing control that sets them apart as a new type of hero.

## 'So What Are You – Man or Superman?': Defining the Genre's New Hero

In the pilot episode of *Smallville*, Lana Lang asks the awkward, love-struck Clark Kent the above question; Clark's response is, 'I don't know yet', although viewers obviously do. While both Clark and Max are fated to achieve greatness in their lives, these stories begin when they are right in the midst of those awkward teenage years. As sixteen-year-olds, they are already wise beyond their years. An analysis of the nature of the hero within these two teen male melodramas provides a better understanding of how these protagonists, as well as their companions – like the programmes themselves – speak to a new trend within the genre. Moving from the personal to the interpersonal, my examination of these two series will highlight issues that mark this new, enlightened male.

Part of the quintessential teenager's life experience is the profound need for a sense of belonging, to feel a part of a group, to be 'normal'. While successfully masquerading as average teenagers (their white skin, healthy bodies and beautiful features help) in high school, Max and Clark are biological aberrations. They are organically outsiders, literally aliens. For Clark this difference means that for the safety of his secret – as well as that of the other characters – he cannot play sports, something which would make him 'cool' in the eyes of his classmates. In the episode 'Leech', however, Clark gets to experience life as a 'normal' teenager when he loses his powers. Even Lana notices, saying: 'You seem more relaxed. Like you haven't got the weight of the world on your shoulders.' At school, Clark easily passes as normal. He is a little geeky, quiet, stays out of trouble and he limits his extra-curricular activities to working on the high-school newspaper and helping his parents on their farm. This notion of 'passing' is made more explicit on *Roswell*. Until Max saves Liz's life, Max and Michael kept to themselves, making the decision that being quiet is the best way to go unnoticed and pass as human. In 'The End of the World', Max tells Liz that he is obligated to protect his race. Over the course of the series, as more characters learn their secret, talk about aliens becomes normalised, but in the world outside their small group of friends, they know they will never be safe. This type of outsider status sets these young men apart, but never goes so far as to position them as the Other, in a cultural or racial sense: they are outsiders with secrets, but their position as heroes within the text never falters.

While their DNA may make them outsiders, the bodies of these new heroes are decidedly more masculine than previous protagonists of the male melodrama such as James Dean or Montgomery Clift. With their soulful eyes, full, pink lips, their dark tousled hair, and their voices filled with adolescent conviction, Jason Behr (who plays Max Evans) and Tom Welling (Clark Kent) are worthy of teen fantasies, even though both of them are grown men, and therefore fully beyond those awkward teenage years (Behr began playing Max at the age of twenty-six, Welling was twenty-four).[11] In 'The Face on the Lunch Box: Television's Construction of the Teen Idol', Gael Sweeney contends that teen idols, principal players in many female teen fantasy scenarios, must be appealing but always in a non-threatening manner.[12]

> Television teen idols must be young, or appear to be so, not too tall, soft (the 'cuddle factor'), long on head hair but sparse of body hair, and sad-eyed like the puppies with which they are so often photographed. In short, television teen idols must be male, but not phallically male. Teen idols offer to girls objects of desire that are heterosexual but not overtly masculine or sexually threatening. These idols channel adolescent desire into a containable space.[13]

Like Sweeney's idols, Max and Clark are sensitive on the inside, but both stand out as significantly more 'hardened' on the outside. Though Max began the series with a 'soft' body, by the second season Behr had bulked up and began doing more shirtless scenes.[14] Even considering their more masculine bodies, Behr and Welling perform their characters with a softness that only makes more clear the paradoxical nature of the contrast. In fact, when they are shown shirtless, it only accentuates their moments as sensitive boys within the scene. The two most obvious examples are when Clark is abandoned virtually naked in a field as part of the school's annual scarecrow prank in the *Smallville* pilot, and when Max is strapped shirtless to an operating table as a specimen for study in 'The White Room'. It is as if their (partial) nudity is yet another trial for these boys to endure. Here is, perhaps, the new idol for a contemporary audience: strong on the outside, soft in the middle.

In addition to the physical appearance/character dichotomy, Max and Clark's contradictory characterisations as teen aliens mark them as both powerful *and* vulnerable young men. Max's gifts rely less on physical strength than emotional power. From sharing memories to the ability to manipulate matter – healing young bodies, stopping bullets, warming food – Max's powers extend from the mundane to the messianic, but they are distinctly rendered through a strength of mind, rather than a strength of body. Clark's powers, on the other hand, are purely physical: by the end of the first season these include speed, strength, x-ray vision, immunity to physical harm or pain and, once, floating in his sleep. By the beginning of season two, he has also picked up heat vision. Though more than willing to employ their superhuman tricks to help people, both boys have learned that protecting themselves and their secret is just as important as saving lives. Both series continually place these young men in threatening situations where someone has suspicions, or even proof, of their unique abilities.

The development of power and vulnerability can be seen as a metaphor for the experience of every teenager. Max and Clark's transformations are like alien puberty: they often feel uncomfortable at first with their growing abilities, and sometimes letting people know about how their bodies are changing makes them more vulnerable (for example, Max's shyness about his exhaustion after intense healing sessions, or Clark's embarrassment after he accidentally triggers his heat vision when thinking about sex). While the powers of both characters are constantly developing, and often becoming stronger, these boys are still not entirely in control of what is happening to their bodies. In some ways, what makes these characters unique among protagonists of the male melodrama is that they make growing up look more like a discovery than an obligation. Of course, alien puberty also seems a bit cooler to audiences than the real, human version.

One thing that does affect both Max and Clark, and adds to their vulnerability, is an abiding sense of guilt. For three seasons, Max continually experiences regret for making Liz keep his secret. Before Max healed Liz, she was a happy, ambitious girl. But saving her changed the course of her life. By the end of Season One, she is skipping school; by Season Two, she sneaks away on road trips; and by Season Three, she holds up convenience stores and her father is threatening her with boarding school. During season three, Max continually wears a leather jacket (the talisman of the Marlon Brando club of wild boys), and Liz begins behaving as a truant.[15] While much of the re-writing of these characters seems like a desperate attempt to keep the show afloat, the justification for their actions is based on the integrity of their characters.[16] They are rebelling for the sake of a larger cause: to help Max discover his past and his destiny. But Max can take no pleasure in this; his deep sense of responsibility ensures that for three seasons viewers will never see him smile.[17] In the first episode of *Smallville*, Clark learns that his landing on earth was accompanied by the extraordinary meteor shower that caused the death of Lana's parents and made Lex bald. In addition, the meteor rocks are responsible for all the strange phenomena in Smallville collected on Chloe's 'Wall of Weird'. Clark could not have prevented the meteor shower, but particularly because he is such a powerful young man, he continues to be haunted by his failure to have intercepted the cataclysmic act that hurt so many people he loves. When Clark first sees Lana's picture up on the 'Wall of Weird', he mutters, 'My fault. It's all my fault.' Because neither boy understands the reasons for their arrival, or the story behind their powers, both carry the burden of their actions like the scars that will never develop on their invulnerable bodies. Perhaps this is the extraterrestrial original sin.

With such power and sense of responsibility comes a depth of character; but for teenagers, it demands of them an exceptional level of maturity. As Clark gains x-ray vision in 'X-Ray', his adoptive mother, in one of her only lectures to him, warns Clark about not using his power for personal pleasure (for example, seeing through Lana's clothes), but for just and right causes (locating kidnapped people inside buildings, and so on). While only a teenager, Max learns that he is a king; with such a weight put on him, he begins to feel overwhelmed by the implications of this responsibility. In the episode 'Ask Not', Max takes special interest in his history class, hoping to learn practical lessons about leadership and decision-making from studying about the young, liberal American presidential icon John F. Kennedy's experience during the Cuban Missile Crisis. While still leaders – it seems alien planets are also patriarchal – these boys are always also accountable for their actions and respectful of the positions of power they hold.

By the nature of their characters, Max and Clark are destined not only for greatness, but also for goodness; they use their powers to be healers and helpers, and to set things right. Even though audiences know Clark Kent's future is mapped out for him as Superman, Clark must still discover this. In 'Hourglass', Clark meets a blind seer who tells him, 'More than once I've touched people, and I've seen such pain and despair. But then you were there, and the pain was gone. I think that's your destiny, Clark. To help people, to save them from fear and darkness.'[18] Even before this, Clark's actions speak to his character as a hero – in particular his adeptness at saving people from vehicular peril.[19] Though he shares certain abilities with his fellow aliens, the gift that makes Max unique is his power to heal people. In 'Panacea' he is even referred to as 'The Healer'. The one time Max cannot save a dying man (for fear he will expose his secret), he is so wracked by guilt that he compensates for his act of self-preservation by healing an entire children's cancer ward at a hospital. These leading boys are innately good; episode after episode, they are forever the self-sacrificing heroes of the melodrama.

Though both *Roswell* and *Smallville* place these young heroes in loving families, their human elders cannot provide much guidance; their adoptive human mothers offer little beyond affection, and their adoptive fathers and male guardians can only serve as protectors. Max's adoptive parents, unaware of his alien status until the final episodes of the third season, are not capable of helping him. Instead, starting in the second season, Sheriff Valenti serves as a father figure for the alien teens. In 'Hourglass', Clark's father tells him, 'Your destiny may be to protect people, but ours is to protect you.' Adoptive mothers within both series are basically impotent: providing meals, offering hugs and telling boys to talk to their fathers.[20] These programmes' sometimes archaic ideas about gender roles are most clearly seen in their representation of mothers: ineffectual and uninvolved, they are not the type of women who could have given birth to such emotionally well-rounded young men. Those mothers, it seems, must be back on their home planets. Instead, the beacons of emotional strength and the teachers of equality and morality are their male guardians. John Schneider, who once played a wild boy heartthrob himself as Bo Duke on *The Dukes of Hazzard*, now stands in as Jonathan Kent, teaching his son a new way to be a dream boy.

This new hero of the melodrama can be sweet and gentle, but he is also comfortable with his masculinity, making him the ideal mate for a budding young feminist. Max and Clark treat the women in their lives with a deep respect – not putting them on a pedestal, but rather looking to them for friendship, guidance and help with their homework. They choose to spend time with young women who are intelligent and ambitious. The young women on these programmes are emancipated from patriarchal relationships: either they live with a strong female guardian, or if they have over-protective fathers, these men are simply ignored. For both boys, the girls of their dreams are fellow classmates: smart, friendly, working young women (both are waitresses) who are, most importantly, brunettes – the ultimate sign that the boys are not just interested in looks.[21] And though there is little sexual gratification for these young men – it seems good girls still don't give themselves up very quickly – there is no question about their virility: when Max kisses Liz, she sees galaxies forming, and when Clark wakes up from a dream about Lana, he finds himself floating above his bed. Though feminist mothers are nowhere in sight in these series, there is hope for strong heterosexual coupling for the next generation.

## Conclusion

Complicated and thoughtful, yet comfortable with his masculinity, the protagonist that Max and Clark represent is an attractive new hero for the teen male melodrama. Both boys are effortlessly in touch with their feminine sides, and much more likely to tend to the emotional needs of the women around them than to act out with anger or violence. Even as virtuous sufferers, there are never any doubts about their heterosexuality – though much has been made by fans of *Smallville* of Clark's mouth-to-mouth meeting with Lex Luthor, Clark himself did not hesitate to give CPR to another man. With this in mind, Max and Clark could be defined as gender-enlightened heroes living within traditionally melodramatic worlds.

Max and Clark can be viewed as a new type of figure of identification for young viewers, similar to Brandon in *Beverly Hills 90210*, Bailey in *Party of Five* or Dawson in *Dawson's Creek*, in that they are sensitive boys seemingly born out of an Abercrombie & Fitch catalogue – but these young men have both a wisdom and a sense of responsibility to humanity beyond their years. Unlike earlier teen melodramas, in this new hybrid of science fiction and teen male melodrama, there are not just the basic youth-oriented obstacles to the hero's happiness. Rather, their angst derives from their sense of (literal) alienation, while at the same time they are called upon weekly to risk exposure of their secrets in order to save their loved ones. Both boys are constantly concerned with how they are viewed by others; as teenage aliens, their deep desire to be seen as 'normal' is more than typically magnified.

Beautiful in their innocence, tragic in their struggle for goodness in the world, these melodramatic heroes are more human than humans. Both victim and saviour, these boys in fulfilling their destinies become enlightened heroes that are somehow more attractive to contemporary audiences. This paradoxical position refreshes the genre of melodrama and presents truly heroic models of teen masculinity.

## Notes

1. In particular, see Robert Lang, *American Film Melodrama: Griffith, Vidor, Minnelli* (Princeton, NJ: Princeton University Press, 1989). For an overview of theories on melodrama, see also Christine Gledhill (ed.), *Home Is Where the Heart Is: Studies in Melodrama and the Woman's Film* (London: BFI, 1987), and Marsha Landy (ed.), *Imitations of Life: A Reader on Film and Television Melodrama* (Detroit, MI: Wayne State University Press, 1991).
2. For a study of the family melodrama, see Thomas Schatz, 'The Family Melodrama', in Schatz, *Hollywood Genres: Formulas, Filmmaking, and the Studio System* (New York: McGraw-Hill, 1981), pp. 221–60, and Thomas Elsaesser, 'Tales of Sound and Fury: Observations on the Family Melodrama', *Monogram*, no. 4 (1972), pp. 2–15. Examples of such melodramas would include *Stella Dallas* (Vidor, 1937), *All That Heaven Allows* (Sirk, 1956) and *Written on the Wind* (Sirk, 1957).
3. The licensing of popular music, in particular in teen-oriented programming, is worth extensive study in its own right. For an overview of the practice, as well as its profitability for networks and music companies, see Daniel Frankel, 'Synergy Sings at the WB: Licensing Pop Music for Series and Promotion Helps Labels and Programmers', *Broadcasting and Cable* (29 July 2002), Special Report, p. 20. See also the essays by Kay Dickinson and Valerie Wee in this volume.
4. Although this is somewhat complicated by Liz's bookended narratives in every episode of the first season of *Roswell*, her diary entries tend to focus on Max, or her relationship with him.
5. One could even argue that these programmes will sometimes go through generic shifts within individual episodes, as well.
6. Timothy Shary, 'The Teen Film and Its Methods', *Journal of Popular Film and Television*, vol. 25, no. 1 (Spring 1997), p. 38.
7. As Robin Wood writes, teen-oriented entertainment holds a particular pleasure for those of us well outside the target demographic. See Robin Wood, 'Party Time or Can't Hardly Wait for That American Pie', *CineAction*, no. 58 (2002), pp. 2–10.
8. Charlotte Brunsdon, '*Crossroads*: Notes on Soap Opera', *Screen*, vol. 22, no. 4 (1981), p. 35. This technique of deferment was first used for the serialisation of novels.
9. For a brief overview of Dean's experience on live television, see Susan Bluttman, 'Rediscovering James Dean: The TV Legacy', *Emmy*, vol. 12, no. 5 (October 1990), pp. 50–7.
10. This changed when Bailey became rebellious and struggled with alcoholism in later seasons. Conversely, Charlie only became more honest and open about his emotions over time.
11. Clark and Max are not actually awkward, they only perform awkwardness, something which audiences seem to prefer in their heroes. As for side characters, like Pete Ross in *Smallville* or Alex Whitman in *Roswell*, true teen awkwardness is allowed, and usually played for its humour.

12. I would argue that these young men, in particular Tom Welling as Clark Kent, have equal sex appeal for gay teens, as well as older audience members of both sexes.
13. Gael Sweeney, 'The Face on the Lunch Box: Television's Construction of the Teen Idol', *The Velvet Light Trap*, no. 33 (Spring 1994), p. 51.
14. This new over-developed body on such a supposedly young boy looked almost unsettling. Max's powers, unlike Clark's, did not include physical strength, or anything that would necessitate this sudden bulking-up.
15. This same symbolism is employed on *Smallville*. In the episode 'Red', Clark has his first interaction with red kryptonite. This derivation of the alien rock leads him to abandon all his inhibitions and act on every impulse, thereby turning Clark into a rebel – leather jacket, sunglasses and motorcycle included.
16. Often when a show becomes exhausted and begins losing viewers, as a last-ditch effort writers will alter a character's behaviour dramatically – something which almost always results in angering audiences. This can be seen in *Roswell*, when Max moves out of his parents' house and begins his sartorial penchant for leather, or when Bailey became an alcoholic on *Party of Five*. Television fans often find pleasure in locating that precise moment a series falls from grace – or, to use the expression made infamous in a *Happy Days* episode and by the website created in its honour, 'jumps the shark'.
17. In fact, in one or two episodes, when I did see him smile, I found it not only surprising, but almost disturbing. Jason Behr has a face that was designed to brood.
18. In a strange mixing of Greek mythology, the blind prophet in 'Hourglass' is not named Tiresias, but Cassandra. Unlike the mythical Cassandra, though, here she prophesies Clark's greatness, not just imminent tragedies.
19. Clark pulls Lex out of a drowning car in 'Pilot'; he drags Lana's boyfriend Whitney out of a burning car in 'Metamorphoses'; he rips a burning door off a car to release the town hermit in 'Hug'; and he steps out of an exploding car and later rushes to save Lana stuck in her truck from the vortex of a tornado in 'Tempest'.
20. In this second season, there seems to be hope for Martha Kent. As I write this piece, Martha has just taken a job off the farm, working for Lionel Luthor. After going against the wishes of her husband, Martha might soon become a more prominent figure in Clark's development as a young man.
21. In fact, Max and Clark are arguably prettier than Liz or Lana.

# 2

# Teen Futures: Discourses of Alienation, the Social and Technology in Australian Science-Fiction Television Series

## Leonie Rutherford

Prior to the present volume, there has been little attempt to theorise the concept of 'teen' television. What might we mean by the 'teen' in teen television studies? Research such as that of Angela McRobbie on print culture locates its definition in the way in which texts *address* and are implicated in the construction of teen subcultures.[1] Alternative definitions might include texts which: are at least partially coded for teen audiences; represent youth subcultures; define problems of teen identity; use actors who are embodied teenagers; and/or meet 'teen' needs according to developmental or social models (the parallel here would be 'young adult fiction' in the publishing market).

These questions are crucial to my analysis. Most of the science-fiction drama series produced in Australia since the mid-1960s have been coded for younger audiences, with an emphasis within the industry on their additional potential to be sold as 'family' viewing. Since the inception of the Children's Television Standards in the mid-1980s, it has been important for commercial broadcasters to meet a quota of designated 'C' certificate (children's) drama. The Children's Television Standards define 'children' as young people up to the age of fourteen:[2] most 'C' certificate drama, therefore, is bound by regulation to 'meet the needs' of viewers in the upper childhood to early teenage years. The Film Australia productions I discuss in this chapter (*Escape from Jupiter*, *The Girl from Tomorrow* and *Tomorrow's End*), as well as such series as Jonathan Schiff's *Ocean Girl*, are all classified by the Australian Broadcasting Authority as 'C' drama. What then is their claim to be considered 'teen' television?

The answer is partially to be found in their intersection with the genre of science-fiction cinema and television. Regardless of the embodied ages of its consumers, science fiction is culturally constituted as a 'young adult' product, in its status as spectacle, celebrating the pleasures of possibility.[3]

More crucially, to maximise audience share and, thus, industry profitability, these dramas are typically double- or triple-coded, cross-written with a range of references which address teen, child and 'family' audiences. Film Australia's productions, in particular, cast 'bankable' adult actors as protagonists, along with the diegetically more prominent teen and child characters. While these series do not foreground fictional youth cultures to the same extent as some of the American serials analysed elsewhere in this volume, they do address questions of teen identity using the particular thematics of science fiction: in particular, the relationship of the individual to technologies and framing discourses of futurity. Unlike series such as *Buffy*, *Beverly Hills 90210* or *Roswell High*, these productions cast actors who are embodied teenagers. One could argue that this deflects the aspirational, desiring gaze of corporeal teenaged viewers; on the other hand, a case can be made that these programmes offer a different perspective on teen subjectivity, one located in a broader set of social and technological discourses.

According to Annette Kuhn the thematics of science fiction typically concern 'societal organisation' and technology.[4] The future is an imaginary space where different models of social organisation may contend. Within this space, teen identity may be represented in transformed relationships to familiar structures of family and other institutions.

Science fiction overwhelmingly prefers the action-adventure mode. However, more speculatively, science-fiction drama explores 'alienness' – of the body and of societal organisation. The exploration of alterity is one of the genre's defining tropes, a trajectory in which points of contact and communication must be found within difference. Potentially, this may construct a politics of exclusion, in which the teenager, troped as alien, may confirm the normative status of adult subjectivity. On the other hand, the teenager, as liminal category, one who is neither child nor adult, may function as an avatar of potential other futures, critiquing social hierarchies and global economic and technological regimes.

### Alien Avatars: *The Girl from Tomorrow*

Through the narrative device of time or space travel, science fiction has developed its own version of the *idiot-savant* – the stranded alien, adrift in a world whose structures and knowledges are unfamiliar. The narrative device of the infantilised alien, often literally an 'alien youth', distantiates the contemporary middle-class world and its culture. For instance, the motif of the 'alien child' is exploited to this effect in Steven Spielberg's 1982 classic, *ET: The Extra-Terrestrial*.

Film Australia's drama *The Girl from Tomorrow* is a slick adventure series with highly developed comic elements. In this series, the alien teen is a fourteen-year-old girl from the year 3000. The backstory is also familiar territory. Gene Roddenberry's *Star Trek* and its sequels have familiarised generations of viewers with a projected history in which human culture evolves from a violent interregnum to an enlightened future. In *The Girl from Tomorrow*, the ultimate future is utopian, with a holistic-mystic technology based on channelling the power of the mind. The intermediate era, which provides the villain of the piece, is a dark age of anarchy and manipulation by tyrannic global corporations.

The strangeness of Alana, 'the girl from tomorrow', also provides a way of interrogating the difference of that liminal stage represented by the teen. The transitional space occupied by the teen in contemporary Western culture is almost erased in the year 3000. Teens and children are represented as part of a sober and conscientious adult continuum. Here the 'child' at school is not part of a segregated and differentiated category. In the first episode of the series, it is revealed that Alana's biological parents live off-world; she is educated in a tranquil garden setting by an almost contemporaneous guardian (the historian Tualista). Already an apprentice healer, with a good deal more responsibility than the children of 1990s' Sydney who are depicted in the programme, Alana's major companion is a wrist-unit computer, PJ, who acts as organiser, friend and helper. The brutal dynamics of identity formation, common to the peer-group culture of the contemporary junior high school, are wholly missing from Alana's pre-time-travel experience.

Contemporary knowledges and social practices are rendered alien through the temporal dislocation of the 'girl from tomorrow'. Tualista's time-travelling history expedition to discover the causes of 'the Great Disaster' is hijacked by a twenty-sixth century buccaneer. As a consequence, Alana is deposited amidst the decay of a Sydney suburban rubbish dump in the year 1990. This plot device provides the vehicle for humour at the expense of the suddenly knowledge-poor Alana, as she negotiates differences in technologies and discourses. A farcical series of misadventures is structured around Alana's literal-minded misreadings of communication utterances whose purpose is manipulative rather than purely informative.

The series contrasts the 'innocent' and earnest Alana with the streetwise contemporary teenager, Jenny Kelly. On the other hand, the way in which Alana, Jenny and her kid brother, Petey, collude to outwit not only the villain, Silverthorn, but also the limitations imposed by parents and teachers, emphasises common youth perceptions and interests, constructing young people as subjects who are forced to inhabit and negotiate an 'alien', adult world.

## Smart Talkin' versus the *Idiot-Savant*: Truth and Contemporary Teen Discourse

In the thirty-first century a benign technology and cooperative governance have done away with the harsh economic, political and structural inequalities of race, class and age. Knowledge and sustenance are freely available to all citizens via 'public information terminals' and communal facilities which provide food, clothing and services. Transported to the year 1990, Alana functions narratively as an inept reader of contemporary institutions. Seeking directions, she asks a passing 'bag lady' where she might find a 'public access terminal': her attempted clarification – 'a public information bank' – heralds a drama of comic misunderstanding. The homeless woman directs Alana to an autoteller machine. The girl from tomorrow is a complete alien to 1990s' structures of exchange. Not only is she oblivious to the street dweller's position of social disadvantage; more crucially, she is ignorant of the function of money as the means of obtaining basic necessities. When PJ, her wrist computer, hacks into the autoteller machine, it disgorges a bundle of banknotes rather than the desired information, but Alana is unable to recognise the use or value of the money. This institutional incompetence is ironic in the light of the next sequence; having unconcernedly given away the cash which would have paid for her consumption, she shoplifts fruit from a 'self-serve' kiosk. The nuances of the commercial exchange have escaped her observation.

As *idiot-savant*, the alien teen renders visible the possessive practices which create social disadvantage through the commodification of basic resources. Alana's incomprehension is coded as an ethical position. She is wise in her ignorance of the practices of monopoly capitalism. This ethical positioning is crucial to the ideological work of the series and its sequel, *Tomorrow's End*. The villain, Silverthorn, and the corrupt corporate moguls of the twenty-sixth century are products of an age in which global monopoly capitalism has brought about planetary degradation and social collapse.

The trope of the alien teen not only functions to expose the crises within categories of economic relations. The system of education is also rendered strange by Alana's gaze. The curricula of the year 3000 are practical, interactive and are organised non-hierarchically. The learning relationship is one of supportive one-on-one guidance of a respected apprentice by a more experienced mentor. In stark opposition to this, in the educational and peer context of the junior high school of 1990s' Sydney, Alana is constructed as alienated, not only from the discourses of her peers, but also from contemporary modes of mediating knowledge. One of the elements associated with the trope of the *idiot-savant* is truth telling in fora where polite euphemism is the norm. Alana does not comprehend the strategies of mendacity and connivance which contemporary teens practise in order to evade adult surveillance and age-specific regimes of confinement. This incompetence codes her as a 'nerd' to her fellow students. Lying to teachers is how teens within the institution of the school conceal transgressive opinions and screen their own non-compliance behind a facade of dutiful attention.

When Jenny Kelly tells the time-traveller that she should 'sit down, shut up' and copy down what the Ancient History teacher says, Alana is characteristically bemused: 'How can anyone learn anything like that?' In her *overt* non-compliance she is coded as deviant. She transgresses school discipline by her open and honest inattention in class, as well as teen codes of *covert* non-compliance through her naive avowal of her lack of interest. Significantly, she merely voices what the mendacious, knowing silence of her peers has always spoken. The regimes of containment shared by the teens underline the universality of the youth experience. The modern 'children' also find educational institutions strange. The world adults have created is 'alien'.

While the drama foregrounds a youth perspective, there is also an adult gaze, however affectionate, in which the difference of 'children' is ruefully acknowledged. The commonplace perception of alterity is troped onto the 'teenager as alien'. This is effected largely through the stereotypical elements in the characterisation of Jenny Kelly, with her purple hair, overloud music and smart-mouthed one-liners at the expense of adult folly. To her mother, Jenny Kelly is an alien child, complete with the characteristic lifestyle markers of difference: divergent investments in fashion, music and subculture-specific linguistic forms.

Jenny is a sign of teenage alienation in general. Hers is a 'protest' femininity,[5] marked by punk inversion of hegemonic codes of beauty, seemliness, truth and duty. Jenny Kelly is alienated from the exemplary femininity of her own school peer group, with its iconography of classic blonde beauty, tanned skin and elegantly braided coiffures. She is an actor in a tragi-comedy of exclusion: the blonde set exclude Jenny from parties; she responds by sending a dead rat as a birthday gift; they respond with a gambit which ensures Jenny's social humiliation. Due to her smart mouth, her genius for extempore fabrication, and her traditionally masculine trait of rebelliousness, Jenny is coded as 'alien' to the exemplary models of sexualised teen femininity.

It was a cliché of another era that parents and teens suffer from a 'breakdown of communication'. The liminal status of the 'alien' child in this programme reveals that effective communication does exist – not in the 'truth-telling' exemplified by Alana, but in the mutually recognised and satisfying discourse of mendacity exemplified in contemporary adult–youth interactions. This transgressive insight is couched in a comic modality and, therefore, rendered less challenging. Adult–teen institutions (family or school) negotiate power relationships through a structure of fabrication and exhortation to (imaginary) duty. This is witnessed in the example of Jenny Kelly's creative tales. Her lies/stories leverage a space free from domestic duty/containment in which extra-curricular expeditions can take place. Jenny gets her way by telling mutually convenient lies. These lies meet the needs of parents and teachers as well as teens. They are not actually believed, but they are connived at because ignorance frees adults from the necessity of further attention and allows them to proceed with their own concerns.

The 'truth-telling' of the girl from tomorrow, on the other hand, is unwelcome because it reveals the necessity of lies in the structure of adult–teen social relations. A teacher's interrogative – 'Are the boys [outside the classroom window] more interesting than my lesson?' – demands a lie. Fabrications demand complicity. In another scene, Mrs B, the rotund, pet-besotted habituée of the Kelly Deli, orders mounds of sweets for herself and her lapdog. Jenny Kelly exhibits a forced politeness. The 'alien' response, however, explodes the structure of adult phantasy. Alana treats Mrs B's rhetorical posturing – 'I don't know why I get so many colds' – as a serious inquiry, delivering a deadpan lecture on the effects of obesity and poor diet on the immune system. In the process she breaks the contract of complicity which structures adult–teen discourse. As Jenny ruefully remarks: 'You get us into more trouble by telling the truth than I do by lying.' The contradictory status of teen fabrication is vindicated in the second series, *Tomorrow's End*. In the 'future noir' of the year 2500, Jenny's talent becomes a socially valued asset in a world where lies are an essential survival technique.

### Parasites or Antibodies: Alien Teen Bodies

If the alienated punk body of Jenny Kelly in *The Girl from Tomorrow* signifies teenage difference from normative adult and exemplary peer styles,[6] the *mise en scène* of *Escape from Jupiter* creates an architecture of space which politicises the difference between adults and youth. The production design creates a binary between surfaces and interiority, a Faustian environment in which the teen's body itself is represented as alien, invasive and disruptive.

Film Australia's *Escape from Jupiter* was co-produced with NHK Japan and the Australian Broadcasting Commission, with a Japanese production designer (Kazuo Sasaki). The series is clearly influenced both by the retro and post-modern stylistics of Japanese *anime* and by a tradition of cinematic futurescapes – consisting of polyglot urban technocultures – which reached its apex in Ridley Scott's 1982 classic, *Blade Runner*. Corporate greed precipitates a planetary holocaust on the mining colony of Io, when engineers fracture the lava core. A paranoid business and defence culture threatens the colony with annihilation in an environment where technology itself becomes inimical to life.

The mining colony of Io is a product of rapacious venture capitalism; the architecture of its world is alien to the energy and curiosity represented by the bodies of the teens and younger children. The *mise en scène* utilises retro stylistics reminiscent of 1950s' iconography of the future, suggesting that Io is a 'hick', somewhat under-resourced, outpost. Combined with this, however, the programme uses state of the art CGI representations of holography and simulacra, celebrating the spectacular aspects of this future's communication and entertainment technologies.

In the form of domes and decaying metallic structures, human habitations hug the exterior of Io, while a red, bifurcated fissure reveals the interior. Shafts penetrate to the site of the 'deep drilling'. 'Deep' penetration to the fiery depths is redolent with Faustian overtones: the greed of the adult social world, associated with opportunistic monopoly capitalism, overreaches prescribed natural limits. The world of the interior is labyrinthine, proscribed to the teenagers and their younger siblings, who are defined as nuisance elements, disruptive to the smooth operation of the corporate machine. Because of the remoteness of the colony, its population consists of worker families. It is therefore also a village, a social formation which produces offspring who are superfluous to the economic imperative. To the director of the mining colony (Duffy), the main protagonists, though clearly around sixteen or seventeen years old, are always stigmatised as rule-breaking 'children': non-adult and non-productive elements.

To Duffy (played to camp perfection by Steve Bisley) the teen body is properly the subject of restraint. However, its creativity and energy cannot be contained by the geopolitical structures of the adult world. Two narrative motifs construct the body of the teen as anarchic. The first is the motif of the lost 'child'; the second involves the coding of corporeal size as either a subversive or redemptive element. The teen's body fits spaces not designed for human traverse; it evades limitations.

For the mining director the 'child's' body is a parasite, disruptive of normal workflow. Duffy's policy of corporeal containment is designed to ensure that production quotas are met efficiently. Teens should not be seen in spaces mapped as workplaces. Neither should they hear adult business; information crucial to the future of the colony is restricted. Nevertheless, throughout the thirteen episodes of the series, the alien body of youth escapes its bounds.

Lost children halt operations at regular intervals. When Kumiko, an attractive sixteen-year-old girl, visits the colony with her parents (mining engineers), she becomes the catalyst for male rivalry between the local teens, Michael and Gerald. Gerald's taunts seduce Michael and Kumiko into an expedition to view the deep drilling. Predictably, an explosion from the fractured lava core precipitates a disaster sequence, amidst an epic landscape of precipices, rockfalls and fiery chasms.[7] The teen bodies are literally and figuratively trapped in spaces created by adult greed.

The younger siblings in the series function as camp-comic stereotypes. Kingston, much like Petey Kelly in *The Girl from Tomorrow*, is an example of the geeky boy genius, with his round glasses and robotic toy dog. Gerald's kid sister, Anna, is more obviously coded as toylike, with her Barbie-doll vestimentary regime of pinks and purples and her headgear with its retro connotations of mouseketeer ears. Her cupie-doll sweetness is clearly no serious threat. A comic effect is, thus, brought into play when the younger children set out to save their more capable teen siblings. The younger children prefigure the role of the teen body as 'antibody', a saving grace which is able to enter the fissures barred to adult forms. The miniature size of the child's body allows an avenue of communication and escape for Kumiko and the male teens.

Linda Mizejewski has argued that the excessively sculptured and constructed form of the bodybuilder in adult science-fiction cinema functions as a special effect.[8] The pumped-up bodies of the Schwarzenegger/Van Damme school are spectacular, rather than functional. They connote the triumph of technology over the natural body. The body that exercise technologies produce is excessive rather than human. In *Escape from Jupiter*, teen bodies, inversely, are less defined and, therefore, more flexible. They are neither cyborgs nor techno-products; rather, by means of their adaptive power, they subvert technologies and institutions which alienate the natural and evolving body.

The 'miniature' body of the teen in this programme functions as a beneficent antibody, entering the gaps in adult and corporate geopolitical architecture. These spaces have immense potential: Michael and Kumiko are able to gain entry to the antiquated space station, KL5, a refuge after the implosion of Io, through an airlock which is too small to admit adult bodies. Due to paranoid corporate policy, normal entry to the station has been prevented. The teen body becomes an optimistic trope of futurity, a signifier of plastic potential able to change and grow to meet the exigencies of survival.

The 'child's' body also penetrates virus-like through architectural gaps to overcome young people's exclusion from adult discourse. They slip through ventilation shafts and hidden passages to eavesdrop on hidden debates about the colony's future. Finally, the fuel and space constraints of the colony's shuttle craft ensure that it is the teens and younger children who must make the quest to Earth to get help for the stranded colonists. Teen bodies have been vilified as alien to corporate culture, yet they are the only bodies ultimately able to redeem it.

## Teens and the Trope of Futurity

As Patricia Holland demonstrates,[9] the prevalence of children and teens in the visual rhetoric of marketing is explained by the traditional connotation of potential. Hope for the future is troped onto the body of the teen. When Alana, the girl from tomorrow, meets two punk teenagers in a subway station she informs them she is from 'the future'. 'Future? What future?' quips the female of the pair. The discontent of the teenagers of the 1990s is an implicit critique of contemporary social and economic regimes which deny them a 'future'.[10] In the programmes analysed in this chapter, teenage anxieties about lack of social agency and 'disinheritance' from a fair share in material resources are projected onto representations of the future. *The Girl from Tomorrow*'s construction of twenty-sixth-century Sydney exemplifies the worst teenage fears concerning the dystopian 'futures' adults have engineered for them.

'One of the most immediate signifiers of the genre of science fiction', according to Janet Staiger, 'is the representation of a known city in which readily distinguishable sections of today's cityscape are present while other parts are rewritten.'[11] The futures of *The*

*Girl from Tomorrow* and *Tomorrow's End* are binary opposites traced across the landscape and architecture of Sydney – dark versus light, space versus constriction, vistas of nature versus vistas of waste and urban degeneration. The Sydney of the thirty-first century appears bucolic, its setting primarily virgin bushland, cool green lawns, pristine beaches and sheltered coves. There are no streets, no cars, no highrise buildings. The few domiciles and facilities are set amidst the green of nature.

The proliferation of space is itself politicised: the polis of the far future appears to be a series of federated villages. The state has a direct democracy (a World Council) and its population is small. Scientists, politicians, historians, teachers and children mix easily in an Edenic setting. The benevolent and ethical atmosphere of Alana's Sydney suggests the seriousness of a secluded religious commune. Children live together in dormitories, with individual, though Spartan, cells as sleeping quarters. The *mise en scène* invokes health and harmony with nature. The denizens all wear sandals and white robes, or loose tunics and trousers in natural fibres and colours. Their major activities like education and training are conducted outdoors in the sunlight; people walk from place to place. There are no dedicated weapons and the societal philosophy is one of non-violence and mutual cooperation.

By the end of the second series, *Tomorrow's End*, the crusade which inspires such austerity and ethical commitment, even in its young people, is disclosed. The planet has been redeemed from a 'Great Disaster' after half a millennium of dedication. The plot of *Tomorrow's End* exploits a common motif in fiction of time travel: the alteration of history. The temporal adventures of the first series have made tragic changes to the subjective timeline experienced by the teens. Alana's remembered 'present' has been obliterated from history. To reinstate the utopian future, the teens have to face the 'future noir' of twenty-sixth-century Sydney. Their task is to identify and prevent the catastrophe which will otherwise obliterate all possible futures.

The world of 2500 is a wasteland. As with the cities in the films analysed by Janet Staiger, the Sydney of the twenty-sixth century is dark:

> [T]he metaphoric implication of an end to civilisation or alienation from natural light pervades the atmosphere . . . darkness and urban-design chaos as bricolage also permit labyrinthine cities where only overhead schematics provide a sense of orientation . . . [T]hey are entropic, characterised by debris, decay and abandonment. Thus these dystopias' city architectures comment on a potential, post-industrial, age-of-communication society. The forecast is not favourable. For the future noir city is more nightmare vision, more anxiety than wish-fulfilment.[12]

The primary metaphor of entropy in *Tomorrow's End* is the ruined arc of the Sydney Harbour Bridge, framing the eerily illuminated bulk of a modernist skyscraper whose eminence suggests an imposing and sinister fortress. The highrise is a survivor from the late twentieth century. In 1990s' Sydney, its mirror-like frontage houses the 'Global and Interstellar Research Institute'. By the twenty-sixth century the Institute has become 'Globecorp', a planet-wide totalitarian regime with its own private army ('GlobeCops'), and digital surveillance systems which monitor and control dwindling resources and an increasingly feral population. An elite few control the planet backed by security forces and a military-style organisation of career minions. These bland corporate cogs cheerfully 'modify/brainwipe' antisocial elements, condemning them to a life as worker-drones for the corporation.

Outside the Corporate Centre the populace is divided into two groups. The first consists of neo-tribal scavengers who evade the surveillance of the GlobeCops by cannibalising the debris of past commodities and technologies. Silverthorn – the time-travelling antagonist of the series – is chief of one such tribe. Their vestimentary code is paramilitary, with breastplates reminiscent of tyre treads, bandoliers of junk metal and battered military helmets rent to reveal bushy growths of unkempt hair beneath. The tribes are a cargo cult: the origin of their clothing (recycled waste) exemplifies the fate of contemporary commodities in this dystopian future. The second group consists of street and slum dwellers who inhabit the pavement level surrounding the Globecorp fortress. These are a heavily monitored social underclass whose resistance, if present, remains covert. The *mise en scène* of this netherworld is reminiscent of the anarchic, poly-racial Los Angeles depicted in Ridley Scott's *Blade Runner*. Globecorp's Sydney underworld is also, if less insistently, a post-modern urban melting pot.[13]

Distrust of corporate techno-futures is also traced in *Escape from Jupiter*. Kumiko's view of the colony she is reluctantly visiting is shaped by consumer culture. The holoscreen she views on the journey disgorges not entertainment but heroic promotions for the mining corporation's colonial enterprise. This scene appears to cite the floating 'babble machines' from *Blade Runner*'s LA, which hover above the streets dispensing, as Staiger puts it, 'not news but ads'.[14] A subject of urban marketing ideology, Kumiko expects the other teens to be 'neanderthals', without style or consumer credibility.

The cityscapes represented in these programmes reflect an anxious engagement with the future of commodity production. Commodities and communications technologies are a source of pleasure for the teens represented. While the dark side of consumer and information culture is traced in the twin spectres of digital surveillance and planetary degradation, a future without entertainment culture and peer fashions would be a reality in which the difference between adolescence and adulthood could be erased. The bland but worthy 'utopian' society of thirty-first-century Sydney presents an austere picture of what such a world might mean for the future of adolescence.

### Organic versus Acquisitive Technologies

The discourse of ecologism is a potent subtext to the television dramas analysed in this chapter. Typically, the junction at which the utopian and dystopian timelines divide is forged by the misuse of technology. Certain kinds of science and its technologies are demonised while others are humanised and embraced as a means of resolving global problems. Anxiety is primarily invested in military and consumerist technologies which lead to environmental degradation and the production of waste.

Valorised knowledges and technologies are coded as organic. Typically feminised and/or infantilised, they are associated with nurturing, healing or play. In *The Girl from*

*Tomorrow*, thirty-first-century technology is made possible by amplifying the potential of the human brain. Its 'transducers' and generators produce no waste products but yield enough energy for both time and space travel. Alana and her female mentors are capable of using this organic power as a weapon, yet they choose to use it to heal – in a medical and an ecological sense. The invention of the transducer is the catalyst which enables the rehabilitation of the planet after the Great Disaster.[15]

Information technology in the service of monopoly capitalism is associated with digital surveillance and curtailment of civil liberties. Conversely, IT may be coded as feminine or toylike. The wrist computer, PJ, in *The Girl from Tomorrow*, is a mentor and friend, complete with a youthful male voice. The 'Helen' computer on the Orca Research Station in *Ocean Girl* is nominatively gendered female; she plays a beneficent and educative role for the young crew of the vessel. Play technologies – from the holographic gaming simulator in *Escape from Jupiter* to the robot dog of the programme's younger male sibling – are optimistically presented.

Technologies appropriated or operated by the teen or child are also recuperated. The ludic space of the special effect in science-fiction cinema, often associated with child characters, has been read as an optimistic sign of the future of technology. Infantilised technology features in the resolution of dystopic regimes in the series under discussion. The girl from tomorrow prevents global nuclear destruction by attaching her computer, PJ, to one of Globecorp's miniature surveillance droids, which has been appropriated as a toy by Jenny Kelly's kid brother. The merging of organic technology (a prototype transducer), the childlike computer and a child's toy is able to deflect the nuclear missile and save the world. A similar narrative motif is found in *Escape from Jupiter*. Kumiko's computer – contemptuously dismissed by Duffy as 'a child's toy' – is launched into space to decoy a rogue defence satellite away from its attack on the KL5 Station. In each case a teenage girl sacrifices her major object of cathexis, her techno-friend. In the hands of adult and corporate culture, technology becomes inimical to life. When operated by teens, however, as play, quest or special effect, it is redeemed.

## Conclusion

In the teen drama series discussed in this chapter, science fiction's speculative exploration of alterity reinforces tropes concerning the *difference* of youth. Generational markers of separation between adult and adolescent culture (such as vestimentary codes, musical and linguistic practices) are linked to the trope of the alien child. Jenny Kelly, with her purple hair and hyperloud music is 'sister under the skin' to the 'girl from tomorrow', whose domestic incompetence results in disasters such as microwaved laundry. Both are misfits, their behaviour inexplicable to harried and bemused parents.

The mismatching of adult and teen subjectivities also functions as an ironic ploy in these narratives. Contemporary institutions – the police, the welfare agencies, media and politics – are rendered strange through the puzzlement of 'alien' teens. The liminal status of the alien or time-travelling teen exposes the crises within contemporary social and economic relations. Camp and comic modalities are used to reinforce an ironic truth: that teens also find these institutions alien.

Youth on other worlds, in other futures, is shown to be *different*. This difference may offer a subversive alternative to constructions of 'exemplary' teen subjectivity. Can teens be educated as social partners by means of a mentor–apprenticeship model? Can misfits challenge the possessive practices which create social disadvantage through the commodification of basic resources? Would a world without the pleasures of consumption be a world in which adolescence itself could not be expressed?

Finally, these series trace anxieties about the technological and ecological future. Left to follow its own trajectory, rapacious venture capitalism threatens to deliver planetary annihilation. The global exploitative regimes designed by adults disenfranchise young people from their share in the promise of 'tomorrow': 'Future? What future?' The future might be utopian, as in *The Girl from Tomorrow*, with an organic, telepathic technology. More probable, these series seem to suggest, are dystopic techno-futures, the culmination of the violent and acquisitive trends of our own era.

## Notes

1. Angela McRobbie, *Feminism and Youth Culture: From 'Jackie' to 'Just Seventeen'* (Basingstoke and London: Macmillan Education, 1991).
2. Australian Broadcasting Authority (2002), *Children's Television Standards 1999*. Reproduced from the Australian Broadcasting Authority's website: http://www.aba.gov.au/tv/content/childtv/standards/#1, cited 13 June 2002.
3. On the infantilisation of spectacular cinema, see Barry Keith Grant, '"Sensuous Elaboration": Reason and the Visible in the Science-Fiction Film', in Annette Kuhn (ed.), *Alien Zone 2: The Spaces of Science Fiction Cinema* (London and New York: Verso, 1999), pp. 22–8.
4. Annette Kuhn, 'Introduction', in Kuhn, *Alien Zone 2*, p. 3.
5. The term is an adaptation of Bob Connell's category, 'protest masculinity'. R.W. Connell, *The Men and the Boys* (Cambridge: Polity Press, 2000).
6. Interestingly, Jenny's body is normalised in her visit to the thirty-first century in *Tomorrow's End*. The holistic technology of the future cleanses the abject elements of her punk persona – signified by the removal of the dye from her hair – and paves the way for Jenny's reintegration into the familial world of 1990 in the closure of the series.
7. The science-fiction film's aesthetics of destruction have been analysed by Susan Sontag in her chapter 'The Imagination of Disaster', in Sontag, *Against Interpretation* (New York: Delta, 1966), pp. 208–25.
8. Linda Mizejewski, 'Action Bodies in Futurist Spaces: Bodybuilder Stardom as Special Effect', in Kuhn, *Alien Zone 2*, pp. 152–72.
9. Patricia Holland, *What Is a Child: Popular Images of Childhood* (London: Virago, 1992), pp. 8–22.
10. Ibid., pp. 100–21.
11. Janet Staiger, 'Future Noir: Contemporary Representations of Visionary Cities', in Kuhn, *Alien Zone 2*, p. 97.
12. Ibid., p. 100.
13. See David Desser, 'Race, Space and Class: The Politics of Cityscapes in Science-Fiction

Films', in Kuhn, *Alien Zone 2*, pp. 80–96. Both Desser's and Staiger's analyses share insights with Fredric Jameson's work on science fiction and post-modernism, most recently in *Postmodernism, or the Cultural Logic of Late Capitalism* (Durham, NC: Duke University Press, 1991).
14. Staiger, 'Future Noir', p. 114.
15. The trope of telepathic or quasi-mystical technology features in another series of the 1990s, Jonathan Schiff's *Ocean Girl*. Merging the genres of science fiction, mythic fantasy and the Robinsonnade, *Ocean Girl*'s narrative juxtaposes the organic science of marine biology with the acquisitive and xenophobic technology of 'Praxis', an organisation vaguely reminiscent of the CIA.

# 3

# Chosen Ones: Reading the Contemporary Teen Heroine

**Jenny Bavidge**

> BUFFY: When this is over I'm thinking pineapple pizza and teen video movie fest. Possibly something from the Ringwald oeuvre.
> ('What's My Line? Part 2', *Buffy the Vampire Slayer*, 2: 10)

This chapter outlines an approach to the teen series *Buffy the Vampire Slayer* that, I believe, has been sorely neglected by the critical writing produced on the programme to date. Analysis of the show has frequently concentrated on its feminist credentials: is Buffy herself a positive role model for adolescent girls, sexually sussed and politically aware, or is she a 'girly girl through and through', as Rachel Fudge suggests?[1] However, such perspectives tend to ignore something fundamentally important about the series: that it enables, and has offered up, an interrogation of the social and cultural construction of female adolescence. That is, over its seasons, *Buffy* has explored how one comes to be – and, indeed, what it means to be – a girl. In this regard, *Buffy* can be seen as the latest in a long line of Western popular cultural artefacts that have concerned themselves with 'girlhood' – a lineage that stretches back to (at least) the nineteenth century.

Buffy, of course, is not merely a teenager, but also a heroine: as such, it is necessary for this chapter to explore the series' intersecting representations of female adolescence and female heroism. The richly intertextual nature of *Buffy the Vampire Slayer* invites us to read its protagonist's daring, courage and bravery in the light of other popular incarnations of female heroism. Indeed, she could be seen as both a product of, and a reaction to, previous representations of heroic women and girls. From such a perspective, her antecedents would seem primarily to be female characters depicted in comics and fantasy television and it is this contextual network which some critics have commented on.[2] Buffy's generic 'female heroine' roots have been traced to a range of sources, contemporary, classical and mythical – and, on occasion, a collision of all three. Her adventures are read by Frances Early, for example, in the light of 'a rebel warrior narrative that harkens back to the mythic and historical tradition of the disruptive woman warrior hero at the same time that it beckons us forward, urging viewers to contemplate a refashioned humanitarian and partly androgynous citizen ideal for the twentieth century'.[3] Rather than following this particular critical trajectory, I wish to consider Buffy as the latest incarnation of a specific tradition of teenage heroine in popular and literary culture: the figure of the 'Anglo-American Girl' (a term I will define shortly). Further, this chapter will suggest that *Buffy*'s insistent foregrounding of the complexities of such a character is a crucial component in the show's wider comments on the social identities of contemporary girls and their cultures.

*Buffy*'s treatment of female heroism is seemingly motivated by series creator Joss Whedon's much quoted desire to see the typical victim of Hollywood slasher movies turn the tables on her aggressors. As such, the programme clearly devotes much energy to recasting and, to a debatable extent, subverting familiar generic signifiers of feminine weakness and victimhood perpetuated by horror and melodrama film and TV targeted at teenage audiences. This aspect of the programme deserves – and has received – substantial critical interrogation. However, attention also needs to be paid to Buffy's connection with representations of girls as figures of social redemption and salvation outside of sci-fi or fantasy genres. The vicissitudes of girlhood, particularly the distinction between good and bad girls, is notably present in much contemporary teen TV. Indeed, in certain respects, such characters as Liz Parker in *Roswell High* or Lana Lang in *Smallville* echo the models of ideal girlhood and the heroic 'Girl' established in the nineteenth century more obviously than vampire-slaying Buffy does.

Here it is necessary to briefly define the 'Anglo-American Girl', as a specific character type (although, in the next section of this chapter, I will sketch a more thorough history of this concept). The term has come to critical prominence in recent years through the writings of, among others, Frances B. Cogan, Catherine Driscoll, Carol Dymhouse, Sally Mitchell and the authors corralled together in a collection of essays by Sharon Mazzarella and N. O. Pecora, all of whom offer accounts of the Girl in cultural history and popular culture.[4] The term is used by these authors (and others) to define a specific model of femininity within wider cultural definitions of girlhood and womanhood, emerging from the eighteenth century onwards. The creation of the Girl is closely bound up with the ideology promoted within the sphere of a developing and separate girls' culture itself, and with discourses concerned with the education, upbringing, social roles and welfare of young women. The Girl is the embodiment of an ideal of female adolescence: her defining characteristics are intelligence, independence and playfulness. Stories in which the Girl features dwell on her education or her struggles, rather than romance; she ultimately turns away from a period of adventurousness, back towards a life of domesticity. Although we can note similar concerns associated with the heroines of the romance and Gothic traditions, the Girl attains her most distinct expression in the late nineteenth and twentieth centuries, in her articulation by literary and popular texts aimed specifically at teenage girls. Key texts in this lineage include the novels of Frances Hodgson Burnett (*The Little Princess*, *The Secret Garden*), Susan Coolidge (*What Katy Did*), Louisa May Alcott (*Little Women*, *Good Wives*), L.M. Montgomery (the *Anne of Green Gables* saga), and the school stories of Angela Brazil and Enid Blyton.

If we read Buffy as the latest manifestation of this 'Anglo-American Girl', then we are clearly placing her in a category distinct from more general feminist approaches to the representation of 'women' or the 'feminine'. And yet, the complex history of 'Girlhood' is, obviously, intertwined with, and inflected by, feminist understandings of women's history and shifting representations. In recent years, for instance, there has been a growing sense in contemporary theories of girlhood that the implicit and explicit 'Be Good' message of literary and popular culture targeted at girls has, in the post-feminist period, been replaced by a distinct, more complex understanding of 'what it feels like for a girl'. This discussion is the latest stage in a long-established debate over the particular nature and place of the Girl, a subject position which is largely defined by the academic, medical, psychological and cultural discourses which have identified her as an object of inquiry. Viewers of contemporary teen TV are, therefore, receptors of often very similar tensions regarding the identity and propriety of their heroines as were the readers of literary, cinematic and popular constructions of the Girl in previous generations.

This chapter suggests that this similar reception occurs because the Anglo-American Girl – whether a kick-boxing ex-cheerleader, a jolly English boarding-school gal or an all-American achiever – is always a generic construction, and, crucially, one which has consistently foregrounded the performative nature of girlhood itself. The debate around the feminist credentials of *Buffy the Vampire Slayer* (or indeed any TV show which depicts girls made strong, by supernatural means or not) is understandably caught up in unravelling the problematic politics of a show which demonstrates many of the contradictions and complexities of third-wave feminism. In so doing, it risks missing one of the most valuable and enabling principles of the show. What *Buffy* does so successfully is dramatise the Anglo-American Girl as a construct – one which is useful, charming and fun, and yet also artificial, potentially dangerous, and possibly doomed. The very metaphysics of *Buffy* underlines this: the Slayer is always a young girl who, when 'called' to her mystical duty, discovers within herself an identity and a destiny which is inescapable and essential. She must be educated and guided, and learn how to channel her powers. Her gifts are redemptive and protective, but, if misused, misplaced or manipulated by the wrong forces, wield enormously destructive power. As such, the Slayer character is, in effect, a correlative to the position of girls in society more generally.

Indeed, existing alongside the show's depiction of the particular nature of Girl heroism is a more general examination of the way in which girlhood is seen to be a series of culturally determined roles and performances. As Catherine Driscoll has suggested, '*Buffy* is as much about feminine adolescence as it is about monsters.'[5] That is, the show has a further reach than the 'high school is hell' metaphor: '*Buffy* . . . is an index for specific technologies of the self – locating the contact or exchanges between disciplinary powers (such as the school, state and parents) and self disciplines (processes of producing a self).'[6] Buffy might yearn to be 'just a normal girl', but finds, much as the teenage Superman does over in *Smallville*, that 'normality' is itself a fictive category.

In the following sections of this chapter, I hope to pick up on, and explore, some of these concerns surrounding the cultural representations of idealised and heroic girlhood – and the ways in which *Buffy the Vampire Slayer* reworks or reinvigorates them. Of course, my discussion is necessarily limited by the length of this chapter. Following a brief overview of the Girl's history, then, I will focus in on two specific areas of interest: the interrelation between female adolescence, practices of consumption and norms of beauty; and the ways in which narratives of Girlhood expose their central characters as negotiating, interrogating and playing with performed roles.

## The Cultural History of the American Girl

>BUFFY: *Whistle while you work/so hard, all day/to be like other girls,/to fit in in this glittering world . . .*
>
> ('Once More, With Feeling', *Buffy the Vampire Slayer*, 6: 7)

Ruth Saxton, in her study of the figure of the Girl in contemporary fiction, admits that she had expected to find that narratives of post-feminist girlhood 'would stand in stark contrast to configurations of girlhood in earlier fiction'.[7] Given the increased visibility and social power of girls and women, such fictions could be expected to reflect and mark a significant break in the roles and images used within, and presented by, narratives of girlhood, and open up a critical space from which to examine the culture which produced them.

> To some extent, this notion has proven correct, in that new fictions of the Girl provide access to a constellation of themes and narrative patterns – including race and ethnicity, sexual orientation, class, female subjectivity, and nationalism – in ways far different than their earlier predecessors of centuries, or even decades, ago. However, despite the important ways in which the texts addressed . . . break open and into older narratives and plots of girlhood, I have found that contemporary literary investigations into the Girl continue to envision girlhood according to tropes and plots familiar since the dawn of novelistic fiction.[8]

Right up to the present moment, the notion of the Girl – her identity, her body and sexuality, as well as her moral, physical and intellectual education – has been recognised as a site around which many of culture's concerns and anxieties cohere. In response to this, what Vallone and Nelson call the 'protean quality' of the Girl as 'simultaneous subject, object and opponent of cultural classification'[9] has been a focus of critical feminist attention, in attempts to trace the roots of such discourses. Particular consideration has been paid to the various idealised or heroic figures offered as points of identification or role models (or conversely, warnings) to adolescent girls in popular biographies of 'great and noble women', in school and college stories, as well as magazines and comic-book narratives. The roles played out in these tales are frequently recognisable from any survey of representations of female activity, including character types such as the domestic angel, the dutiful daughter or the helpless romantic heroine.

However, the texts which seek to define and describe the Girl as a particular kind of focus are more varied than this implies. They may include, for example, the Girl as fighter for the cause of personal morality, temperance or chastity; they may focus on the physical prowess which proves a healthy mind and body; they may also champion female communities such as all-girl schools and colleges and display a growing regard for academic achievement in the idealisation of the college girl. The new breed of heroines of nineteenth- and early twentieth-century American, British and Canadian fiction, such as

Pollyanna, Rebecca (of Sunnybrook Farm), Frances Hodgson Burnett's Mary Lennox and Sara Crewe, Jo March, Katy Carr or Anne Shirley, through to Enid Blyton's schoolgirls, typically yearn for and, for a temporary period, experience success outside of the domestic sphere. Their relationships with boys are marked by jolly comradeship rather than romance, and love affairs are sensibly postponed until the appropriate life-lessons have been learned, and the appeal of the domestic has asserted itself over the desire for fame and fortune in the wider world. Education, growing self-knowledge and sometimes loss and tragedy, temper impulsiveness and ambition and gently turn the Girl homewards. Sense is valued over sensibility in such stories; youthful romance and energy is seen to be channelled into usefulness and clear-sightedness. Speaking specifically of the American Girl, Lynn Vallone notes:

> The active, intelligent, playful, and loving tomboy, a popular conception of nineteenth-century girlhood, embodies, in part, the ideals of Real Womanhood and conduct ideology, even as she strains against their boundaries. She will become, with time and training, a capable American woman.[10]

The style of these novels, as Henry Jenkins has pointed out, contrasts with the 'purple prose' and 'adventure island' settings of boys' books of the same period, tending instead to 'describe naturalistic environments, similar to the realm of readers' daily experience'; further, 'the tone is more apt to be confessional than confrontational'.[11] Even the more melodramatic or romantic stories from this era retain a similar style, setting and narrative trajectory. Often, however she manages it, the heroic Girl of these stories will prove to be the salvation of her community or family and particularly, of her father or father figure. This popular narrative model is, of course, not exclusive to the novel and transfers easily to other media: we find it in the stage and film versions of the story of Little Orphan Annie and the standard plotlines of Shirley Temple films, for example.

Interestingly, Joss Whedon's favourite book, according to an interview with one of *Buffy*'s writers, is Burnett's *The Little Princess*, a classic of the genre.[12] In this 1903 novel, Burnett's much put-upon Sara is orphaned when her rich father dies. She is left alone and powerless, but for an innate sweet nature (which will inevitably bring her reward), her ability to be fiercely imaginative and her drive to keep alive a deep faith in her own worth in the face of wicked adults and contemptuous schoolgirls (who are not unlike Buffy's cheerleader-tormentor Cordelia). Everyone can find their 'inner princess', Sara insists, although Burnett implies that some princesses are more real than others.[13] It is Sara's virtues of compassion and charity which prove to be her salvation, and also enable her to enrich the life of her surrogate father.

Contemporary popular culture has also promoted this version of girlhood, even to very young girls. In her studies of the representation and the viewing and reading practices of pre-teen girls, Walkerdine suggests that the characters of stories in *Bunty* and *Tracey*, British comics aimed at girls aged six to eleven, are always marked as being 'selfless, helpful'. Their triumph over adversity comes from precisely these qualities, and also from learning to turn 'the other cheek'.[14] Such stories and models of heroism develop into the narratives McRobbie describes as appearing in magazines such as *Jackie* or *Just Seventeen*, which Walkerdine's readers would graduate to, stories wherein the heroine 'replaces all vestiges or traces of adolescent sexuality . . . with concepts of love, passion, and eternity'.[15] Third-wave feminism has not improved the situation: in McRobbie's latest accounts of the representation of women in popular culture, 'emancipation has become depoliticized and individualized' and 'slim blondeness is the zenith of young women's aspirations . . . [F]eminism finds no place in the world of "TV blondes".'[16]

There are certainly parallels to be drawn and lines to be traced from the cultural moment of the Anglo-American Girl of the late nineteenth century to Buffy the slim, blonde, Californian princess. Certain themes recur: the importance of education; the difficulty of splitting duties between home and work; and, perhaps primarily, the search for what it means to be a girl – that is, whether it's something she's 'born with' or an identity she can paint on along with her mascara. In the following two sections of this chapter, I wish to explore two specific aspects of girlhood that *Buffy the Vampire Slayer* engages with: first the ideals of beauty and consumption which are associated with female adolescence; and second, notions of victimhood, roleplaying and performance.

## Demonising Popular Culture: Buffy and Lolita

> DAWN: My sister thinks I'm staying at your house.
> JANICE: Oh. The Mominator thinks I'm staying at yours. Can't believe they fell for that one. Like, own a TV?
>
> ('All the Way', *Buffy the Vampire Slayer*, 6: 6)

The Anglo-American Girl is not only a source and symbol of optimism within Western culture. She is also a possible point of weakness: a potential victim, willing or otherwise, of the projections or temptations of the corrupt adult world. As such, her representation can operate as a model, warning adolescent girls how *not* to behave. Often, nineteenth- and early twentieth-century novels for girls closely followed and reflected the guidance and admonitions of conduct and advice books.[17]

This process seems only to have accelerated and intensified in the contemporary media, where the ass-kicking Girl is also always a lipsticked lovely (as the Maybelline cosmetics advert states, 'Maybe she's born with it . . .').[18] The use of make-up, and its association here with performative identity, is a crucial component in the constitution of Girlhood, as it links exemplary female adolescence with ideals of beauty and consumption. As Saxton argues:

> The body of the young girl – whether athlete or potential Miss America – is the site of heated battles, not only among parents, teachers and coaches, but also among those who would exploit her sexuality, lure her to internalize their fantasies and purchase their products. . . . Told to develop her mind, she is simultaneously bombarded with messages that reinforce the ancient message that her body is the primary source of her power, that she is primarily decorative, that she should have a model's body, that she should be beautiful within a narrow range of cultural stereotypes.[19]

The Girl's link with pop culture is thus figured as imprisonment and entrapment, rather than the emancipation latterly claimed for Girl Power-style consumer choice – and it is imprisonment figured specifically as the direct result of adult manipulation and projection. This may partly explain the suspicion many teen TV adolescents have of adults: indeed, the uneasiness with which the teen characters of Buffy observe the adult world has been noted in a number of articles.[20]

How does *Buffy the Vampire Slayer* configure the relationship between these elements, circulating around the construction of the Girl – adult manipulation, standards of feminine beauty, the intoxicating nature of popular culture? As a starting point, it is worth noting that, with her tweedy, English, literary mentor, her devotion to sugary junk foods, pop culture and fashion, Buffy has shades of Nabokov's Lolita about her (although of course, unlike Humbert Humbert, Giles is scrupulously decent). Indeed, the particular antagonism in *Buffy* between a heavy-handed, patriarchal and anachronistic European culture (embodied in the heartless and incompetent Watchers' Council) and lighter (if not safer) America recalls the widespread critical reading of *Lolita* as a text about the clash of Old World literary values and New World consumer culture.[21] Lolita's victimhood is associated with her seduction by the popular culture she adores, figured as a slavish devotion to mass culture, itself feminine, frivolous and empty, and most often associated with teenage girls.[22] However, while Buffy is often linked with the kitsch delights of pop culture, she is never condemned for it. Buffy catches Giles out in an episode in which she can mind-read, when she hears him think, 'Look at her shoes. If a fashion magazine told her to, she'd wear cats strapped to her feet' ('Earshot', 3: 18). In an earlier episode, she and Giles argue over the music she listens to while training:

GILES: I know music. Music has notes. This is noise.
BUFFY: I'm aerobicizing. I *must* have the beat.
GILES: Wonderful. You work on your muscle tone while my brain dribbles out of my ears.
('The Dark Age', 2: 8)

Giles' Series One 'stuffy librarian' image becomes more layered in later episodes where he's revealed to be an ex-punk and rock fan with a dubious record collection.[23] Indeed, rather than popular culture itself being presented as debasing, Buffy's own inability to participate fully in the popular culture, particularly the *girl* culture around her (for example, her love of ice-dancing is rarely indulged), is intended more to arouse the viewer's sympathy than to invite condemnation.

## Performing Girlhood

XANDER: Hey, Red. What you got in the basket, little girl?
BUFFY: Weapons.
('Fear Itself', *Buffy the Vampire Slayer*, 4: 4)

Given the complexity of the figure of the Girl and the various intertwinings of cultural representations of girlhood, how does a contemporary product of popular culture mediate the heroic girl? Indeed, given that the category of heroism is equally contested, is such a role still possible? Again, looking at *Buffy*'s treatment of its antecedents shows the tension created by a narrative format that is both referring to a generic tradition of victimhood and self-consciously reinventing it as it goes along. Red Riding Hood, who could perhaps be seen as the original incarnation of Carol Clover's 'Final Girl', is a figure who has appeared more than once in the diegesis of Buffy.[24] Jack Zipes's illuminating study of the history of this particular girl, around whom there is an obsessive amount of interest (latterly elevated within contemporary advertisements, as Zipes notes, to her 'commodified appearance as a sex object'[25]), shows how the tale is used within our 'rape culture' as a warning to girls who veer too far from the path. The oral origins of the tale have a happy ending, with Red Riding Hood rescuing herself, and there are conflicting versions through the years between those which end with the the heroine being eaten up, and others which have her escaping and defeating the wolf. Most renderings of the story, however, according to Zipes, have 'transformed a hopeful oral tale about the initiation of a young girl into a tragic one of violence in which the girl is blamed for her own violation'.[26] Zipes is able to include in his collection several modern versions of the tale in which the tables are turned on the wolf,[27] and mentions Angela Carter's celebrated reworking, 'The Company of Wolves', in which Red Riding Hood abandons boring domesticity and runs off with the Wolf instead. However, 'for the most part', he suggests, 'the traditional images have prevailed and continue to be circulated by a culture industry primarily interested in making profits by gambling with our subliminal sexual phantasies and reinforcing male notions of rape'.[28]

Zipes argues that 'the changes made in the discourse about the fictional helpless girls dubbed Little Red Riding Hood – her discipline and punishment – indicate real shifts, conflicts, and ruptures in the Western civilizing process'.[29] While Buffy dresses as Red Riding Hood in the Halloween episode of Season Four, 'Fear Itself', she really becomes such a girl in the episode 'Helpless' (3: 13), when she faces a particularly horrible wolf, her powers gone, made into a 'real girl' at last, although without her consent.[30] Her vulnerability as she walks the streets after dark, tormented by catcallers, eventually attacked and having to be rescued by Giles, is marked by her red coat. This episode is one which, in hindsight, has more of the uneasy edge of the later Season Six, in that there is real danger of Buffy's rape by this particularly unpleasant demon, who is 'profiled' in the manner of a serial killer and is reported to have tortured and killed his female victims.[31] Even here, however, the aspect of girlhood which is most difficult to claim as 'performed', physical vulnerability, is overcome by the kind of intelligent strategy traditionally adopted by the Red Riding Hoods who survive.

Buffy's Slayer identity distances her from the other 'destinies' of girlhood she might otherwise have adopted. Audiences have watched her experiment with a series of roles and costumes, adopted and dispensed with, not always at will. In 'Homecoming' (3: 5), Cordelia and Buffy's battle to be crowned Queen sends up the beauty pageant of glamourised girlhood, with the kind of 'feminist camp' which Patricia Pender identifies as one of the show's rhetorical strategies.[32] Such storylines underline the frequent anxiety about appearances and popularity expressed in the show, but also point out the performative nature of this kind of girl, a theme which is also expressed in the number of episodes which deal with forces of mind-control, possession and doubles. In 'Never Leave Me' (5: 15), Buffy unmasks a *Stepford Wives*-inspired villain who has created a 'perfect' robotic girlfriend who will always look pretty, enthusiastically praise her boyfriend/owner and never refuse to 'put out'. What could have been a one-off 'Villain of the Week' storyline is, in fact, extended through Seasons Five and Six, as a robotic Buffy is created, who has all the Slayer strength of the 'original', but also displays a ridiculous level of girlish subservience. While the 'Buffybot' episodes *are* camp, there is also a deep diegetic uneasiness about the misogynist impulse behind the scheme, a disquiet intensified in a later episode in which the creator of the girlfriend robot finally murders a girl he has tried to hypnotise into similarly subservient behaviour. The need for girls and women to be on their guard against such controlling forces and assuming the role of girlish helplessness is a message frequently repeated in *Buffy*, appearing, for example, in episodes such as 'Ted' (2: 11) and 'Beauty and the Beasts' (3: 4).

Another episode which explores this theme is 'Halloween' (2: 6), in which on Halloween, the annual event described by Buffy herself as 'come as you aren't night', our heroine is transformed by her enchanted costume into an eighteenth-century girl. As she swoons, shrieks and trips her way through the episode, complete with lacy pink dress and tumbling locks, Buffy discovers that being a girl is no fun, and is dangerous to boot. Having worried prior to her transformation that her boyfriend Angel (a 240-year-old vampire) is turned off by her modern lack of girlish propriety and grooming, she is gratifyingly told that the girls Angel used to know were 'boring'. In fact, she discovers the reason why the category of the Girl, as envisioned in the nineteenth century, has become all but redundant. According to Vallone and Nelson:

> Much of the tension surrounding the Girl . . . clearly emanates from her ambiguity of position: by virtue of her status (position, inexperience, supposed purity and so forth) she is a girl – but what if these status indicators were absent? In other words, what happens if femininity turns out to be learned rather than innate? This very tension becomes not only a motive for the cultural controlling of girlhood, but also an energy source enabling girls – as they moved over into the category of 'young women' – to gain a measure of control on their own part. Without the Victorian Girl then, the contemporary woman becomes in some ways unimaginable.[33]

By defining herself *against* certain categories of girlhood and re-creating those which are still haunting popular culture, Buffy formulates new versions of old myths. She becomes a contemporary manifestation of the teen heroine, often confronted with many of the same issues, albeit within different contexts (the tension between social and domestic duty, erotic desire versus family). But the most radical movement the show makes is its explicit engagement with femininity as performance and its questioning of the traditional narrative trajectories of female heroism. Although at the point of writing, we are unable to say for sure what Buffy's eventual fate will be, the fantastical metaphysics of the show demand and enable a different end for its Girl heroine than was possible for her forebears, or is likely for her contemporaries in other teen TV shows. This has been recognised by

Catherine Driscoll, who points out that *Buffy* 'exceeds the teen TV genre' in its parodic use of the generic 'frustrated romance' narrative: 'Buffy remains an exception to the generic convention of romance as growing up because she cannot proceed to any absorbing future domesticity. The destiny articulated for Buffy is magical and deathly rather than heteronormative bliss.'[34]

In this way, Buffy eludes the traditional narrative modes by which the contradictions of the Girl identity were resolved in earlier fiction for girls, and although she may yet meet a sticky end, it is unlikely to be one of Red Riding Hood-style punitive narrative closure.

## Conclusions

The Girl continues to be an ambivalent creation in her cultural context and for her intended audience, retaining her ability to act as a redemptive or threatening figure. Both heroic and vulnerable, she continues many of the negotiations begun by earlier Girls, but with a post-modern, arguably post-feminist twist.

That such representations might be produced by teen TV is perhaps surprising, given that the expectations of the genre have been relatively low in terms of innovation or narrative experimentation, expectations associated not just with television aimed at teenagers, but also films of the same type. Such narratives tend to celebrate difference and individuality, while encouraging an ultimate reconciliation with societal codes of propriety. Contemporary teen TV has tended to walk this conservative path. Indeed, teen TV has often aimed either to 'understand' the alienated teen, or to proffer distraction from genuine social concerns. *Buffy* does not adopt either of these polemical strategies, and the show's address to its audience in relation to the treatment of 'issues' has been particularly innovative.

As Rhonda Wilcox has argued, the logic of the show cannot allow for the kind of 'special' episodes which feature 'unmediated presentations of social topics such as AIDS or alcoholism', common in series such as *Beverly Hills 90210* or *Party of Five*.[35] The open-ended quality of serial television is often (partially) curtailed by such definitive moral statements, whereas *Buffy*'s self-reflexivity has enabled the show to retain a 'protean' narrative form which aptly reflects its depiction of, and attention to, shifting gender identity. *Buffy* does not need to employ the 'very special issue' formula of other teen TV to discuss the problems of the contemporary girl, because it can approach these struggles through its generic references to the vulnerability of girls and the problematic nature of their identity. The show returns again and again to its most dynamic theme, the insistent protest against the violence done to 'real' girls and women. It does so through the limitless potential of fantasy narratives, but especially through reference to the past and present trials of the Girl-as-heroine, consistently showing that to be 'just a girl' is often an epic task in itself.

## Notes

1. Rachel Fudge, 'The Buffy Effect: Or, a Tale of Cleavage and Marketing', *Bitch: Feminist Responses to Pop Culture*, vol. 10, no. 18 (1999), p. 21. A number of different positions on this topic have been articulated in the two recent collections of articles on the series: see Roz Kaveney, ed., *Reading the Vampire Slayer: The Unofficial Critical Companion to Buffy and Angel*

(London: I.B. Tauris, 2001), and Rhonda V. Wilcox and David Lavery, eds, *Fighting the Forces: What's at Stake in Buffy the Vampire Slayer* (Lanham, MD: Rowman & Littlefield, 2002). *Buffy*'s feminist credentials are also frequently pursued on the discussion list attached to the e-journal *Slayage* (archived at http://www.slayage.tv/). See also Irene Karras, 'The Third Wave's Final Girl: *Buffy the Vampire Slayer*', *Thirdspace*, vol. 1, no. 2 (March 2002), archived at http://www.thirdspace.ca.

2. Catherine Johnson, for instance, has compared Buffy to the 'highly feminised action heroes in series like *Charlie's Angels* . . . and *Wonder Woman* . . .': Johnson, '*Buffy the Vampire Slayer*', in Glen Creeber (ed.), *The Television Genre Book* (London: BFI, 2001), p. 42.
3. Frances Early, 'Staking Her Claim: Buffy the Vampire Slayer as Transgressive Woman Warrior', *Journal of Popular Culture*, vol. 35, no. 3 (Winter 2000), p. 26.
4. See Frances B. Cogan, *The All-American Girl: The Ideal of Real Womanhood in Mid-Nineteenth Century America* (Athens: University of Georgia Press, 1989); Carol Dymhouse, *Girls Growing up in Late Victorian and Edwardian England* (London: Routledge and Kegan Paul, 1981); Sally Mitchell, *The New Girl: Girl's Culture in England, 1880–1915* (New York: Cornell University Press). For accounts which address the Girl in contemporary culture, see Sharon Mazzarella and N. O. Pecora (eds), *Growing up Girls: Popular Culture and the Construction of Identity* (Boston, MA: Peter Lang, 1999), and Catherine Driscoll, *Girls: Feminine Adolescence in Popular Culture and Cultural Theory* (Columbia, NY: Columbia University Press, 2002). Driscoll's thesis is a Foucauldian 'genealogy of girlhood' and an examination of the defining discursive practices which have created the category of the girl. For a general overview of the critical lineage of the term, see Ruth O. Saxton's introduction to *The Girl: Constructions of the Girl in Contemporary Fiction by Women* (London: Macmillan, 1998), pp. xi–xxix.
5. Driscoll, *Girls*, p. 233.
6. Ibid.
7. Saxton, *The Girl*, p. xi.
8. Ibid.
9. Lynne Vallone and Claudia Nelson, 'Introduction' in Vallone and Nelson (eds), *The Girls' Own: Cultural Histories of the Anglo-American Girl, 1830–1915* (Athens: University of Georgia Press, 1994), p. 5.
10. Lynne Vallone, *Disciplines of Virtue: Girls' Culture in the Eighteenth and Nineteenth Centuries* (New Haven and London: Yale University Press, 1995), p. 119.
11. Henry Jenkins, 'Complete Freedom of Movement: Video Games as Gendered Play Spaces', in Justine Cassell and Henry Jenkins (eds), *From Barbie to Mortal Kombat: Gender and Computer Games* (Cambridge, MA: MIT Press, 1998), p. 281.
12. Nancy Holder, 'Interview with Tracey Forbes', in *Buffy the Vampire Slayer: The Watcher's Guide, Vol. 2* (New York: Pocket, 2000), p. 339. In 'Tough Love' (5: 19), Tara refers to 'Miss Minchin's Select Seminary for Girls', the school at which Burnett's heroine Sara Crewe suffers.
13. When Sara is recognised and delivered from her lowly life, she is restored to princess status, while her fellow sufferer, kitchen-maid Becky, is also rescued and earns her reward as promotion, to the position of Sara's maid.

14. For a discussion of these pre-teen girls, see Valerie Walkerdine, *Daddy's Girl: Young Girls and Popular Culture* (Basingstoke: Macmillan, 1997).
15. Angela McRobbie, '*Jackie* Magazine: Romantic Individualism and the Teenage Girl', in McRobbie, *Feminism and Youth Culture* (London: Macmillan, 2000, 2nd edn), p. 92.
16. Angela McRobbie, 'Sweet Smell of Success?: New Ways of Being Young Women', in McRobbie, *Feminism and Youth Culture*, p. 203 and *passim*.
17. See Vallone, *Disciplines of Virtue*, *passim*, for an account of the close relationship between didactic fiction for girls and non-fiction conduct books.
18. The actress who plays Buffy, Sarah Michelle Gellar, appears in adverts for Maybelline cosmetics, the tagline for which is 'Maybe she's born with it/maybe it's Maybelline'. Beauty, grooming and 'etiquette' books, from nineteenth-century 'Girls' Own' papers to contemporary magazines have helped to define the very nature of what being a girl is. For example, around the time the teenager was being 'invented' by the culture industry, advice books were defining the nature of '*teenliness*': 'You achieve the state of teenliness when you appear and act your most attractive self', suggests Mary Sue Miller in *Here's to You Miss Teen!: A Guide to Good Grooming and Poise* (Philadephia, PA and Toronto: The John C. Winston Company, 1960), p. 205. Readers are also warned that 'everybody knows that a girl must conform to high standards of grooming, or she is lumped in with the bad eggs' (p. 7).
19. Saxton, *The Girl*, p. xxi.
20. See J. P. Williams, 'Choosing Your Own Mother: Mother–Daughter Conflicts in *Buffy*', in Wilcox and Lavery (eds), *Fighting the Forces*, pp. 61–72; and Sarah E. Skwire, 'Whose Side Are You on Anyway? Children, Adults and the Use of Fairy Tales in *Buffy*', in Wilcox and Lavery (eds), *Fighting the Forces*, pp. 195–204.
21. See, for instance Alfred Appel, Jr: 'Tristram in Movielove: "Lolita" at the Movies', in *Russian Literature TriQuarterly* (Ann Arbor, MI), vol. 7 (1973), pp. 343–88; John Haegert, 'The Americanization of Humbert Humbert', in Harold Bloom (ed.), *Lolita* (New York: Chelsea House, 1993), pp. 120–33; Carl Proffer, *Keys to Lolita* (Bloomington: Indiana University Press, 1968).
22. Rachel Bowlby offers an alternative reading which defends the pleasure to be taken in the consumer world, and Lolita's 'glad as an ad' 'poetic' response to it, in her *Shopping with Freud* (London: Routledge, 1993), pp. 65–71.
23. For a survey of the uses of musical references in *Buffy*, see S. Renee Dechert, '"My Boyfriend's in the Band!": *Buffy* and the Rhetoric of Music', in Wilcox and Lavery (eds), *Fighting the Forces*, pp. 218–26.
24. Carol Clover, *Men, Women and Chainsaws: Gender in the Modern Horror Film* (Princeton, NJ: Princeton University Press, 1993). See also Driscoll's discussion in *Girls*, pp. 226–32.
25. Jack Zipes, *The Trials and Tribulations of Little Red Riding Hood* (London: Routledge, 1993, 2nd edn), p. 8.
26. Perrault's 1697 version, which was the first printed version of the tale, ended with the following moral verse: 'One sees here that young children/Especially young girls/Pretty, well brought-up and gentle/Should never listen to anyone who happens by,/And if this occurs, it is not so strange/When the wolf should eat them.' In Zipes, ibid., p. 93.
27. As in James Thurber's 1939 version 'The Girl and the Wolf', which parodies the Perrault

original: 'it was not her grandmother but the wolf, for even in a nightcap a wolf does not look any more like your grandmother than the Metro-Goldwyn lion looks like Calvin Coolidge. So the little girl took an automatic out of her basket and shot the wolf dead. Moral: It is not so easy to fool little girls now as it used to be.' In Zipes, ibid., p. 229.
28. Ibid., p. 356.
29. Ibid., p. 93.
30. Buffy describes her sudden weakness to Giles:

> BUFFY: I have no strength, no co-ordination. I throw knives like . . . like . . .
> GILES: A girl?

As Barbaccia notes, Buffy equates 'normal' with 'helpless'. See Holly G. Barbaccia, 'Buffy in the Terrible House', *Slayage 4*, archived at http://www.middleenglish.org/
31. See Barbaccia's comments on this episode's parodic use of slasher genre motifs: ibid., *passim*.
32. Patricia Pender, '"I'm Buffy and You're . . . History": The Postmodern Politics of *Buffy*', in Wilcox and Lavery (eds), *Fighting the Forces*, p. 39.
33. Vallone and Nelson, 'Introduction', in Vallone and Nelson (eds), *The Girl's Own*, p. 9.
34. Driscoll, *Girls*, p. 233.
35. Rhonda V. Wilcox, '"There Will Never Be a 'Very Special' *Buffy*": *Buffy* and the Monsters of Teen Life', *Journal of Popular Film and Television*, vol. 27, no. 2 (1999), p. 16.

# 4

# Dawson's Creek: 'Quality Teen TV' and 'Mainstream Cult'?

## Matt Hills

If part of teen identity, and part of teen TV, involves managing the wider stigmatisation or even pathologisation of 'the teen' in adult society, then *Dawson's Creek* attempts to powerfully revalue discourses of 'the teenager'. By stressing teen agency and articulacy, *Dawson's Creek* seeks to align itself with cultural systems of value that credit individual agency, self-mastery and self-expression. It carries out these textual moves by 'therapeutising' its teen characters and their relationships, drawing on discourses of therapy and on what Anthony Giddens calls therapy's 'expressions of processes of reflexivity'.[1]

Stressing character reflexivity is one way that *Dawson's Creek* constructs itself as quality teen TV. In the first part of this chapter I will consider how the show depicts different types of intimate relationships, leading many of its online fans to champion either the Joey/Pacey relationship or that of Dawson/Joey. This variation means that *Dawson's Creek* cannot be reduced only to matters of teen romance; instead it introduces reflexivity into its depicted relationships, contrasting different types of romance. This, I want to suggest, gives the show's format a flexibility and sophistication that form part of its bid for cultural value.

I will then move on to consider a further way in which *Dawson's Creek* seeks to textually and intertextually position itself as quality teen TV: through the issue of TV authorship. By stressing its links with creator Kevin Williamson and his work elsewhere, early *Dawson's Creek* nominated Williamson as its author, distinguishing itself from notions of TV as ephemeral, industrially manufactured, trashy or non-cinematic. The show has therefore sought to elevate itself above a devalued 'teen TV' status both textually (via its representations of relationships and character reflexivity) and intertextually (by aligning itself with Williamson's other, high-profile work in teen horror cinema). These bids for 'quality teen TV' status have also been connected with the show's scheduling – designed in the USA and the UK to attract a crossover teen/adult audience.

Contemporary cult TV such as *The X-Files* and *Buffy the Vampire Slayer* is often revalued by its fans as authored: *Buffy* by creator-executive producer-sometime-writer-director Joss Whedon and *The X-Files* by a similarly hyphenated Chris Carter. Such cult TV also inspires dedicated, active fandoms which often fragment around favoured characters or character relationships. Both my discussion of different relationship types and their different fan followings (in the first part of this chapter) and TV authorship (in the second part) suggest that *Dawson's Creek* is akin to cult TV, given its online fandom and its textual markers of quality. In the third part of my discussion I will therefore ask whether *Dawson's Creek* can be meaningfully thought of as cult TV. Although the programme has not been discussed as 'cult' in secondary texts such as the UK magazine *Cult Times*,[2] or indeed in other publicity, I will suggest that its 'quality teen TV' affinities with cult TV mark it out as an example of a 'mainstream cult'.[3] This type of text supports an active, online fan culture and carries textual and intertextual markers of quality TV *without* necessarily being inserted into the 'intertextual network' of texts[4] that are described by fans — and in secondary texts (fanzines, publicity) — as 'cult'.

## Quality Teen TV (I): Reflexivity and the Depiction of Relationships

*Dawson's Creek* reflects changes in social norms of love and relationships in Western cultures of 'late modernity', and does so via its focus on key character relationships. The sociologist Anthony Giddens has analysed love relationships in *The Transformation of Intimacy* (1992), distinguishing between what he terms 'romantic love' and 'confluent love' or the 'pure relationship':

> The clash between the romantic love complex and the pure relationship takes various forms . . . Romantic love depends upon projective identification . . . Projection here creates a feeling of wholeness with the other, no doubt strengthened by established differences between masculinity and femininity, each defined in terms of an antithesis . . . Confluent love is active, contingent love, and therefore jars with the 'for-ever', 'one-and-only' qualities of the romantic love complex.[5]

'Romantic love' — the 'one true love' of soulmates with its discourses of magic and destiny — is hence contrasted by Giddens to the actively worked-on and worked-out 'confluent love' of the pure relationship. Giddens defines the 'pure relationship' as referring

> to a situation where a social relation is entered into for its own sake, for what can be derived by each person from a sustained association with another; and which is continued only in so far as it is thought by both parties to deliver enough satisfactions for each individual to stay within it.[6]

The 'pure relationship' is devoid of institutional/social features or sanctions that might compel its continuation (such as a social pressure to remain married), and it can therefore 'be terminated, more or less at will, by either partner at any particular point'.[7] This type of relationship, entered into entirely for its own benefits, and capable of being ended immediately when either partner is dissatisfied, is viewed by Giddens as having 'close connections with the reflexive project of self'.[8] Who and how we love is, in his view, subject to constant processes of self-monitoring in contemporary Western societies, whereby people consistently ask themselves 'Am I happy in this relationship?', 'Am I getting what I want from this relationship?' and 'Should I stay with this other person?' Such a perspective 'therapeutises' personal relations, making them a matter of chronically recurrent, reflexive self-interrogation, self-articulation and self-expression. Giddens sees this process as a positive one, since it moves people from undemocratic ideals of romantic love in Western societies (which often translated into the oppression of women in the past) to more democratised and non-coercive ideals of the 'pure relationship'. Whereas tradition and social sanctions may previously have kept people trapped in unhappy relationships blighted by power imbalances and by a lack of mutuality, the 'pure relationship' tends toward more egalitarian relations.

I have spent some time establishing what is meant by the 'pure relationship' and 'confluent love'. How can these terms help us to reflect on *Dawson's Creek* as quality teen TV? I want to suggest that a major part of the show's textual sophistication and appeal for fans is the way that its depicted romances fail to correspond to Giddens' apparent opposition between (traditional) 'romantic love' and (modern/contemporary) 'confluent love'.

It could be argued that, in fact, the show corresponds only too well to Giddens' analytical separation, and that it charts the collapse of romantic love as a viable option before developing an alternative 'pure relationship'. Romantic love is represented through the 'soulmate' status of Dawson and Joey's relationship, and the fact that their 'lives are destined to be intertwined' (Joey, in episode 213, 'His Leading Lady'). This 'destiny' is also alluded to by a character, Devon, who plays a thinly veiled version of Joey ('Sammy') in one of Dawson's films. As Scott Andrews says, quoting from the show, Devon's point is that 'Sammy and Wade, and by extension Joey and Dawson, are "soul mates who will be for ever [sic] connected by an overpowering transcendent love"'.[9]

If the Dawson/Joey (D/J[10]) relationship is viewed as a rather unremarkable pop-cultural representation of 'true love', then what might we make of the show's transition into (and back out of) a Joey/Pacey (J/P[11]) relationship? This, by contrast, could be viewed as an example of 'confluent love'; here is a 'pure relationship' actively entered into for its own rewards, whereas Dawson and Joey's relationship emerged problematically out of their pre-puberty friendship. While D/J stand for traditional, romantic love, the active choosing of J/P indicates a new phase in the programme, and a (partially) revised view of how relationships might work reflexively through self-mastery and 'opening-out' to the other. If this reading were sustainable, then fans of the show who favour the Dawson/Joey relationship, who according to Darren Crosdale are 'D/Jers – believers in the everlasting "soulmates" status of Dawson and Joey', could be characterised as regressively supporting ideologies of romantic love. By contrast, Crosdale's 'J/Pers – believers in the relationship between Joey and Pacey'[12] could be viewed as progressively supporting a democratising and reflexive 'pure relationship'.[13]

Although this interpretation is tempting, it is far too tidy. It splits audiences, and phases of the show, into 'good' and 'bad' objects, and demonstrates a profound lack of analytical flexibility. Rather than simply 'applying' Giddens' romantic/confluent love opposition to *Dawson's Creek*, I want to suggest that one aspect of the programme's bid for 'quality' status lies in how it *combines* supposedly conflicting versions of traditional and late-modern relationships. I am not arguing that Giddens' theoretical model is thus wrong – though it may be, I remain open on this question – only that Giddens identifies two very different types of romantic relationship. And by dramatising a clash between these types of love relationship, *Dawson's Creek* avoids affirming clichés of teen romance while making romance a matter both of apparent predestination ('soulmates') and mature reflexivity ('talking through one's hopes and fears in and for a relationship').

D/J is the relationship that the show opens with: it is the focus of the pilot episode and the defining problematic of the series' ongoing narrative. If *Dawson's Creek* could be described as possessing an 'endlessly deferred narrative'[14] – by which I mean a narrative question that is central to the programme's format and so can never be entirely resolved or displaced without reinventing/destroying the programme concerned – then this would have to be the Dawson/Joey relationship. Whether in its 'can-friends-be-lovers' phase, its 'can-ex-lovers-be-friends' phase, its 'can-a-not-quite-ex-going-out-with-my-best-friend-still-be-a-friend' phase or its 'how-the-hell-do-we-redefine-our-friendship-now' phase, this relationship provides the show with its spine and continuity. Although other soap-operatic storylines are introduced, and other (treacherous) partnerships are established across the seasons, the issue of Dawson and Joey remains narratively present and diegetically potent. And rather than simply representing 'romantic love' in Giddens' schema, the masterstroke of the show is that this relationship captures aspects of both 'romantic' and 'confluent' love. The D/J relationship displays qualities of 'romantic love' repeatedly; for example, in the episode 'The Scare' (episode 109), one character, Ursula (who it is comedically implied may have some kind of sixth sense), immediately senses that Dawson and Joey should be together. But allied to this 'one true love' ideal, Dawson and Joey reflexively articulate and work on their relationship, attempting over and over again to negotiate their self-identities through and in relation to one another. And they are repeatedly shown as being involved in an egalitarian relationship, caring for one another and supporting each other in an almost mirroring fashion. A major appeal of *Dawson's Creek*, on this reading, is that its 'endlessly deferred narrative' splices together romantic 'one true' and confluent 'working through' types of love relationship. The D/J relationship is an endless problematic given the 'therapeutising' of Dawson and Joey's mature, reflexive discussions, and given the show's serial need not to exhaust or collapse this narrative. By depicting different types of reflexive love relationships, and combining aspects of traditional and pure relationships, *Dawson's Creek* bids for quality status through its textual and romantic sophistication.

In the next section I want to reflect on another way in which *Dawson's Creek* has been constructed as 'quality teen TV': via discourses of authorship. This, along with the show's textual emphasis on sophisticated and variant versions of romance, represents an audacious piece of textual positioning, given that teen texts, especially those likely to appeal to teenage girls, are routinely culturally devalued.[15] Reflexivity and the 'therapeutising' of teen activities are central to the way that *Dawson's Creek* bids for cultural value via authorship, just as I have argued that they are important to the way that the programme depicts its key relationships.

## Quality Teen TV (II): Reflexivity and *Dawson's Creek* as Authored

An injunction to 'communicate', and thus find one's place, is central to the world view encapsulated by *Dawson's Creek*. In the series, teen characters insistently focus on analysing and expressing their feelings about one another. Characters thus take up what Ian Parker has described as 'the concepts that psychoanalytic texts employ' as these 'are relayed through culture . . . [T]his . . . discourse constitutes places for subjects to come to be . . . [such] as a teenager filled with frustration at authority',[16] or for that matter, the teenager as self-analyst needing to articulate his/her desires and self-identity. Sometimes this analysis might arrive through therapy that is explicitly marked as such (as was the case for Jen Lindley in episodes 415 through to 418), but typically it is a feature of everyday life and everyday, casual conversation in *Dawson's Creek*. Indeed, this prevalence of self-analysis is such that Scott Andrews' *Troubled Water: An Unauthorised and Unofficial Guide to Dawson's Creek* includes the heading 'All Things Freud' in its episode guide, a line that is itself taken from self-referential dialogue appearing in episode 323, the Season Three finale 'True Love'.[17] And when, in an earlier narrative turning point, Dawson kisses Joey, Pacey responds with the comment: 'After years of gratuitous self-examination, you finally did it, you acted' (from 'The Kiss', episode 201).

A typical stereotype of the teenager is indeed the image of an inarticulate, frustrated, if not rage-fuelled, not-quite-yet-adult. But if, as Jen says in episode 415 ('Four Stories'): 'I'm not sure I'm the kind of person who would benefit from therapy. I might just be too self-aware for the likes of you', and if as has been commented elsewhere, 'self-awareness is the Capeside disease',[18] then the 'problem' of adolescence in Capeside is certainly not one of clumsy self-expression or of hormonally induced confusion. Barbara Hudson suggests that the very real problem

> of adolescence *as defined by adult society* is that it is a time of uncontrolled appetites, a time when teenagers need protecting against themselves if they are not to damage their chances of reaching respectable adulthood; the problem of adolescence for teenagers is that they must demonstrate maturity and responsibility if they are to move out of this stigmatised status, and yet because adolescence is conceived as a time of irresponsibility and lack of maturity, they are given few opportunities to demonstrate these qualities which are essential for their admission as adults.[19]

In marked contrast to this, the teens in *Dawson's Creek* avoid stigmatisation and pathologisation by virtue of 'communicating' with one another and their parents and/or siblings. Although they may occasionally *behave* in irresponsible or immature ways, their talk is always resolutely mature and responsible in its pursuit of open channels of communication and reflexive self-understanding. Indeed, as Clare Birchall discusses in Chapter 13 of this volume, the characters' 'hyper-articulacy' can be read as indicating 'a fear of unconscious work, for . . . everything gets articulated, everything gets brought into the open, and, equally, nothing is allowed to slip back, perhaps irrevocably, into the underworld of unconsciousness'.[20]

In other words, *Dawson's Creek* represents its characters as if they *are* consistently rational and self-present. By contrast, actual teens (and adults, for that matter) tend to perform their identities publicly as 'rational' simply because this is culturally valued, while remaining aware of themselves as sometimes behaving irrationally. While agreeing broadly with Birchall's conclusions, I want to avoid pre-empting her work on nostalgia by moving my own argument onto a slightly different terrain.

*Dawson's Creek*'s 'hyper-articulacy' occurs in part, I want to suggest, due to the programme's bid for cultural value. Its teens become 'hyper-articulate' because by making this move, the programme can align itself with cultural ideals of self-transparency, reflexivity and agency. Quality teen TV is, perhaps, not only about textual self-reflexivity or self-referentiality, it is also about the reflexivity that teen characters display.

And, significantly, both of these qualities – media-pervaded, post-modern self-reflexivity and therapy-saturated character reflexivity – are combined through the unifying 'author-function'[21] of Kevin Williamson as *Dawson's Creek*'s creator, pilot writer and executive producer (on Seasons One and Two). It is Williamson's construction and mediation as a TV auteur, also buttressed and sustained by his extremely successful work in teen horror cinema, that extends the status of 'authored' quality teen TV to *Dawson's Creek*. The characters' Williamson-esque propensity for self-analysis means that they are represented not just as smart teens, but also as teens who are grappling with, and realising, questions of their own powers to make a difference and to work reflexively at personal relationships. Teen reflexivity and agency are consistently emphasised in *Dawson's Creek*; this works to sustain Williamson's construction as a TV auteur as well as supporting the programme's alignment with broader cultural systems of value (where 'rationality' and 'reflexivity' are valorised terms). Such an emphasis carries connotations of 'sophistication' at the level of textual self-reflexivity and at the level of characters' reflexivity/relationships, and demonstrates why *Dawson's Creek* has been so important to US and UK broadcasters. In the UK it has been a flagship component in Channel 4's 'T4' strand, thus being explicitly branded as 'teen TV', but also contributing to Channel 4's 'sophisticated' corporate identity, as Janet McCabe has observed (my own emphasis in italics):

> Reliance on American syndicated material has helped Channel 4 build its corporate identity. . . . *Acquisition of such dramas from the US, programmes defined as literary-based, generically ground-breaking, tending towards liberal humanism, and made by those with a 'quality' reputation . . . for 'yuppie, TV-literate baby boomers' (Feuer 1995: 8) sits well with Channel 4's remit* that encourages diversity and experimentation . . . Far from merely copying lessons learnt from the American networks, Channel 4 has bought in these dramas to serve the interests of its own network identity.[22]

As Will Brooker notes, '*Dawson's Creek*'s . . . context in terms of American television scheduling is significantly different from its British context within Sunday morning's "T4" schedule'.[23] In the USA *Dawson's Creek* Season One was broadcast on WB at 9 p.m. due to concerns over its sexual content and the sentiment that it might not be suitable for the 8 p.m.–9 p.m. 'family hour', before being shifted to this very time slot in its later seasons. It is thus more heavily institutionally marked as 'teen TV' in its UK context. However, despite differences between US and UK scheduling decisions, both the 8 p.m. prime time US timeslot and the Sunday morning UK slot permit the show to be constructed as 'teen' viewing that can also be appreciated by 'adult' viewers. In the USA, this audience coalition is possible as the show has been linked to discourses of 'family TV' via its scheduling. In the UK, this audience combination can occur because adults are likely to be available to view TV on a Sunday morning (not being at work). And it is also significantly the case in the UK that Sunday morning or early afternoon television is not culturally/conventionally marked out as a scheduling block corresponding to 'kids' TV' in the way that, say, 'Saturday morning TV' has become synonymous with specific formats aimed at a child and youth audience. *Dawson's Creek*'s demographic, textual and scheduling appeals are thus 'crossover' in the sense of bidding for pre-teen through to thirtysomething audiences.

The stretching of 'teen TV' into the domains of authored, 'quality TV' and across a coalition of teen/adult audience demographics has been used as one explanation of *Dawson's Creek*'s reliance on articulate, therapeutised teen agents. As Steven Jay Schneider has remarked:

> Williamson['s] specialty lies in the creation of characters who appeal to different sectors of the audience at the same time . . . teenagers who sound like Gen X-ers. . . . [S]ophistication . . . is a function of their enculturated self-awareness. As Williamson puts it:
>
>> I think that our target audience today is just so savvy, so I try to write all of my characters so that they are self-aware. They've all lived through the psycho-babble of the eighties . . . Even if their behaviour is not that of an adult, they can sure talk like one. That's certainly true in *Scream* and [*I Know What You Did Last*] *Summer* and in *Dawson's Creek*. You could dub that show *Thirty Something*, even though they (the characters) are fifteen. I'm really having fun with that.[24]

In an article predominantly concerned with Kevin Williamson's work in the 'neo-stalker' horror subgenre (on the *Scream* franchise, *I Know What You Did Last Summer* and *Halloween H20* ), Schneider concludes that

> today's teens are not the ones who 'lived through the psycho-babble of the eighties'. At least not in comparison with the Gen X-ers, who were fully cognizant the whole time. It seems that, by effecting a fusion of two generations in his adolescent characters [both in his horror film work and in *Dawson's Creek*], Williamson has found a voice that appeals to them both.[25]

However, this bid for 'quality TV' status – linked to the creator-executive producer-writer 'hyphenate' role initially adopted by Kevin Williamson – has also formed a basis for criticism of *Dawson's Creek*. Darren Crosdale, author of *Dawson's Creek: The All New Official Companion* (2001), puts the following question to executive producer, Paul Stupin: 'When the show first aired in 1997, Michael Krantz wrote in *Time* magazine, "Williamson's kids may talk like therapists but they act like guarded and wounded 15-year-olds . . ." Do you think that was ever an apt description, and is it apt now?'[26]

Criticism of *Dawson's Creek* has thus often focused on the criterion of emotional realism; can teens actually articulate their feelings as well as they do on the show? Williamson's bid to combine Gen-X and teen voices, and thus to garner both these audiences for a self-reflexive text featuring reflexive teen characters, has resulted in an accusation that the show is forced or artificial (insufficiently realist, in other words) in its representation of teenagers as teen agents. Paul Stupin tries to evade such criticism by accepting that the show's teen agents are an idealisation, something 'better' than we may be, but that we (the audience) nevertheless share certain types of feelings, regardless of our demographic:

> [Stupin:] Well, our characters have always been very articulate and particularly adept at expressing themselves. But one thing we have always tried to do is make sure that the emotions and feelings they express are indicative of feelings we have all probably gone through. Our characters feel the same things we all do, they are just better at expressing them.[27]

Stupin both accepts and amends the 'non-realist' charge, converting teen articulacy into a front for more 'universal' emotional experiences. He thus preserves the sense that although *Dawson's Creek* is about teens, it may also appeal, quite legitimately, to a Gen-X or older audience. The character reflexivity on the show is re-framed and neutralised by Stupin as a diegetic skill – the characters are 'adept at expressing themselves' – rather than as a head-on challenge to the show's realism.

In this section I have argued that the way *Dawson's Creek* 'therapeutises' its teen characters as hyper-reflexive has been consistently read through and in relation to the figure of Kevin Williamson as the show's creator/auteur. This link between teen reflexivity and named/branded authorship has been made in secondary texts such as *Time* magazine ('Williamson's kids') and in academic articles on Williamson such as Steven Jay Schneider's work. The link between reflexivity and authorship has also been made in the text of *Dawson's Creek* itself, especially in the Season One episode 'The Scare' (109). In Chapter 6 of this collection, Valerie Wee notes the importance of intertextuality in 1990s' teen TV, analysing this very episode of *Dawson's Creek*: '"The Scare" . . . was stylistically and conventionally similar to the cinematic *Scream*, going as far as to replicate, in large part, the narrative conventions, characters and visual style of that landmark teen-oriented film.'[28] I suspect that Wee overstates similarities between 'The Scare' and *Scream* (it could be argued that the TV episode recontextualises the conventions and devices of *Scream* within the *Dawson's Creek* format, largely neutralising the affective structure of the teen horror film). However, what I want to note here is that links between Williamson's horror work and his role on *Dawson's Creek* are foregrounded most centrally in 'The Scare'. At no other point in the series is Williamson's role as auteur so insistently emphasised textually and intertextually. Perhaps not coincidentally, given its powerfully 'authored' status, this episode is one of four contained on the 'Best of Seasons One and Two' DVD/videos. Its inclusion indicates that it is simultaneously viewed – at least in publicity discourses and merchandising surrounding the show – as a marker of the programme's quality and as a marker of Williamson's authorship. Thus, while this episode may be usefully analysed as an instance of cross-media synergy, stylistic blurring and borrowing, or even (as Wee notes) brand awareness of 'Kevin Williamson', none of these scenarios quite captures the relevance and centrality of 'quality TV' to such phenomena.

It is hence in 'The Scare', in the first season of *Dawson's Creek*, and at a time when issues of quality would have been crucial to securing the show's future, that the programme comes closest to highlighting, and seeking to cement, its links to *Scream et al.* via the author-function of Kevin Williamson. It is in this relatively early episode that the programme displays an anxiety about stressing its influences and its 'cinematic' status, and through this, a need to display itself as quality teen TV. The episode can be read as a thorough-going attempt to play up Williamson's involvement with the show, and thus construct or pre-programme intertextual links to his film successes, despite the fact that, ironically, Williamson himself did not write the episode (it is credited to Mike White).

In the final section of this chapter, I will explore whether the ways in which *Dawson's Creek* operates uneasily or insecurely as 'quality teen TV' might also allow us to describe it as a 'mainstream cult' programme. Cult TV often hails from horror/fantasy and science-fiction genres.[29] What claim, then, might a realist teen drama focused on reflexive relationships have to being 'cult'?

### Quality Teen TV as 'Mainstream Cult'?

> [A]n alternative perspective . . . that . . . has been neglected by writing on the teen series . . . [is] that of the intersection between the teen series and cult television. Considering the fact that fans of cult media are often stereotyped as adolescent . . . it seems surprising that teen TV has not been examined as an object of cult interest: many of its fans *really are* adolescent.[30]

Here, then, is one answer to the question posed above: *Dawson's Creek* could perhaps be considered as a type of 'mainstream cult' given the way in which it depicts relationships, allowing its online fans to split into sub-subcultures or micro-communities that support different characters or couples, and given the way that it constructs Williamson-esque teen characters linked to discourses of authored, 'quality TV' both by fans and in much publicity.

Cult TV tends to be linked to stereotypes of nerdy, geeky, infantile fans, or to the genres of science fiction/fantasy, but teen audiences (displaying more-or-less intense fandoms) often form a key part of cult TV and film audiences, and so too do 'crossover' transgenerational audiences of the type attracted by *Dawson's Creek*. Furthermore, cult TV is often constructed, in publicity and by its fans, as authored/idiosyncratic. Notions of 'cult TV' as TV art hence partially overlap with industry definitions of quality TV. The manner in which cult TV fans often follow their favoured TV show across different media, through tie-in books, fan fiction and websites, is also displayed by *Dawson's Creek*. In fact, its televisual text has been extended through official online stories that fill in the gaps between seasons, such as the 'Summer Diaries' available online that deal with Pacey and Joey's adventures between Seasons Three and Four, as well as through 'Dawson's Desktops', another online feature at www.dawsonscreek.com that constructs intimacy between fans and characters via '"characterised" proliferations of the text', giving fans access to the main characters' PCs.[31] As John Caldwell has commented:

Both the WB and Fox have authored intricate sites to cultivate fan cultures for their hit and cult series *Buffy the Vampire Slayer* and *Dawson's Creek* (WB) and *The X-Files* and *The Simpsons* (Fox). . . . television, far more than film, has succeeded at converging fan activities, e-commerce and online merchandizing as an intricate part of their television shows.[32]

Note that each of the shows referred to by Caldwell has some claim to being described as cult TV in secondary texts/publicity/fan practices, except for *Dawson's Creek*. Although the other named shows have teen, fan and teen-fan followings, they fit into the 'intertextual network' of shows dubbed 'cult' by virtue either of a fantasy aspect to their narrative worlds or the artificial 'other-worldliness' and satirical knowingness of *The Simpsons*. *Dawson's Creek* lacks these textual qualities, even if it shares the story arc format or 'series memory' of *The X-Files* and *Buffy*, as well as these shows' interests in thwarted, blocked or failed relationships.

However, the strongest case for *Dawson's Creek* as a 'mainstream cult' remains non-text-based; it is based, in fact, around the show's online fandom. Even while it is not labelled as cult TV in publicity and fan discourses, *Dawson's Creek* has a socially organised fandom with its own communal identities and languages (such as the 'D/J or J/P fans') that is strikingly similar to fan factions surrounding shows labelled 'cult' (*The X-Files* has fans called 'shippers' who focus on the Mulder/Scully relationship, and *Buffy* has fans who continue to lament the passing of Buffy/Angel as a couple, as well as a fan faction who are pro or anti a Spike/Buffy pairing). Such fans of *Dawson's Creek* represent what a cluster of writers have dubbed or discussed as the 'mainstreaming' of fandom.[33] Theorists argue that the Internet has made it easier to form socially organised fan cultures, encouraging and sustaining fandoms around a wider variety of TV shows than would have been the case in the past. Consider the following views:

[Henry Jenkins:] New fandoms emerge rapidly on the web . . . As fandom diversifies it moves from cult status towards the cultural mainstream, with more Internet users engaged in some form of fan activity.[34]

[Kirsten Pullen:] More fans are able to take part in fan activity, and fan cultural production is more readily available to a larger community. However, fans do not always interpret texts, fan production, or fan positions and identifications similarly. Though the internet may have begun to mainstream fandom, it has not necessarily created a single, unified fan position or practice.[35]

[Janet H. Murray:] In the past this kind of attention [to detail and continuity] was limited to series with cult followings like *Star Trek* or *The X-Files*. But as the Internet becomes a standard adjunct of broadcast television, all program writers and producers will be aware of a more sophisticated audience, one that can keep track of the story in greater detail and over longer periods of time.[36]

However, it evidently doesn't follow that because a TV programme has an online fandom, it will automatically be described as 'cult' in magazines and other secondary texts that are linked to already-established fan cultures which specifically celebrate their tastes and 'intertextual networks' of telefantasy as 'cult'. What we see in the 'mainstream cult' *is a cultural power struggle for and over legitimacy between different fan cultures* rather than between, say, fans and producers. Certain texts – teen TV that cannot be linked to 'cult' forms such as superhero comics, science fiction/fantasy or horror – are denied entry to the 'cult' intertextual network. This means that texts that are closer to culturally conventional female interests (including soaps as well as much teen TV) are relatively delegitimated and denied cult status despite their dedicated fan followings. One fan audience (for cult TV) therefore takes up a position of cultural power relative to another (for types of teen TV), attempting to deny that such teen TV can be viewed as authored, sophisticated and so on. The irony of this is, of course, that fans of what is labelled cult TV value their own media tastes by drawing on discourses of authorship, while seemingly striving to deny that this move can have relevance for other, non-cult fandoms.

What this also indicates is that 'quality TV' need not be viewed as such by all audiences; shared norms of quality (textual sophistication, reflexivity, authorship) can be drawn on in publicity, and utilised by fans of a TV programme, even while being denied or delegitimated by other audience factions (non-fans/critics/academics). Quality, therefore, is not simply 'in' the text (despite certain cues being generally culturally significant). It is produced discursively and intertextually and, as such, it can be read selectively by audiences in different cultural/social contexts. *Dawson's Creek* is 'quality teen TV' for its fans and for those who accept certain publicity intertexts or intertextual cues (as I have here) but it can continue to be devalued by fans of cult TV, if not by TV critics and no doubt some TV scholars. What texts can do is bid for the notion of quality or cultural value by aligning themselves textually and intertextually with norms of 'quality'; and it is this process that I have explored in the case of *Dawson's Creek*.

Although the extent to which *Dawson's Creek* (online) fans are representative of the show's wider audience remains an important question,[37] this should not dissuade us from considering the fan culture built around the show. Will Brooker has concluded, on the basis of a relatively small-scale but revealing piece of audience research, that many *Dawson's Creek* fans do not map out or create their own intertextual networks around the programme. Instead they follow

> the pattern . . . cannily mapped out by WB and its media alliances. They know that Joey wears American Eagle and J. Crew, they know that Pacey is in *Skulls* and Dawson in *Varsity Blues*, they know that the show's music is available on two soundtracks, and they show no sign of resisting as their participatory culture is neatly structured for them, with intertextual spin-offs and cross-promotions clearly linked up and signposted like stores in a shopping mall.[38]

Again, this could lead us to consider *Dawson's Creek* as a type of 'mainstream cult', insofar as its intertextualities are potentially pre-programme rather than emerging through fans' grassroots interests as they move from favoured text to text.

But this should not be taken to imply that 'mainstream cults' are somehow more tainted by commerce or consumerism than are media cults-proper. It can hardly be argued that shows like *Buffy* and *The X-Files*, granted 'cult' status in *Cult Times* magazine, are somehow anti-commercial or anti-consumerist, especially given the vast ranges of merchandising that exist around each show. Rather, the distinction I am making here is between fan cultures that construct their own intertextual links between programmes (arguably, the very category 'cult' was originally constructed by fans) and fandoms that largely follow intertextual links put in place by the media industry to court such fans.

In this discussion I have suggested that *Dawson's Creek* is constructed as sophisticated, quality teen TV via its textual combination of 'romantic' and 'confluent' love, as well as in its use of character discourses of 'reflexive' therapy and its use of self-referentiality/self-reflexivity. Given its dependence on the author-function, its 'endlessly deferred narrative' of soulmates talking things through, its textual extensions on the web and its active (online) fan culture of J/Pers or D/Jers, *Dawson's Creek* is fascinating teen TV. But it surely also merits recognition as a 'mainstream cult' and as 'quality teen TV'. The real difficulty I have highlighted here is that 'quality' cannot simply be read off from the texts of teen TV, just as 'cult' status cannot be textually decided or defined in isolation from audience activities and intertexts. Both 'quality' and 'cult' TV therefore form part of struggles over cultural value that take place between different fan audiences as well as between producers and audiences and within the wider culture. 'Quality teen TV' remains a problematic category because it threatens to disrupt established cultural power relations that associate all things teen with negative stereotypes such as 'not-quite-adult'. Bidding for quality thus means representing teenagers as mature, reflexive and 'adult', while also appealing to older, non-teen audiences through scheduling. The 'mainstream cult' is no less problematic, since it threatens to disrupt the subcultural power of fans of cult TV, challenging their own (rather insecure) bids for cult-as-quality-TV by illustrating that these bids hinge on marking out devalued others (types of teen TV or conventionally 'feminised' genres such as soaps). 'Quality teen TV' and the 'mainstream cult' are certainly awkward, ungainly categories. But as ways to make sense of *Dawson's Creek*, they illustrate how issues of cultural value and representations of teen life are true soulmates, inseparable to the end.

## Notes

Many thanks to the editors for their guidance with this piece, and to Amy Luther for reading an earlier and rather tangential draft.

1. Anthony Giddens, *The Transformation of Intimacy* (Stanford, CA: Stanford University Press, 1992), p. 64; see also Anthony Giddens, *Modernity and Self-Identity: Self and Society in the Late Modern Age* (Cambridge: Polity Press, 1991), p. 180.
2. Indeed, in a recent conference paper, Glyn Davis observes quite rightly that *Dawson's Creek* is 'a teen series that *Cult Times* clearly doesn't see as "cult"' ('*Dawson's Creek* and *Roswell High*: Teen TV as/and Cult Television', paper presented at the 'Analysing Series and Serial Narrative' conference, Liverpool John Moores, 16/17 November 2002), p. 6, despite the fact that *Charmed*, *Smallville*, *Buffy* and *Roswell* are constructed intertextually as 'cult' by this UK magazine.
3. Although I borrow this term from Gunnar Sæbø, 'Between Ubiquitous Media Event and

Teenage Fan Phenomenon: Notes on the Mainstream Cult of James Cameron's *Titanic*' in Philippe Le Guern (ed.), *Les Cultes Médiatiques* (Rennes: Presses Universitaires de Rennes, 2002), pp. 283–307, I do not use it in quite the same way. His account labels texts as mainstream cults if they are culturally ubiquitous, like blockbuster films, but are consumed intensely, repeatedly and ritualistically by fans (*Titanic* and *Star Wars* would be good examples of these mainstream cults or 'cult blockbusters': see also Matt Hills, '*Star Wars* in Fandom, Film Theory and the Museum: The Cultural Status of the Cult Blockbuster' in Julian Stringer (ed.), *Movie Blockbusters* (London: Routledge, 2003), pp. 178–89). My own use of the term does not require cultural ubiquity, but does gesture towards a shift in cult status, whereby cult cannot easily be equated with 'anti-mainstream' or 'minority' fan tastes, instead becoming co-opted as part of a recognisable consumerist option.

4. Henry Jenkins, *Textual Poachers* (London: Routledge, 1992), p. 40.
5. Giddens, *The Transformation of Intimacy* p. 61.
6. Ibid., p. 58.
7. Ibid., p. 137.
8. Ibid., p. 90.
9. Cited in Scott Andrews, *Troubled Waters: An Unauthorised and Unofficial Guide to Dawson's Creek* (London: Virgin, 2001), p. 125, again referring to episode 213.
10. This relationship is often abbreviated as 'D/J' in online fan discussions.
11. Again, this relationship is often abbreviated in online fan discussions to 'J/P' or 'P/J'.
12. Both quotes are taken from Darren Crosdale, *Dawson's Creek: The All New Official Companion* (London: Ebury Press, 2001), p. 139.
13. It is worth noting that the terms 'D/J' and 'J/P' are not created by Darren Crosdale. They circulate within online fan discussion, sometimes being transposed as P/J for Pacey/Joey fans, e.g. as in the posting 'What about Joey and Pacey back togheter [*sic*] again?' on the WB *Dawson's Creek* discussion board (http://www.talk.thewb.com). This posting begins 'I know I'm not the only P/J fan here' (Laura Weinreb, posted 11–14 15:40). Many responses then refer to being fans of Pacey and Joey, while one posting explicitly contrasts these fans to others who want Dawson and Joey to be together: 'I don't understand the people who love dawson and joey . . . I mean it's disgusting to see them kiss, it's like they're being forced to have their lips kissed. Pacey and Joey are the romance of all romances!!' (JoEyFaN04, posted 11–15 20:44).
14. Something that I have previously described as a characteristic of cult TV: see Matt Hills, *Fan Cultures* (London: Routledge, 2002), pp. 134–5.
15. See Melanie Nash and Martti Lahti, '"Almost Ashamed to Say I Am One of Those Girls": *Titanic*, Leonardo DiCaprio, and the Paradoxes of Girls' Fandom' in Kevin S. Sandler and Gaylyn Studlar (eds), *Titanic: Anatomy of a Blockbuster* (New Brunswick, NJ: Rutgers University Press, 1999), pp. 64–88.
16. Ian Parker, *Psychoanalytic Culture* (London: Sage, 1997), pp. 7–8.
17. See Andrews, *Troubled Waters*, pp. 265–6.
18. Ibid., p. vi.
19. Barbara Hudson, 'Femininity and Adolescence' in Angela McRobbie and Mica Nava (eds), *Gender and Generation* (London: Macmillan, 1984), p. 36, my italics.

20. Clare Birchall, '"Feels Like Home": *Dawson's Creek*, Nostalgia and the Young Adult Viewer', this volume, pp. 186–7.
21. This phrase is originally Michel Foucault's (see Michel Foucault, 'What is an Author?', *Screen*, vol. 20, no. 1 (Spring 1979), pp. 13–33). For an excellent discussion of the TV 'author-function', see John Tulloch and Henry Jenkins, *Science Fiction Audiences: Watching Doctor Who and Star Trek* (London: Routledge, 1995), pp. 186–91.
22. Janet McCabe, 'Diagnosing the Alien: Producing Identities, American "Quality" Drama and British Television Culture in the 1990s' in Bruce Carson and Margaret Llewellyn-Jones (eds), *Frames and Fictions on Television: The Politics of Identity within Drama* (Exeter: Intellect, 2000), p. 145.
23. Will Brooker, 'Living on *Dawson's Creek*: Teen Viewers, Cultural Convergence, and Television Overflow', *International Journal of Cultural Studies*, vol. 4, no. 4 (2001), p. 465.
24. Steven Jay Schneider, 'Kevin Williamson and The Rise of the Neo-Stalker' *Post Script*, vol. 19, no. 2 (2000), pp. 85–6.
25. Ibid., p. 86.
26. Crosdale, *Dawson's Creek*, p. 123.
27. Ibid.
28. Valerie Wee, 'Selling Teen Culture: How American Multimedia Conglomeration Reshaped Teen Television in the 1990s', this volume, p. 93.
29. See Hills, *Fan Cultures*, p. 138.
30. Davis, '*Dawson's Creek* and *Roswell High*', p. 3.
31. John Caldwell, 'New Media/Old Augmentations: Television, the Internet, and Interactivity' in Anne Jerslev (ed.) *Realism and 'Reality' in Film and New Media* (Copenhagen: Museum Tusculanum Press, 2002), pp. 258–9; see also Brooker, 'Living on *Dawson's Creek*', p. 469 and Crosdale, *Dawson's Creek*, pp. 135–8 for an interview with Arika Mittman, the producer of 'Dawson's Desktops'.
32. Caldwell, 'New Media/Old Augmentations', pp. 257–8.
33. See, for example, Janet H. Murray *Hamlet on the Holodeck* (Cambridge, MA: MIT Press, 1997); Kirsten Pullen, 'I-love-Xena.com: Creating Online Fan Communities' in David Gauntlett (ed.), *web.studies* (London: Arnold, 2000), pp. 52–61; Henry Jenkins, 'Interactive Audiences?' in Dan Harries (ed.), *The New Media Book* (London: BFI, 2002), pp. 157–70.
34. Jenkins, 'Interactive Audiences?', p. 161.
35. Pullen, 'I-love-Xena.com', p. 60.
36. Murray, *Hamlet on the Holodeck*, p. 85.
37. Brooker, 'Living on *Dawson's Creek*', p. 468.
38. Ibid.

# Part II

## Consumption

# 5

# 'So Who's Got Time for Adults!': Femininity, Consumption and the Development of Teen TV – from *Gidget* to *Buffy*

## Bill Osgerby

### 'Wholesome as a Peach'?: Girls, Grrrls and Teen TV

Gidget was hardly an icon of feminist defiance. Played by a winsome Sally Field in an eponymous ABC TV sitcom launched in the USA in 1965, fifteen-year-old Gidget (the character's 'real' name was Frances Lawrence) in many ways represented a model of conventional teen femininity. Domesticity and romantic obsessions were perennial features of the Gidget universe, while the character's nickname (a jokey fusion of 'girl' and 'midget') implied a childlike purity and playful innocence. Little wonder, then, that *TV Guide* should enthuse over Gidget's weekly pranks and adventures, one reviewer describing the chirpy teen as being 'wholesome as a peach'.[1] At the same time, however, the character often had a sparkle of rebellious independence. And in some ways her madcap escapades pointed towards a brand of femininity based less around compliance and family-oriented domesticity than a relish for autonomous and active fun.

Many feminist critics have been relatively optimistic in their accounts of contemporary popular depictions of teenage girls and texts aimed at audiences of young women. Angela McRobbie, for example, has identified a 'new' emphasis on young women's 'personal choice', 'self-confidence' and 'individual identity' in *Just Seventeen*, *More!* and other British magazines geared to the teenage girls' market.[2] Surveying contemporary 'girlie culture' more widely, McRobbie identifies a shift towards 'sex, having fun and enjoying a sense of freedom' – with mainstream commercial culture eschewing representations of 'ladylike' sweetness and innocence in favour of constructions of teen femininity predicated on energy, independence and pleasure.[3] In American culture, too, many feminist commentators have detected a move from 'girl' to 'grrrl' culture, with representations of rebellious and autonomous girlhood emerging across a range of popular texts. The Warner Bros. TV series *Buffy the Vampire Slayer* (1997–), for example, has won many feminist plaudits. Buffy, the lead character, has been identified as a 'transgressive woman warrior',[4] an embodiment of 'strength, power and assertiveness'[5] who often destabilises gender power structures by being 'a supremely confident kicker of evil butt'.[6]

Gidget, in contrast, did not do a lot of butt-kicking. Nor did she have the sexual audacity and bold irreverence of the commercial 'girlie culture' discussed by McRobbie. At the same time, however, *Gidget* and the plethora of other 'teen girl' TV shows that appeared in America during the early 1960s did not simply construct young women as passive and submissive. Instead, these series – along with British teen TV programmes of the same period – provided important spaces where the elaboration of active and independent feminine identities sometimes took place. Rather than being the bearers of monolithic ideologies of domesticity or any uniformly oppressive 'code of romance',[7] therefore, these texts were characterised by many tensions and contradictions. In particular, their privileging of hedonism and commodity consumption can be seen as offering enticing glimpses of a femininity distinguished by an ethos of dynamic self-expression and autonomous pleasure – an ethos that has been amplified and extended in contemporary cultural texts such as *Buffy*.

## Screening the 'Junior Miss': Young Women and the Growth of American Teen TV

The rise of 'teen' programming in American TV schedules was indebted, at least in part, to market economics. TV series appealing to teenage audiences and depicting the exploits of jaunty teens were a bankable proposition because young people had come to represent a powerful economic force after World War II. A youth-oriented commercial market had first taken shape in the USA during the 1920s and 1930s, but during the 1940s youth began to emerge as an especially influential consumer group. This growth was partly the consequence of demographic trends, with wartime increases in the birth rate and a post-war 'baby boom' ensuring that the American teen population rocketed from ten to fifteen million during the 1950s, eventually hitting a peak of twenty million by 1970. At the same time, a major expansion of education provision saw the proportion of US teenagers attending high school rise from around 60 per cent in the 1930s to virtually 100 per cent during the 1960s – a shift that helped accentuate the identifiability of young people as a distinct generational cohort.[8] But even more significant than this was the growth of young people's economic muscle. Wartime demand for labour had brought a rise in levels of youth employment and young people's earnings had grown as a consequence. Peacetime saw a decline in full-time youth employment, but the growth in young people's spending power was sustained by a combination of part-time work and parental allowances, some estimates suggesting that young Americans' average weekly income had risen from just over two dollars in 1944 to around ten dollars by 1958.[9]

For many, the purchasing power of American youth had become an astonishing phenomenon, an awestruck 1959 edition of *Life* magazine announcing the arrival of 'A New $10-Billion Power: the US Teenage Consumer'. As the magazine explained, American youth had now 'emerged as a big-time consumer in the US economy . . . Counting only what is spent to satisfy their special teenage demands, the youngsters and their parents will shell out about $10 billion this year, a billion more than the total sales of GM [General Motors].'[10]

It is hardly surprising, then, that commercial interests scrambled to stake their claim in the teenage goldmine. The range of products geared to the young was literally boundless, consumer industries interacting with and reinforcing one another in their efforts to woo the lucrative youth market. Hollywood was especially keen to capitalise on booming youth demand. As Thomas Doherty (1988) has shown, the decline of adult cinema audiences during the 1950s forced the American film industry to target new markets, with young cinemagoers singled out for special attention, the 'teenpic' industry coming of age as numerous studios cranked out quickly made, low-budget features aimed at a youth audience. The developing medium of television also began to address the youth market more directly. TV broadcasters were drawn to young audiences partly by a desire to pull in advertisers keen to milk teenage spending. But the rise of teen TV was also part of the television industry's attempts to experiment with different kinds of programme format. This was especially true of the ABC network. Since its bigger and more established rivals (CBS and NBC) were best placed to exploit the mass TV audience, the younger and smaller ABC developed a strategy of competition in which it courted more specialised markets, the network developing a reputation for programming aimed at youth and young families with children.

Local stations also played their part in the growth of American teen TV. For example, premiering in 1946 on WRGB (a local station in New York state), the youth talent show *Teen Canteen* was one of the earliest attempts at a TV series aimed at teenagers. Other teen-talent shows followed, including *Paul Whiteman's TV Teen Club* (ABC, 1949–54), together with teen-oriented variety shows such as *Teen Time Tunes* (Dumont, 1949), teenage quiz shows such as *Junior High School Quiz* (CBS, 1946), and discussion programmes such as *Teenage Book Club* (ABC, 1948) and *Today's Teens* (WENR–Chicago, 1951).[11] During the early 1950s, meanwhile, shows featuring pop performers and their fans became a staple of local TV stations' afternoon and Saturday morning schedules, examples including *Teen Twirl* (WNBK–Cleveland, 1955) and *Teen Club Party* (WGN–Chicago, 1957). Most famous, however, was the Philadelphia-based *American Bandstand*. Launched by WFIL–Philadelphia in 1952, by 1957 the show's success had prompted a transfer to the ABC network where its audience figures could touch twenty million.

Programmes like *Teen Twirl* and *American Bandstand* attracted a diverse youth audience, though the recipe of music and dance had an especially strong appeal for young women. Indeed, teenage girls were a potentially lucrative market that advertisers (and the programmers striving to attract them) were eager to reach. Young women had emerged as an influential consumer group during the 1940s, their economic significance confirmed by the huge success of *Seventeen* magazine. Conceived as a publication geared to the college girl market, *Seventeen* was launched in 1944, with its first edition selling out within two days. Its circulation shot up to over a million by 1947 and soared to two-and-a-half million by 1949.[12] Into the 1950s and 1960s young women remained a potent economic force – prompting teenage marketing guru, Eugene Gilbert, to report in a 1959 edition of *Harper's Magazine* that:

> The junior miss leads the way in endorsing 'separates', 'man-tailored' shirts, ballet slippers, and skintight 'stem' skirts or ballooning layers of petticoats. She has built seamless leotard

tights … into a multi-million-dollar industry [and] one manufacturer of girls' clothing who started out eighteen years ago with a $4,000 investment has, by concentrating on teen-age preferences, blossomed into a $30 million business with six factories around the country and a listing on the American Stock Exchange.[13]

During the 1950s teenage life was a firm feature of many American TV soap operas and family-based sitcoms. As Mary Celeste Kearney observes, shows such as *The Adventures of Ozzie and Harriet* (ABC, 1952–66), *Father Knows Best* (CBS/NBC, 1954–62), *Leave It to Beaver* (CBS, 1957–8; ABC, 1958–63) and *The Donna Reed Show* (ABC, 1958–66) all featured teenage characters who became increasingly central to storylines over the course of the 1950s.[14] In many of these series, together with school-based sitcoms such as *Mr. Peepers* (NBC, 1952–5) and *Our Miss Brooks* (CBS, 1952–6), it was adolescent boys who were centre stage. Indeed, in the first prime-time TV show to focus consistently on teenage characters – *The Many Loves of Dobie Gillis* (CBS, 1959–63) – it was boys who were in the limelight, the series regaling audiences with the comedic antics of the luckless Dobie and his beatnik buddy, Maynard. But teenage girls were also a tangible TV presence. As Kearney demonstrates, for example, the early 1950s saw the launch of both *A Date with Judy* (ABC, 1951; 1952–3) and *Meet Corliss Archer* (CBS, 1951–2; syndicated 1954–5).[15] Sitcoms based on the lives of high-school bobby-soxers, both *Judy* and *Corliss Archer* had started life as 1940s' radio series and were subsequently adapted into live-action TV shows. Indeed, during the early 1950s both *Judy* and *Corliss Archer* appeared across a wealth of different media formats (including radio and TV series, stage plays, books, magazines and films). Kearney argued that this demonstrates how contemporary trends towards synergy and inter-dependence within the entertainment industry should be seen as part of a much longer history of 'transmedia exploitation'.[16]

During the late 1950s and early 1960s American TV networks sought to tap further into the market of the 'junior miss', with a succession of sprightly sitcoms centred on teenage girls. The first, *Too Young to Go Steady* (NBC, 1959), focused on the life and loves of fourteen-year-old Pam Blake (Brigid Bazlen) and her transition from tomboyish girlhood to ladylike maturity. A similar theme underpinned *Peck's Bad Girl* (CBS, 1959–60), though in this case twelve-year-old Torey Peck (Patty McCormack) was decidedly more precocious. *Margie* (ABC, 1961–2) was ostensibly set in the 1920s, though the trials and tribulations facing teenage Margie Clayton (Cynthia Pepper) and her flapper chum, Maybelle (Penney Parker), were strangely familiar to 1960s teens – troubled romances, conflict with parents and hassles at school. In *Fair Exchange* (CBS, 1962–3), meanwhile, hands-across-the-sea 'hilarity' was the order of the day, scenes alternating between New York and London as the programme chronicled the experiences of two teenage girls whose families had agreed to 'swap' them for a year.

A greater success was *The Patty Duke Show* (ABC, 1963–6). The series saw Patty Duke, fresh from her award-winning role in the motion picture *The Miracle Worker* (1962), star in a dual role. As Patty Lane she was an all-American teenager who chewed gum and dug Paul Anka and slumber parties, while as the more reserved Cathy she was Patty's newly arrived Scottish cousin, identical to Patty in all but her bagpipes and highland burr. The show proved the longest-running of the 1960s' 'teen girl' sitcoms, its popularity boosted by guest appearances from pop heartthrobs such as Bobby Vinton and Frankie Avalon. Less enduring were *Karen* (NBC, 1964–5) and *Tammy* (ABC, 1965–6), programmes whose appeal capitalised on their 'exotic' locales – sixteen-year-old Karen Scott (Debbie Watson) enjoying the fun and sun of Southern California, while eighteen-year-old Tammy Tarleton (also Debbie Watson) switched between a down-home life on her family's Bayou houseboat and her job as a secretary to a wealthy plantation owner.

Like the earlier *A Date with Judy* and *Meet Corliss Archer*, *Tammy* can be seen as an early example of commercial 'transmedia exploitation'. The central character had originally debuted in the cinema, with Debbie Reynolds starring as the backwoods lass in the movie *Tammy and the Bachelor* (1957), while the TV series was followed by two more outings to the silver screen, this time with Sandra Dee taking the lead in *Tammy Tell Me True* (1961) and *Tammy and the Doctor* (1963).[17] Gidget, too, can be seen as a 'transmedia' phenomenon. The fresh-faced Californian teen had first appeared in Frederick Kohner's 1957 novel based on the true-life adventures of his surfer daughter, Kathy. Then, in 1959, Kohner's novel got the Hollywood treatment. In *Gidget*, Columbia Pictures' romantic beach 'n' surf comedy, Sandra Dee (again) featured in the title role as an irrepressible teen who persuades her affluent parents to buy her a surfboard so she can surf 'just like the guys'. A box-office hit, *Gidget* was followed not only by the film sequels *Gidget Goes Hawaiian* (1961) and *Gidget Goes to Rome* (1963 – both starring Deborah Walley as Gidget), but also by ABC's TV series and a deluge of books, comics, records and mountains of other Gidget paraphernalia.

The torrent of 'teen girl' TV shows produced during the late 1950s and early 1960s, then, was just part of a wider business machine geared to reaping profit from a new, lucrative consumer market. Indeed, in an attempt to maximise the pulling (and selling) power of its schedule, ABC created a prime-time 'teenage block' in its 1964–5 season, with *The Patty Duke Show* and pop jamboree *Shindig!* screened back-to-back on Wednesday evenings.

For many in the nascent women's movement, this kind of commercial culture was manipulative and oppressive. Most obviously Betty Friedan, in her classic *The Feminine Mystique* (1963), depicted women in post-war America as being seduced into submissive quiescence by capitalist marketeers, a malaise exemplified by the 'new vacant sleepwalking, playing-a-part quality of youngsters who do what they are supposed to do, but do not seem to feel alive or real in doing it':

> Like a primitive culture which sacrificed little girls to its tribal gods, we sacrifice our girls to the feminine mystique, grooming them ever more efficiently through the sexual sell to become consumers of things to whose profitable sale our nation is dedicated.[18]

Friedan did not discuss the relationship between young women and teen TV directly, but it is hard to imagine her as an avid fan of *A Date with Judy* or *The Patty Duke Show*. And, undeniably, there was room to criticise such series. The earlier 'teen girl' shows, especially, could be interpreted as offering representations of femininity that were passive, conformist and subordinate through their emphasis on the importance of 'winning a man' and their depiction of a woman's place as being 'in the home'. As Kearney observes of *A Date with Judy* and *Meet Corliss Archer*, for example, these series tended to confine their female protagonists to the family home and domestic roles, and foregrounded their future identities as spouses and parents.[19] In shows such as *Too Young to Go Steady* and *Peck's Bad Girl*, meanwhile, girls' integration into the world of heterosexual relations was a recurring theme, with the young protagonists habitually presented as boy-obsessed and desperately anxious about their appearance. At the same time, however, as much as these series reproduced traditional ideologies of passive femininity, Kearney points out that their characters also showed an independence and assertiveness that 'suggested that as they aged they most likely would pursue additional goals, including college and work outside the home'.[20] And, in later shows such as *Patty Duke* and *Gidget*, these elements of dynamism and autonomy became more pronounced.

The inherent tensions and open-endedness of *The Patty Duke Show* are highlighted in Moya Luckett's (1997) insightful analysis of the series. For Luckett, the narrative device of having Duke play two characters – the zany Patty and the more sober Cathy – created 'a doubling, a *disruption* of identity' that implied 'the extreme mutability of the teenage girl's identity'.[21] Moreover, by contrasting the bouncy Patty with her bland boyfriend Richard (Eddie Applegate) and her nerdy younger brother Ross (Paul O'Keefe), the show offered a relatively positive depiction of teen femininity that was vibrant and confident.[22] And, as in many of the 1960s' 'teen girl' sitcoms, same-sex friendship was a central theme in *Patty Duke*. This was partly a strategy through which the programme-makers could avoid dealing with the still relatively taboo subject of girls' sexuality – emphasis on characters' friendships with female friends displacing the potentially risqué subject of relationships with boys. Nevertheless, the consequence was that the narrative ultimately expelled male figures 'in order to underline the importance and pleasure of female bonding'.[23]

Many of the same elements were also prominent in *Gidget*. But, whereas in *Patty Duke* the tensions of teen femininity were played out through the interplay of two characters – Patty had her alter ego Cathy – in *Gidget*, Luckett argues, the theme was articulated through the programme's narrative strategies. Most episodes of *Gidget* opened with a voiceover from the heroine and closed with her directly addressing the audience, these confessional asides underlining the contradictions surrounding the character's negotiation of her feminine identity in the week's adventure.[24] And, as in *Patty Duke*, it was Gidget's relationship with her best friend, Larue (Lynette Winter) that was central to the series rather than any romantic interest. Indeed, young male characters were fairly marginal to the show. For most of the series Gidget's boyfriend, Jeff (Stephen Mines), was studying at Princeton and seldom seen. For the fast-talking, wisecracking Gidget it was not romantic commitment but fun and independence that were the priority. In one episode ('In and Out with the In-Laws'), for example, Gidget is horror-struck at the possibility of marriage when Jeff arranges for her to meet his mother and father ('Sort of halfway going steady is one thing – but meeting a fella's parents is something else!').

*Gidget* also routinely cast boys as foolish buffoons. In 'Ego-A-Go-Go', for example, Gidget resolves to boost the self-esteem of high-school geek Norman 'Derf the Nerf' Derfner (guest star Richard Dreyfuss) by asking him on a date. The gesture, however, backfires and 'Derf the Nerf' is transformed into a conceited twit. Gidget was certainly interested in boys, but rather than any oppressive 'code of romance', the central theme of the show was Gidget and Larue's yearning for fun in the sun and their struggle for freedom from interfering adults such as Gidget's over-protective sister, Anne, and her husband (a maddeningly over-analytical psychologist). This striving for autonomous fun, in fact, was a theme that recurred across Gidget's varied media manifestations, the cover of the first *Gidget* comic cheekily proclaiming 'So Who's Got Time for Adults!'[25]

The world of 1960s' 'teen girl' TV celebrated a femininity based around hedonism and friendship, but these delights were not open to everyone. As Luckett observes, when teenagers were featured at the centre of a show, 'they were always white and middle-class. Working-class and ethnic teenagers were not simply ignored but unapologetically displaced from attention on the grounds they were not significant.'[26] Indeed, possessing relatively little financial power, these groups were of little interest to TV programmers and advertisers.

The teenage market that emerged in America after World War II was pre-eminently white and middle class. Increases in African-American high-school enrolment brought black and white youth together as never before,[27] while the growth of rock 'n' roll testified to important processes of inter-ethnic cultural exchange. Nevertheless, according to Palladino, embedded racism and economic inequality ensured that throughout the 1950s and early 1960s 'black teenagers remained invisible as far as mainstream society was concerned'.[28] Teenage spending power was concentrated in the affluent suburbs, where the post-war prosperity of the American middle class afforded their children a life of significant material comfort with negligible financial commitment. In 1947, for example, market research produced for *Seventeen* magazine revealed the middle-class character of the teenage market, with 63 per cent of the readers' fathers working as company executives, professionals, or owning their own business.[29] And throughout the 1950s and 1960s a steady stream of social scientific research pointed to social class as a significant force within American youth culture, sociologist Jessie Bernard observing in 1961 that 'teen-age culture' was essentially the culture of a 'leisure class':

> Youngsters of lower socioeconomic classes are in the teen-age culture only in their early teens. They are more likely than children of higher socioeconomic class to enter the labor force or the armed forces or to get married soon after high school and, thus, to disappear into the adult world. This exit from the teen-age world by youngsters of lower class background means that those who remain are disproportionately from the higher socioeconomic class background.[30]

It was the wallets of this 'leisure class' that primarily interested American advertisers and TV programmers of the 1950s and 1960s. Hence the teen TV shows of the period addressed the lives and experiences of the white middle class almost exclusively. *A Date with Judy* and *Meet Corliss Archer*, for example, were set in sedate, middle-class households. In *Too Young to Go Steady* Pam Blake's father was an attorney, in *Peck's Bad Girl* Torey Peck's father was a research physicist, while Gidget's father was a widowed college professor – all representing solidly middle-class family backgrounds. *The Patty Duke*

*Show*, meanwhile, was set in the affluent New York suburb of Brooklyn Heights, and Patty's father was a newspaper editor. Tammy Tarleton was the partial exception. A simple country girl, Tammy lived on a ramshackle boat with her bumpkin relatives, Southern-fried stereotypes Grandpa Mordecai, Uncle Lucius and Cousin Cletus. Nevertheless, even 'poor but honest' Tammy enjoyed generous helpings of the good life when she was whisked away by wealthy plantation man John Brent to work as his secretary.

## 'Oi'll Give It Foive . . . But I Won't Boiy It!': Young Women and the Growth of British Teen TV

The socio-economic bedrock to the teenage market in post-war Britain differed from that in America. The growth of teenage spending in Britain was slower and less spectacular than in the USA but, like their American cousins, British youngsters enjoyed augmented disposable income during the 1950s and 1960s. Routinely cited in an array of official reports, as well as a multitude of books, newspapers and magazines, research conducted for the London Press Exchange by Mark Abrams suggested that youth, more than any other social group, had prospered in 1950s' Britain. Abrams calculated that since 1945 young people's real earnings had risen by 50 per cent (roughly double the rise in that of adults), while youth's 'discretionary' spending had risen by as much as 100 per cent – representing an annual expenditure of around £830 million.[31] Furthermore, Abrams maintained that this spending was concentrated in particular consumer markets (representing, for example, 44 per cent of total spending on records and record players and 39 per cent of spending on bicycles and motorcycles) which, he concluded, represented the rise of 'distinctive teenage spending for distinctive teenage ends in a distinctive teenage world'.[32]

But, whereas the heart of America's 'distinctive teenage world' was middle-class suburbia, the youth market that emerged in Britain was different. While Abrams conceded that higher standards of living in post-war Britain had meant that some class barriers had 'tended to lose their clarity',[33] he insisted that among young people class boundaries remained pronounced. In particular, Abrams judged that 'teenage demand' was 'typical only of working class teenagers' and 'largely without appeal for middle class boys and girls'.[34] The 'teenage market', Abrams insisted, was 'almost entirely working class' and that 'not far short of 90 per cent of all teenage spending [was] conditioned by working class taste and values'.[35]

In Britain, the rise of the commercial youth market was largely the outcome of shifting patterns of working-class employment. The intensification of long-term trends in the British economy – the decline of heavy industries, the movement of capital into lighter forms of production (especially the manufacture of consumer goods), the expansion of production-line technologies, trends towards 'de-skilling' and the movement of labour out of direct production and into distribution and service – registered an impact on the workforce as a whole, but had the greatest consequences for young workers.[36] De-skilling and production-line technologies created a demand for a flexible, though not especially skilled, workforce and (cheaper to employ than adults) young people were an ideal source for this labour. Indeed, rather than undertaking a period of relatively poorly paid training or apprenticeship, many youngsters much preferred the relatively high immediate rewards offered by unskilled and semi-skilled work. It was, then, the new spending power of these relatively affluent, working-class youngsters that spurred the growth of the commercial youth market in Britain during the 1950s and early 1960s.

Gender inequalities ensured young women's earnings were significantly less than those of their male peers, but during the 1950s and 1960s most working girls still possessed a margin of disposable income for personal consumption. In fact, many of the new 'teenage' products were specifically targeted at girls, while many established products and brands (especially cosmetics and toiletries) re-pitched themselves to appeal to the 'teen girl' market. Indeed, surveying 'The Teenage Revolution' in 1965, Peter Laurie could confidently assert: 'The real dynamo behind the teenage revolution is the anonymous teenage girl . . . Although girls spend less than boys, the dominant sales efforts for clothes, records, and cosmetics is aimed at girls.'[37]

The British media's response to the rise of the teenage market was varied. Radio, for example, reacted slowly. Until the 1960s rock 'n' roll could be heard only by tuning in to the American Forces Network or Radio Luxembourg, since it was largely ignored by the BBC as a consequence of 'needle time' restrictions[38] and officialdom's mandarin disdain for a music it deemed crassly commercial. The younger medium of television, however, responded more swiftly. Initially, pop music programmes such as *Hit Parade* (BBC, 1952), *TV Music Shop* (ITV, 1955) and *Off the Record* (BBC, 1956) were muted in their appeal to youth. By the later 1950s, however, a more fully formed, youth-oriented genre was emerging. Partly, this was a consequence of institutional change. Under the terms of the 1954 Television Act, TV companies had been obliged to suspend broadcasting between the hours of six and seven in the evening. Known colloquially as 'the Toddlers' Truce', the pause was intended to allow parents to put their children to bed without any distraction.[39] But, at the instigation of ITV (Britain's first commercial channel, launched in 1955), the 'Truce' ended in 1957. As a result, programmers were forced to look for shows that could fill the vacant slot quickly and cheaply. The urgency of this demand afforded sudden opportunities to new production talent and programme formats, effectively laying the way for new TV series aimed squarely at a youth audience.

British TV saw no teen sitcoms in the vein of *The Many Loves of Dobie Gillis*, and little of this US fare made it across the Atlantic to British schedules. In Britain, the pop show format was a bigger hit.[40] The brainchild of Oxford graduate, Jack Good, *Six-Five Special* led the way. Launched on the BBC in 1957, *Six-Five Special* picked up audiences approaching eight million by showcasing contemporary pop talent such as Tommy Steele, 'Little' Laurie London and Adam Faith. But the programme was hardly a bubbling cauldron of teenage rebellion. Making concessions to an adult audience, *Six-Five Special* included variety turns and film extracts, and had the older and obviously 'professional' Pete Murray and Jo Douglas as presenters – their supervisory presence ensuring an air of control and sensible maturity.[41] Leaving the BBC, Good developed a more quick-fire format for ITV with *Oh Boy!* (1958).[42] Broadcast live from the Hackney Empire, *Oh Boy!* proclaimed itself 'the fastest show on television', generating the excitement of a live performance through its stunning choreography and slick camerawork. In 1959 the BBC hit back with *Juke Box Jury*. Here, a conservatively suited David Jacobs introduced excerpts from recent record releases to a celebrity panel who would give their opinions, awarding the disc the status of 'hit' or 'miss'. And the programme, itself, was a resounding hit. With a format that could appeal to both teenagers and their parents, *Juke Box Jury* was attracting audiences of twelve million by 1962.

As in America, teenage girls were a sizeable (possibly the biggest) segment of the audience for pop TV shows. But young women also became a significant presence in the programmes themselves. However, whereas the middle-class composition of the US youth market called for the heroines of American teen TV to have unambiguously bourgeois credentials, the more working-class character of the British teenage market ensured that the young women who fronted British teen TV were constructed as ordinary, down-to-earth 'girls next door'.

In 1959 Susan Stranks had been featured as a 'typical teenager' on the first panel of *Juke Box Jury* – the perky nineteen-year-old enlisted to give 'a teenager's view' of the week's pop offerings. British TV's first true princess of pop, however, was Janice Nicholls. Sixteen-year-old Nicholls sprang to fame on ITV's *Thank Your Lucky Stars* (1961–6), a show launched as a response to the BBC's *Juke Box Jury*. At first, *Thank Your Lucky Stars* simply featured appearances by pop performers, but 1962 saw the introduction of a 'Spin a Disc' segment along the lines of *Juke Box Jury*, with a teenage panel awarding marks out of five to the latest pop releases. Nicholls, from the Midlands industrial town of Wednesbury, was one of the first panellists. She had originally harboured ambitions of working as a telephonist at an engineering firm based in her street, but on *Thank Your Lucky Stars* she became a celebrity. Straightforward and unassuming, Nicholls was a hit with audiences and became a fixture of the series, her broad Black Country accent making her frequent verdict 'Oi'll give it foive . . .' a national catchphrase.

But British teen TV's ultimate 'Joanne Public' was Cathy McGowan – the garrulous queen of ITV's pop flagship, *Ready, Steady, Go!* (1963–6). Initially, the programme harked back to earlier traditions of teen TV, with avuncular compere Keith Fordyce always waiting in the wings to make sure the party did not get out of hand. Increasingly, however, Fordyce looked out of place. Trading on the beat music boom and the rise of mod subculture, *Ready, Steady, Go!* eschewed concessions to an adult audience, instead revelling in the music, fashions and tastes of the 'happening' youth scene. Steadily, therefore, Fordyce was edged out in favour of his bubbly co-host, McGowan. A nineteen-year-old secretary from Streatham, London, McGowan was picked as a 'typical teenager' to help present the first series of *RSG!*, but she ultimately made the programme her own and eventually became the show's solo presenter. McGowan's appeal lay in the accessibility of her image. Certainly, she was chic and attractive, but at the same time she seemed just like any other teenage girl – sparky, fun and gushing with breathless enthusiasm for pop music and fashion. As pop historian Nick Cohn explains:

> She was amateur. She kept stumbling on her lines, stammering and blushing, grinning pointlessly. 'This is a Super record', she'd say, 'with a Swinging beat by a smashing artist . . .'. And when someone truly famous came on her show . . . she'd get tongue-tied and agonized, she'd flutter just like any fan. That was the point – she was just like some fan. She wasn't

some middle-aged DJ with a toupee and a plastic smile, she was almost a teenybopper herself, and she was genuinely thrilled because she met pop stars. So young girls could watch her and they'd think, 'That Cathy McGowan, she's like me, I'm like her, we both want Elvis Presley's autograph. And look at her, she's on TV. That means I could be on TV myself'.[43]

By the mid-1960s Cathy McGowan had become a cultural icon. With the sale of Cathy McGowan shirts, jeans, stockings, record players and even a movable Cathy McGowan doll, she became a figurehead of 'swinging' Britain, an emblem of what was widely heralded as a new era of exciting style and prosperity. More generally, John Davis convincingly argues that the period saw images of young women come to occupy a central position in the British 'youth spectacle' – changing perceptions and representations of femininity seeming to encapsulate a broader collection of uplifting social and cultural transformations (affluence, meritocracy, social dynamism) that many saw as transforming post-war Britain.[44] Indeed, alongside Nicholls and McGowan, the early 1960s saw a battalion of 'girls next door' plucked from obscurity by the British media and promoted as avatars of the exciting cultural moment. Fourteen-year-old Helen Shapiro, for example, was filmed waving goodbye to her friends at Clapton Girls' School as she embarked on a career as a singer and star of light-hearted pop movies such as *Play It Cool* and *It's Trad Dad* (both 1962). In the grittier world of 'kitchen sink' drama, Rita Tushingham made her debut in *A Taste of Honey* (1961) and went on to play a series of stoical working-class girls in films such as *That Kind of Girl* (1963), *A Place to Go* (1963) and *The Leather Boys* (1963), as well as featuring in 'swinging London' romps such as *The Knack* (1965) and the satirical *Smashing Time* (1966). And, significantly, Shapiro and Tushingham together shared the Variety Club of Great Britain's award for 'Most Promising Newcomer' in 1962. In the world of fashion, meanwhile, Mary Quant's designs pioneered a sensibility that was vibrantly youthful, and in 1962 pictures of teenage model Jean Shrimpton sporting a sleeveless Quant dress were splashed over the inaugural cover of the *Sunday Times* Magazine. Four years later the trend was further emphasised, the *Daily Express* promoting sixteen-year-old model Lesley Hornby, better known as 'Twiggy', as 'The Face of 66' – an articulation of femininity that was young, glamorous and excitingly modern.

## Weird Sisters: Femininity, Consumption and the Traditions of 'Teen Girl' TV

There were, then, both similarities and differences between the teen TV that developed in America during the 1950s and 1960s and that which emerged in Britain during the same period. On both sides of the Atlantic the rise of TV programming aimed at teenagers was constituent in, and indicative of, the growing significance of youth as a consumer market. But, whereas in America the rise of teenage spending was related to the prosperity of the suburban middle class, the British youth market was much less bourgeois. Instead, the growing spending power of British youth was chiefly indebted to the transformation of working-class labour markets. Hence the British and American varieties of teen TV were distinguished by contrasting forms of representation and modes of address. In American teen sitcoms like *Gidget* and *The Patty Duke Show*, the protagonists were drawn from well-heeled stock, their adventures addressing the lives and culture of relatively privileged teens. In contrast, the comparatively humble backgrounds and provincial accents of Janice Nicholls, Cathy McGowan and the other 'girls next door' of British pop TV, spoke to the experiences of youngsters from working-class (or, at most, lower-middle-class) backgrounds.

Significantly, however, young women were central to teen TV shows in both Britain and America during the 1950s and 1960s. Their pre-eminence was indebted to the profound changes in gender relations taking place in both countries. In both Britain and America gender inequalities remained pronounced, but in both countries women – and *young* women especially – were beginning to benefit from higher levels of disposable income and wider opportunities in employment and public culture. In media representations, therefore, it was hardly surprising that young women were frequently configured as being at the sharp end of social and cultural transformation – teenage girls often constructed as the living, breathing embodiment of post-war affluence and the widening horizons of commodity consumption.

In other respects, too, the kinds of femininity elaborated in American teen TV shows such as *Gidget* and those distinctive of the British 'pop girl' phenomenon were broadly similar. In both contexts teen femininity was characterised by a kind of 'consumerist hedonism', young women using the products and resources of commercial youth culture to carve out a space for self-expression and personal pleasure that was independent of parental (and often masculine) authority.

Of course, in some senses critics like Friedan were justified in their hostility to the institutions of consumer capitalism. The commercial market is, in many respects, inherently manipulative and exploitative, while access to the pleasures of consumption is limited by processes of exclusion and structural inequality (witness the white, middle-class exclusivity of the world portrayed in *Patty Duke*). Indeed, as McRobbie notes, cultural theorists have sometimes lost sight of the 'miseries and exclusions' of consumerism, dwelling over-eagerly on its 'delights, pleasures and achievements'.[45] At the same time, however, acknowledgement must still be given to the way 'attachments to goods and to the "social life of things" can be productive of new social identities'.[46] With this in mind, we can concede that the 'consumerist hedonism' served up in 1960s' 'teen girl' TV sitcoms and fast-paced, pop extravaganzas was neither radical, nor especially transgressive. But, at the same time, the images of femininity offered in shows like *Gidget* and *Ready Steady Go!* still pointed towards some enticing possibilities for the production of 'new social identities' through their celebration of fun, self-confidence and autonomy.

By the end of the decade, however, the heady atmosphere of 1960s' teen TV was beginning to wane. Certainly, throughout the 1970s and 1980s, both in Britain and America, many teen-oriented sitcoms, pop shows and dramas continued to be produced, some of which (for example, *The Facts of Life* (NBC, 1979–88)) continued to foreground teenage girls. But, as demographic trends brought a decline in the teenage populations (and their potential spending power) on both sides of the Atlantic, TV programmers increasingly turned their attention to other age groups. By the end of the 1990s, however, teen TV was making a comeback, as demographic shifts and economic trends once again combined to highlight young people as a lucrative and influential consumer market.

During the late 1990s, the youth populations of both Britain and America began to increase as the children of the 'baby boom' generation came of age. In Britain, projections suggested that there would be 5.6 million teenagers in 2010 – 800,000 (or 16 per cent) more than in 1992.[47] For market research gurus this represented exciting new vistas of commercial opportunity, Market Assessment International (MAI) hailing the arrival of 'Millennium Youth' or the 'M-Generation' who were 'richer than any previous generation – if measured in terms of possession of consumer durables and personal disposal income'.[48] In the USA, developments seemed even more dramatic. By 2000 the US teenage population stood at 31.6 million, nearly 6 per cent higher than the 'baby boomer' peak of 29.9 million in 1976. Even more than their British cousins, American marketers were energised at the prospect of this verdant consumer territory, youth-market specialists Teen Research Unlimited (TRU) whetting commercial appetites with the news that between 1996 and 2002 teen spending had climbed from $122 billion to $172 billion a year.[49] Amid this wider resurgence of the teenage market, then, teen TV also experienced a renaissance as programmers competed for the attention of advertisers eager to reach the flourishing youth market.

As in the 1960s, young women were especially prominent in the new generation of teen TV shows. But things had changed since the days of *Patty Duke*. Political struggles around gender and ethnicity had left their mark, so that much greater cultural and ethnic diversity was apparent. Young African-American women, for example, were central characters in sitcoms such as *Sister, Sister* (ABC/WB, 1994–9) and *Moesha* (UPN, 1996–). Teenage girls' sexuality, meanwhile, was still treated with caution but was much less taboo. For example, the teen drama *Beverly Hills 90210* (Fox, 1990–2000) explored issues such as teen pregnancy, safe sex and date rape as it charted the lives and loves of Brandon Walsh (Jason Priestley) and his sister, the petulant Brenda (doubly petulant Shannen Doherty). In shows such as *Buffy the Vampire Slayer*, moreover, a 'girl power' ethic has been firmly embraced, with the representation of a femininity that is intelligent, confident and powerful.

It would, however, be misleading to see contemporary images of feminine 'empowerment' in texts such as *Buffy* as marking an abrupt 'quantum shift' in popular representations of teenage femininity. Such programmes are better understood as developing out of a longer 'teen girl' TV tradition whose accent on freedom and fun *always* gestured towards a femininity that was independent and active. In these terms, without Gidget there would – quite possibly – have been no Buffy.

## Notes

I would like to acknowledge the generous help of Mary Celeste Kearney in my research for this chapter.

1. 'Gidget', *TV Guide*, 28 May 1966, p. 16.
2. Angela McRobbie, '*Jackie* and *Just Seventeen*: Girls' Comics and Magazines in the 1980s', in McRobbie, *Feminism and Youth Culture: From 'Jackie' to 'Just Seventeen'* (London: Macmillan, 1991), p. 175; Angela McRobbie, '*More!*: New Sexualities in Girls' and Women's Magazines', in McRobbie, *In the Culture Society: Art, Fashion and Popular Music* (London: Routledge, 1999a), p. 46.

3. Angela McRobbie, 'Pecs and Penises: The Meaning of Girlie Culture', in McRobbie, *In the Culture Society*, pp. 124 and p. 129.
4. Frances H. Early, 'Staking Her Claim: *Buffy the Vampire Slayer* as Transgressive Woman Warrior', *Journal of Popular Culture*, vol. 35, no. 3 (Winter 2001), pp. 11–17.
5. Susan A. Owen, '*Buffy the Vampire Slayer*: Vampires, Postmodernity, and Postfeminism', *Journal of Popular Film and Television*, vol. 27, no. 2 (Summer 1999), p. 25.
6. Alyssa Katz, '*Buffy the Vampire Slayer*', *Nation*, 6 April (1998), p. 35. At the time of writing (2002), scholarly enthusiasm for the Slayer of Sunnydale is proliferating, many accounts highlighting *Buffy*'s depiction of an empowered and frequently transgressive feminine subject. See, for example, several of the contributions to Roz Kaveney, *Reading the Vampire Slayer: An Unofficial Critical Companion to 'Buffy' and 'Angel'* (London: Palgrave, 2001), Lisa Parks and Elana Levine (eds), *Red Noise: Buffy the Vampire Slayer and Critical Television Studies* (Durham NC: Duke University Press, 2005, forthcoming) and Rhonda Wilcox and David Lavery (eds), *Fighting the Forces: What's at Stake in Buffy the Vampire Slayer* (Lanham, MD: Rowman & Littlefield, 2002).
7. Angela McRobbie, '*Jackie*: An Ideology of Adolescent Femininity', in Bernard Waites, Tony Bennett and Graham Martin (eds), *Popular Culture: Past and Present* (London: Croom Helm, 1982), p. 270. In her early contribution to the study of commercial girl culture, McRobbie coined the phrase 'code of romance' to denote 'an ideological bloc of mammoth proportions, one which imprisons [girls] in a claustrophobic world of jealousy and competitiveness' (ibid., p. 265).
8. John Modell, *Into One's Own: From Youth to Adulthood in the United States 1920–1975* (Berkeley, CA: University of California Press, 1989), pp. 225–6.
9. Dwight Macdonald, 'A Caste, a Culture, a Market', *New Yorker*, 22 November (1958), p. 60. See also Eugene Gilbert, *Advertising and Marketing to Young People* (New York: Printer's Ink, 1957), p. 21, Tables 1–6.
10. *Life*, 31 August 1959, p. 77.
11. See Mary Celeste Kearney, 'Teenagers and Television', in Horace Newcomb (ed.), *The Museum of Broadcast Communications Encyclopedia of Television* (Chicago, IL: Fitzroy Dearborn, 2003, forthcoming).
12. Kelly Schrum, '"Teena Means Business": Teenage Girls' Culture and *Seventeen* Magazine, 1944–50', in Sherrie Inness (ed.), *Delinquents and Debutantes: Twentieth Century American Girls' Cultures* (New York: New York University Press, 1998), p. 139.
13. Eugene Gilbert, 'Why Today's Teen-Agers Seem So Different', *Harper's Magazine*, November (1959), p. 77.
14. Kearney, 'Teenagers and Television'.
15. Mary Celeste Kearney, 'Television', in Miriam Forman-Brunell (ed.), *Girlhood in America: An Encyclopedia* (Oxford: ABC–CLIO, 2001), pp. 659–66; Mary Celeste Kearney, 'Recycling Judy and Corliss: Transmedia Exploitation Practices and the Teen-Girl Entertainment Market, 1940s–1950s', in John McMurria (ed.), *Screen Teens: Film, Television and Youth Culture* (Philadelphia: Temple University Press, 2004).
16. Kearney, 'Recycling Judy and Corliss'.
17. In 1967 episodes of the *Tammy* TV show were edited together for a third movie release, *Tammy and the Millionaire*.

18. Betty Friedan, *The Feminine Mystique* (Harmondsworth: Penguin, 1982, orig. pub. 1963), p. 203.
19. Kearney, 'Recycling Judy and Corliss'.
20. Kearney, 'Television', p. 661.
21. Moya Luckett, 'Girl Watchers: Patty Duke and Teen TV', in Lynn Spigel and Michael Curtin (eds), *The Revolution Wasn't Televised: Sixties Television and Social Conflict* (London: Routledge, 1997), p. 101.
22. Ibid., p. 95.
23. Ibid., p. 103.
24. Ibid., pp. 101–2.
25. *Gidget*, Dell Comics, April 1966.
26. Luckett, 'Girl Watchers', p. 100.
27. Between the early 1940s and the late 1950s the percentage of African-American students who finished high school virtually doubled. See James Gilbert, *A Cycle of Outrage: America's Reaction to the Juvenile Delinquent in the 1950s* (Oxford: Oxford University Press, 1986), p. 19.
28. Grace Palladino, *Teenagers: An American History* (New York: Basic Books, 1996), pp. 175–6.
29. Cited in Kelly Schrum, '"Teena Means Business"', p. 139.
30. Jessie Bernard, 'Teen-Age Culture: An Overview', *The Annals of the American Academy of Political and Social Science*, vol. 338 (November 1961), p. 2.
31. Mark Abrams, *The Teenage Consumer* (London: Press Exchange, 1959), p. 9.
32. Ibid., p. 10.
33. Mark Abrams, *The Newspaper Reading Public of Tomorrow* (London: Odhams, 1964), p. 57.
34. Mark Abrams, *Teenage Consumer Spending in 1959* (London: Press Exchange, 1961), p. 10.
35. Abrams, *The Teenage Consumer*, p. 13.
36. A concise overview of the impact of economic change on employment patterns among British youth is provided in Kenneth Roberts, *Youth and Employment in Modern Britain* (Oxford: Oxford University Press, 1995).
37. Peter Laurie, *The Teenage Revolution* (London: Anthony Blond, 1965), p. 151.
38. Since the 1930s an agreement between the BBC and representatives of the record industry and the Musicians' Union had limited the time available for the radio broadcast of commercially produced records.
39. See John Hill, 'Television and Pop: The Case of the 1950s', in John Corner (ed.), *Popular Television in Britain: Studies in Cultural History* (London: BFI, 1991), p. 90.
40. The pop programme was probably more attractive to British programmers because it was cheaper to produce than sitcoms or drama series. Commanding bigger budgets, in contrast, American stations had the freedom to explore a range of different teen TV formats.
41. Hill, 'Television and Pop', p. 93.
42. Subsequently, Good developed the pop vehicles *Boy Meets Girl* (1959–60) and *Wham!* (1960) for ITV, then adapted the *Oh Boy!* format for a stateside audience, producing *Shindig!* (1964–6) and *Hullabaloo* (1965–6) for the ABC and NBC networks respectively.
43. Nick Cohn, *AwopBopaLooBopALopBamBoom: Pop from the Beginning* (London: Paladin, 1970), p. 185.

44. John Davis, *Youth and the Condition of Britain: Images of Adolescent Conflict* (London: Athlone Press, 1990), p. 159.
45. Angela McRobbie, 'Bridging the Gap: Feminism, Fashion and Consumption', in McRobbie, *In the Culture Society*, p. 36.
46. Ibid., p. 37.
47. Barrie Gunter and Adrian Farnham, *Children as Consumers: A Psychological Analysis of the Young People's Market* (London: Routledge, 1998), p. 5.
48. Market Assessment International, *Millennium Youth 1999* (London: Market Assessment Publications, 1999), p. 4.
49. Teen Research Unlimited, 'Teens Spent $172 Billion in 2001', Teen Research Unlimited Press Release, 25 January 2002.

# 6

## Selling Teen Culture: How American Multimedia Conglomeration Reshaped Teen Television in the 1990s

### Valerie Wee

In May 1998,[1] fans of the teen-oriented WB television network watched an episode of the popular teen drama *Dawson's Creek* entitled 'The Scare' which paid particular homage to the highly successful and popular teen-slasher film, *Scream*. Released in December 1996, *Scream* featured a group of high-school students menaced by a knife-wielding serial killer. 'The Scare', like its filmic predecessor, was a clever, ironic treatment of the teen-slasher genre. 'The Scare' featured the TV show's characters engaged in lengthy, self-conscious discussions deconstructing the similarities between the incidents in the show and those in the film. The intertextual relationships between the texts were enhanced by the fact that Joshua Jackson, a member of the *Dawson's Creek* cast, had a small role in *Scream 2*, while guest star Scott Foley was slated to appear in *Scream 3*, the final instalment in the *Scream* trilogy. Furthermore, *Dawson's Creek* was the creation of Kevin Williamson, who had scripted the *Scream* franchise.

In September 1999 an episode of the teen-oriented television sitcom *Sabrina the Teenage Witch* featured pop star Britney Spears in a guest appearance. Entitled 'There's No Place Like Home', the episode revolved, in part, upon Sabrina's (Melissa Joan Hart) great wish to attend the singer's concert. Spears' appearance included a performance of her single '(You Drive Me) Crazy', which had been released just days before the *Sabrina* episode aired. The release of the single and the broadcast of 'There's No Place Like Home' also coincided with the opening of *Drive Me Crazy* in American movie theatres, a teen film starring Sabrina herself, Melissa Joan Hart. This particular instance of cross-promotional synergy culminated with the episode's end credits screened against Spears' *(You Drive Me) Crazy* music video, which featured the pop songstress cavorting with Melissa Joan Hart. This music video was simultaneously enjoying conspicuous exposure on MTV, the cable music channel that caters primarily to the teen demographic – the very same demographic vital to the commercial success of Spears, Hart, *Sabrina* and *(You Drive Me) Crazy* (both the song and the movie).

During the 1999–2000 television season, WB premiered *Popstars*, a reality series (with shades of *The Monkees*) that tracked the creation of a girl-group called Eden's Crush. The series, produced in association with pop producer/songwriter David Foster, featured a week-by-week exploration of the group's formation, from the multiple rounds of auditions to the selection of the final five members, the rehearsals for their musical performances, the recording of their first single and the filming of the group's music video. The WB further promoted the group by having them appear and perform on other WB teen television series such as *Sabrina the Teenage Witch*. The enterprise was yet another case study in synergy. The Time-Warner-owned WB network broadcast the creation of the group and provided invaluable on-air promotion for their album and single, while WEA/London-Sire Records, part of the Warner Music Group, which is a division of Time-Warner, produced and released the group's album. With this intense degree of promotional commitment, Eden's Crush's first single, 'Get over Yourself', went to number one in the American music charts. The song's video also went into heavy rotation on MTV, gaining Eden's Crush, *Popstars* and the WB additional exposure with the cable network's teen audience.

The three examples mentioned above exhibit some of the characteristic markers that distinguish teen television in the late 1990s. These markers include:

- The increasingly synergistic connections between teen television shows and other teen-oriented media texts, including film, music, and music videos.
- The growing tendency for teen stars and creative personnel to 'cross over' between different media.
- The turn towards post-modern 'hyper-'intertextuality, as evidenced by the collapsing boundaries between film, television, music and music video texts as well as the intense intertextual referencing that occurs between these multimedia texts.

Why have these characteristics surfaced in the 1990s' teen television text? What conditions have brought about these developments? This chapter argues that commercial, economic and industrial exigencies play a significant role in constructing, shaping and manipulating the cultural. Rather than addressing issues concerning viewer response and identification, or topics of representation and the like, I will focus on the complex relationship between industrial context and media text. The following pages highlight the qualities inherent in popular American teen television texts of the late twentieth century and relate them to the industrial, technological and marketplace developments that characterised the American culture industries during that period. I will show that attempts to understand the nature of late 1990s' American teen television must take into account the state of the culture industries and how their economic interests shaped commercial teen TV texts.[2]

## Media Conglomeration and the Intensification of Multimedia Synergy in the 1990s

As highlighted above, late 1990s' teen-oriented media texts were a complex mix of various media forms including film, television and music videos. Certainly, teen culture has historically been characterised by blendings of different media texts. Rock 'n' roll acts have appeared on television and contributed to film soundtracks, and teen personalities have appeared on film, television and cut records since the 1950s.[3] Scholars including

Jeff Smith, Thomas Doherty and Alexander Doty have noted that cross-media collusive practices, particularly between the film and music industries, have been practised in some degree since Decca Records acquired Universal Pictures in 1952. However, the early instances of cross-promotional synergy in the 1950s through to the 1970s tended to focus primarily on the marriage of film and music soundtrack. In contrast, the cross-media marketing and promotional activities in 1990s' teen-oriented culture was marked by an unprecedented degree of intersection across multiple forms of media and distribution outlets. This particular movement was motivated by the American media industries' unprecedented acceleration towards multi-media conglomeration during which media corporations expanded their holdings and interests across film, television, music, publishing, retail and the Internet.

This development had its roots in the wave of media consolidation and conglomeration that began in the 1980s.[4] The period was marked by a series of high profile mergers between communications and entertainment behemoths intent upon expanding their interests across multiple media outlets. Rupert Murdoch's News Corp., which began with a base in publishing, initiated the shift towards heightened multimedia conglomeration when it purchased 20th Century-Fox in 1985 and launched the Fox television network a year later. In 1986, Warner Communications, with its film, television and music holdings expanded its multimedia interests by merging with publishing giant, Time Inc. Subsequently, Sony expanded into film, television and music when it purchased Columbia and CBS Records in 1989. Viacom, whose ownership interests included radio, cable and television services, acquired Paramount Studios in 1994, and bought out Blockbuster Video a year later. 1995 also witnessed Disney's purchase of Cap Cities, which owned the ABC television network, and Seagram's buyout of MCA/Universal. In the late 1990s, Universal united with Vivendi, Viacom purchased CBS and Time-Warner joined with AOL.

One key consequence of this escalating media consolidation was the emergence of a handful of multimedia giants that controlled a steadily increasing range of media outlets and products. An intriguing consequence of the culture industries' turn to conglomeration was the growing fragmentation of the market and the multiplication of media texts and products. As multimedia conglomerates continued to expand further into new entertainment media and technology, they became more active and efficient in parsing out and exploiting the existing media/entertainment markets. Expanding multimedia corporations such as News Corp., Time-Warner and Viacom became better poised to manipulate and profit from the continual expansion of the product line, and adapted new ways to promote and sell.

Within teen culture, this resulted in an ever-expanding list of teen products in a variety of media, all of which originated from a single hit product. As Thomas Schatz points out, the shift to conglomeration, the increasing degree of deregulation, and the evolution of new technologies and new media, changed the entertainment landscape:

> The ideal [entertainment product/text] today is . . . [a] promotion for a multimedia product line, designed with the structure of both the parent company and the diversified media

marketplace in mind.... the New Hollywood has been driven (and shaped) by multipurpose entertainment machines which breed movie sequels and TV series, music videos and sound track albums, video games and theme park rides, graphic novels and comic books, and an endless array of licensed tie-ins and brand-name consumer products.[5]

This practice of spinning out an entertainment product across multiple media outlets, the better to exploit the numerous branches of a multimedia corporation, highlights another of the key trends characteristic of the American culture industries in the late twentieth century: synergy. Multimedia conglomeration and the interest in synergy encouraged the culture industries to exploit the promotional and marketing opportunities that accrued from blurring the boundaries of media texts rather than maintaining the integrity of a media figure as a commodity in a single medium.

When Britney Spears guest-starred on *Sabrina*, the incident pointed to the highly intertwined nature of the film, television and music industries' focus on attracting and harnessing the teen market. Here, a hugely popular teen pop star (Spears) who did not have an established acting presence on television, outside her music video appearances that are primarily restricted to MTV, crossed over into television. As such, *Sabrina the Teenage Witch*, Britney Spears, her album ... *Baby One More Time*, the film *Drive Me Crazy* and its soundtrack were all involved in mutually beneficial promotional and marketing exercises. This crossover resembled the ties that bound the *Scream* film series to the *Dawson's Creek* episode which allowed the film franchise to benefit from the promotional exposure on a hit television show, even as the television show itself actively set out to attract the very teenagers who were responsible for the success and popularity of the slasher film franchise.

Another key factor that distinguished this late 1990s' practice of synergistic franchising from previous teen cycles was the simultaneity of the multiple product launches. In the late 1990s, many teen texts were concurrently devised as a teen film with the potential to spawn film sequels, a television series with the possibility for spin-offs, soundtracks and music videos, even extending into merchandise including clothing, books and magazines from their very inception. In contrast, past teen cycles adopted a hierarchical approach to repackaging activities – a hit teen film would generate a television show, whose success would lead to merchandising deals, where these activities tended to be played out in a linear, chronological process. *Dawson's Creek/Scream*, *Sabrina*/Spears/*Drive Me Crazy* and *Popstars* were all simultaneous launches that functioned in very different ways than the media roll-outs of teen films in the 1960s, television shows in the 1970s or music videos in the 1980s, which had a clear hierarchy of intents and interests and explicitly positioned a single media text as the origin of the process.[6]

In an effort to cater to a teenage market that has access to an ever-expanding range of media platforms, the late 1990s' culture industries engaged in focused efforts to exploit and franchise any and all teen-oriented properties they owned. Yet another successful teen-oriented franchise was News Corp./20th Century-Fox's *Buffy the Vampire Slayer*. Interestingly, *Buffy* was originally a moderately successful film released by the studio in 1992. In 1996, Fox resurrected *Buffy* as a television show. The television show went on to generate a television soundtrack, and was simultaneously repackaged into a wide and assorted range of related media/commodity products. The product line included the original film on which the series is based, videos and DVDs of the television show (which were produced and distributed by 20th Century-Fox), the show's soundtrack, books, magazines and comics based on the show (published by News Corp.), a *Buffy*-inspired clothing line, dolls and posters, a computer game, and many other items.

The complex interrelationships between the increasingly convergent film, television, music, publishing and fashion industries directly shaped the nature of these texts. Soundtracks, music videos, trailers, fashion, magazine features and television appearances were just some of the many components circulating and functioning as both related and competing intertexts. As Wyatt notes, these promotional aspects tended to 'multiply the meanings from the texts in order to increase the audience base', a strategy that has been successful for several decades.[7] In many cases, it was hard to distinguish between the text and the commercial for the texts since most of the articulations functioned in both capacities. Hence, a teen television show was never just a television show in the 1990s, but one part of a steadily expanding series of media products.

In addition to product multiplication, the synergistic and cross-promotional activities characteristic of 1990s' teen culture also revolved around the development of the crossover[8] appeal of specific teen-identified personalities.

## Crossover

Crossing over was by no means new or unique to teen culture. Stars such as Elvis Presley, Annette Funicello and Pat Boone, all crossed over between music, film and television appearances. But the activity became particularly prevalent in its own specific ways in the 1990s. During this period, the most successful people were those who appeared to move seamlessly between the media of film, television and music. This was true of the stars as well as the 'star' producers and creators. In fact, 1990s' teen culture was founded, marketed and appeared to revolve around a rather finite set of teen stars and personalities, many of whom consistently worked across a variety of entertainment media, often simultaneously. Melissa Joan Hart (*Sabrina*), Sarah Michelle Gellar (*Buffy*) and Joshua Jackson (*Dawson's Creek*), like many of their peers, successfully transferred their television success onto the big screen, appearing in many of the most popular teen films of the 1990s, while they were also appearing on their television shows. According to producer Neal Moritz, 'The recognizability of these actors makes them valuable . . . they have a built-in awareness [with the teenage audience], and [their work on television indicates that] they're a proven commodity.'[9] The interaction between these teen actors and their film, television, and even musical projects provide further insight into how synergy functioned. In casting an established teen television star in films, the film and television texts attempted to exploit the star's teen-oriented following, hoping that the star would draw his/her teenage fan base to the new project.

The ability to shift between these media had a definite impact upon the nature of the teen text, particularly at the level of plot and characterisation. Teen stars Jennifer Love Hewitt and Brandy were two personalities who starred in television series, and had recording contracts and film careers. Both women's television shows acknowledged and exploited their singing talents by constructing plots that allowed them the opportunities for musical performances. These musical sequences helped to promote their singing careers and sell their CDs.

The practice of cross-over was not restricted to on-screen talent but extended to creative personnel as well. In fact, teen culture's propensity for synergy and crossover contributed towards an increasingly blurred line between the film and television media themselves. While film-makers' involvement in television was not necessarily a new or unique development, it evolved into a late 1990s' teen television trend, one that particularly characterised the teen-identified WB television network's relationship with feature film-makers. Jordan Levin, the president of WB, recognised that the network's teen audience 'demands a cinematic styling . . . because the 12- to 34-year-olds are [avid] movie-goers'.[10] Consequently, attracting 'fresh talent from the feature business' made good sense if the network hoped to distinguish itself as specifically teen-oriented and sell itself to that audience.[11]

The WB network began aggressively luring film-makers to television based on the belief that, if teenagers were the most dedicated film-goers at the time, they could also evolve into devoted television watchers, and what better way to lure them to both media than to ensure that teenagers had access to the very same brand names both at home and in the movie theatre? Hence, many of the creators, producers and scriptwriters most clearly associated with teen culture were people who comfortably, and successfully, shifted between television and film. Both Kevin Williamson, who went from scripting the film *Scream* to creating *Dawson's Creek* for television, and Joss Whedon, who began in music videos and then worked on films including *Speed* (1994), *Toy Story* (1995) and *Alien Resurrection* (1997) and who was responsible for *Buffy the Vampire Slayer*, were the network's early successes. Subsequently, WB entered into a series of development deals with creative personnel from feature backgrounds. Many of WB's teen television shows had ties with feature film personnel. *Felicity* creators J. J. Abrams and Matt Reeves began in films, the former as a scriptwriter with films such as *Regarding Henry* (1991) and *Armageddon* (1998) to his credit, the latter as the director of *The Pallbearer* (1996). The producers and creative individuals on WB's teen TV series *Young Americans* included production designer Vince Peranio, who collaborated with John Waters on many of his films, and also worked on *Blair Witch II* (2000), and camera operator Aaron Pazanti, who worked on the Oscar-winning *American Beauty* (1999).

This cross-media mobility accelerated through the 1990s and led to a growing convergence in style and aesthetics across teen-oriented films, television and even music videos. In fact, one of the key qualities of teen-oriented texts in the late 1990s was the degree of stylistic and narrative consistency that flowed across different texts and different media. In the past, fairly obvious distinctions existed between, for instance, film and television that marked each as a separate medium. By the 1990s, however, these boundaries disintegrated as many teen television shows were shot on film in a single-camera filmic format offering the rich, organic visuals characteristic of the filmic, rather than televisual, image.[12] Further stylistic mixing occurred on the level of thematic content and narrative structure. This is evident in the *Dawson's Creek* episode 'The Scare', which was stylistically and conventionally similar to the cinematic *Scream*, going as far as to replicate, in large part, the narrative conventions, characters and visual style of that landmark teen-oriented horror film. This trend was matched by the increasing congruence between film, television and the once distinct MTV-music-video style. The Britney Spears/*Sabrina* incident was just one example of a teen text that consciously disregarded the distinctions between the television sitcom and music video format, their respective visual styles and narrative strategies. These activities allowed media corporations to extend the promotional opportunities of each television text.

This stylistic and aesthetic convergence across media, the intense and increasingly seamless degree of media mixing, the intertextual references, the loss of historical and chronological distinctions between texts/images/narratives so that they all appear contemporary, all point to another characteristic of the 1990s' teen text, one that occurs across the range of entertainment media: the tendency towards post-modern 'hyper-'intertextuality.

## Post-modern 'Hyper-'intertextuality

1990s' teen culture displayed an amplified propensity for the post-modern. Having recognised the 1990s' teen audience's heightened media and cultural literacy, which were built upon an obsession with popular entertainment and movies in particular, many of WB's teen shows consistently utilised intertextual pop-culture references in an attempt to attract and profit from this target audience's interests. The unprecedented degree to which the network's shows quoted, and frequently spoofed, both past and current popular culture was another trait of WB's teen television format.

Intertextual referencing in general is not unique to late 1990s teen texts. Many teen texts, including the exploitation films of the 1950s and 1970s, have engaged in the activity. In those earlier cases, however, the references tended to be either opportunistically derivative or tongue-in-cheek moments of subtext that often amounted to inside-jokes. In contrast, the current situation is distinctive because the referencing is not restricted to the occasional passing allusion. Rather, in the 1990s' instance, the referencing functions *as text*. Entire episodes of teen television shows and films engage in self-conscious, highly self-reflexive discussions and commentaries on the nature and conventions of other media texts. WB's teen series obsessively and self-reflexively discuss other media texts. In the 1990s, these instances of intertextuality were motivated and driven by overt technological, economic and synergistic imperatives.

According to Jim Collins, 1980s' television displayed an accelerated shift towards self-reflexivity and semiotic excess. Both these aspects revolved around the appropriation and absorption of other popular entertainment texts through the re-circulation of iconic or familiar images, multiple references to popular texts and/or the adoption of generic plot lines. Collins attributes the rise of this particular post-modern moment to a variety of interrelated conditions. One precondition involved 'the proliferation of signs and their endless circulation' in the 1980s and after, a situation 'generated by the technological developments associated with the information explosion (cable television, VCRs, digital recording, computers, etcetera)'.[13] These technological developments allowed the media industries to extend the shelf-life of media products indefinitely. Consequently, texts from past classical eras continued to be available and accessible to audiences along with more recently released material. This has resulted in a condition where what Umberto Eco calls the 'already said', continues to circulate, even as newer texts began to cite and rephrase the 'already said'.[14] Thus, as new texts joined older ones, all of which remain indefinitely accessible, they offered numerous and competing messages and signs which often referenced and re-circulated signs from older media texts.

I would argue that the media industries' shift to multimedia conglomeration and horizontal integration, as well as the accompanying commitment to exploiting all available media forms, directly contributed to the post-modern situation. As already noted, multimedia conglomeration encouraged the stylistic and aesthetic integration of previously distinct media forms. In addition, evolving new technologies continued to add to the media texts already in circulation. With increased access to media and technology, 1990s' teenagers surpassed previous generations in their capacity for media-oriented hyperconsciousness – emerging as the most culturally literate and media-saturated cohort ever encountered. These developments presented a cultural environment that encouraged the intensification of post-modern elements within popular cultural texts.

For instance, *Dawson's Creek* habitually paid homage to both past and contemporary popular films. 'The Scare''s homage/parody of *Scream* has already been mentioned. Other examples include an episode entitled 'Escape from Witch Island' (1999), in which the four main characters spend the night on a deserted, reportedly haunted island, with the intention of creating a video-documentary investigating the legend behind the haunting. Not only is the episode rife with stylistic and narrative references to the phenomenally successful film *The Blair Witch Project* (1999), the characters in the television series are seen obsessively and self-reflexively discussing the complex ways in which their experiences relate to the film and its conventions. Another episode, entitled 'Detention' (1998), borrows and discusses narratives, situations and plot points from the cult 1980s' John Hughes' teenpic *The Breakfast Club* (1985).[15] Like the film, the episode revolves around the teenage characters' experiences during a day in detention, which is spent with a group of misfits. The episode 'The Storm' pays homage to the hit Warner Bros. film *The Perfect Storm* (2000). While out sailing, Pacey and Jen are caught in a vicious storm, leading to numerous instances of dialogue that cite the film and its plot points while they wait for their friends to rescue them. Each of these episodes engaged in a significant amount of hyperconscious dialogue revolving around discussions of the films, with numerous self-aware quips regarding the similarities between the films and their experiences.

*Buffy* has also consistently referenced such diverse popular culture texts as *Jaws* (1975),[16] *The Usual Suspects* (1995), *Dracula* (1931, *et al.*) and *Star Trek: First Contact* (1996) among others. Often, the references tend to be almost glib and sometimes even obscure. In one episode, when Giles, a firm believer in demonic and occult manifestations, offers a rational, logical explanation for a potentially bizarre occurrence, Buffy responds with 'I can't believe that you, of all people, are trying to Scully me' – citing *The X-Files* and that show's scientifically and rationally inclined character, Dana Scully ('The Pack', 1997).[17] In a later instalment, faced with the need to battle a demonic monster of huge proportions, Xander quips, 'We're going to need a bigger boat', a line borrowed directly from *Jaws* ('Graduation Day', 1999).[18] Often, these references (to *Jaws*, *The Breakfast Club* and *Dracula*, among others) helped expose a new teen audience to these older media texts. The continued circulation of these texts (via video or cable), particularly among a new generation of consumers, meant their continued profitability for the multimedia conglomerates. *Buffy*'s intertextual referencing was not restricted merely to dialogue but also included stylistic and aesthetic borrowings as well. Many of *Buffy*'s episodes directly mimic the lighting, editing, style and *mise-en-scène* of teen horror movies.

As Caldwell notes, the refusal to distinguish between the older and more contemporary films, reducing every citation 'to a series of perpetual presents' is central to postmodernism.[19] This intensification of post-modernist intertextual elements within late twentieth-century popular teen culture was inextricably tied to issues of marketing, promotion, commodification and consumption.

## Conclusion

This chapter has focused entirely on American teen culture and American teen television and how these cultural texts were shaped by industrial developments. This perspective is important because the contemporary cycle of American teen culture is engaged in targeting a global teen market. Historically, past cycles of teen culture were largely conceptualised and targeted to a national, 'local' North American market.[20] When American media products travelled to other parts of the world, they were imported by locally owned distributors and exhibitors. Over the years, however, the American culture industries evolved into multinational corporate entities that could efficiently distribute teen culture across national borders, expanding the global possibilities, profitabilities and influence of American teen culture.

In the 1990s, a handful of American-based, American-owned, multinational multimedia corporations began amassing increased global power and influence. The continual merging of media institutions, accompanied by the increasing turn towards global cultural exchange and international cultural flows – much of it aided by the rise of the practically borderless World Wide Web – ushered in an era in which cultural texts and their representations of American teen culture became even more accessible to international audiences. With that came the opportunity for the enhanced economic exploitation of an expanding worldwide market.

These developments suggest that we are on our way to witnessing the rise of a global teen culture that embraces and shares a host of similar media products. The American culture industries' strategies with regard to teen culture raise some interesting implications regarding the politics of narrowcasting and niche targeting a global teen market. The hegemonic impact of these American media products is already unavoidable and will inevitably grow stronger. When we consider the impact of commercial American teen culture on its audience, we must recognise that the television and media industries are driven by, and respond to, primarily commercial and marketplace imperatives. The culture industries are targeting teens in response to industry and advertiser interests and demands rather than out of any altruistic motivation to service the global teen audiences' entertainment needs. Consequently, these multimedia entertainment conglomerates largely offer very specific inscriptions of teen-/youth-oriented programming that overwhelmingly emphasise Western, capitalist, middle-class values and ideologies. The distribution of these texts around the world places native cultures and non-US values and interests at risk. As John Tomlinson notes, a global culture threatens 'native' cultures because it involves 'the simultaneous penetration of local worlds by distant forces, and the dislodging of everyday meanings from their 'anchors' in the local environment'.[21] As American teen culture achieves global influence, Western, capitalist values and ideologies will gain ever-increasing influence over entire generations of youth, supplanting the native values of their national cultures.

Furthermore, these American teen texts also reflect industry-oriented values that emphasise capitalism and consumerism. While teenagers are largely sophisticated media readers and users, the fact remains that these texts will inevitably exercise some influence on their audiences. As such, we need to pay considerably more attention than we have so far on how dominant industrial and advertisers' interests shape textual content. The observations and arguments expressed here are largely speculative; however, they provide a preliminary overview of the key developments that will impact upon teen culture in the twenty-first century.[22]

## Notes

1. In this chapter, all film release dates and television broadcast dates refer to the United States.
2. While I will focus on the teen television text in my discussion, it is worth noting that the characteristics mentioned above are not unique to television but describe teen media culture in general.
3. Elvis Presley, Patty Duke, Annette Funicello and Frankie Valli are some teen stars who successfully crossed over between film, music and television in the 1950s and 1960s.
4. See Thomas Schatz, 'The New Hollywood', in Jim Collins, Hilary Radner and Ava Preacher Collins (eds), *Film Theory Goes to the Movies* (New York and London: Routledge, 1993), pp. 8–36 and Justin Wyatt, *High Concept: Movies and Marketing in Hollywood* (Austin, TX: University of Texas Press, 1994). The media industries' expansion beyond film into other commercial, entertainment-oriented areas did not begin in the 1980s. Indeed, Hollywood's film studios had a history of mergers and acquisitions reaching back into the 1960s and earlier. However, the 1980s' wave of mergers and acquisitions is significant because it marked the industry's shift away from loose diversification, in which studios expanded into a wide and sometimes non-media-related range of corporate activities, towards a strategy of tight diversification, in which these same studios began divesting themselves of their non-media holdings while expanding their interests into strictly media, entertainment and information-oriented industries. Warner Communications' changing industrial activities provide a prime example of this shift in corporate practice. Before the 1980s, Warner Communications was a loosely diversified transindustrial conglomerate with diverse holdings in a range of 'leisure-oriented' industries including entertainment, cosmetics, sports teams, toys, restaurants and other non-media firms. In 1982, the corporation decided to restructure and consolidate its interests in entertainment-oriented media. Consequently, Warner sold off

its interests in Atari, Warner Cosmetics, the Franklin Mint, Panavision and the New York Cosmos soccer team. This allowed Warner Communications to focus its interests on the production and distribution of film and television programming, recorded music and publishing. See Tino Balio, 'Adjusting to the New Global Economy: Hollywood in the 1990s', in Albert Moran (ed.), *Film Policy: International, National and Regional Perspectives* (New York: Routledge, 1996), pp. 23–38 and Eileen Meehan, '"Holy Commodity Fetish, Batman!": The Political Economy of a Commercial Intertext', in Roberta E. Pearson and William Uricchio (eds), *The Many Lives of the Batman: Cultural Approaches to a Superhero and his Media* (New York: Routledge, 1991), pp. 66–89 for more information on Warner Communications' vertical and horizontal diversification.

5. Thomas Schatz, 'The Return of the Hollywood Studio System', in Erik Barnouw *et al.* (eds), *Conglomerates and the Media* (New York: The New Press, 1997), p. 74.
6. Some might argue that these activities are not distinctly teen-oriented, and can be applied to almost all media experiences/texts/audiences in this period. While I acknowledge that media in general do engage in synergistic practices, I contend that the degree and range with which teen-oriented media texts access and exploit each other for promotional and marketing purposes are extreme enough to distinguish them from the more general media cultures.
7. Wyatt, *High Concept*, p. 44.
8. The early definition of crossover concentrated upon issues of race and was used to describe incidents in which non-white, usually African-American, entertainers transcended their racial 'identities' and 'crossed over' into the mainstream. I am not using the term in this particular definition. Rather, I use 'crossed over' in its more recent incarnation: to describe the practice of transcending the boundaries separating the different entertainment media and 'crossing over' (or crossing between) them. Therefore, an entertainer 'crosses over' when s/he moves between working in the film, television and music industries, rather than being restricted to a single one.
9. Annette Cardwell, 'Generation Next: Recent Hits Have Studios Screaming for More Teen Flicks', *The Boston Herald*, 23 September 1998, p. 55.
10. Jenny Hontz, 'Pic Scribes Flocking to Web Deals', *Daily Variety*, 31 August 1998, p. 1.
11. Ibid.
12. This stylistic convergence flowed both ways. Writing in 1991, Timothy Corrigan noticed that big-budget films were attempting to recuperate their large budgets by ensuring the product's viability across ancillary markets particularly on television, whether on video, pay-per-view, or for eventual network broadcast. 'This accounts', Corrigan notes, 'for the common, easy mobility of actors and directors between television and film (usually bringing television styles with them)'. See Timothy Corrigan, *A Cinema Without Walls: Movies and Culture After Vietnam* (New Brunswick, NJ: Rutgers University Press, 1991), p. 23.
13. Jim Collins, 'Television and Postmodernism' in Robert C. Allen (ed.), *Channels of Discourse, Reassembled* (Chapel Hill, University of North Carolina Press, 1992, 2nd edn), p. 331.
14. Umberto Eco, postscript to *The Name of the Rose* (New York: Harcourt Brace Jovanovich, 1984).
15. The 1990s' teenage audience may not have watched *The Breakfast Club* during its theatrical release; however, they would probably have seen the film either on video or in cable re-runs.

16. Like *The Breakfast Club*, *Jaws* is another popular staple available on video and cable.
17. Significantly, *The X-Files*, like *Buffy*, was produced and owned by 20th Century-Fox.
18. Acknowledging the obscurity of some of the references, and sensing yet another avenue for profit, a series of books entitled *The Official Watcher's Guide* was published. These books identified and explained each pop-cultural citation for the edification of its teen audience.
19. John Thornton Caldwell, *Televisuality: Style, Crisis, and Authority in American Television* (New Brunswick, NJ: Rutgers University Press, 1995), p. 206.
20. I am not suggesting that these earlier teen products did not reach an international audience, only that they were not consciously constructed with a global audience in mind.
21. John Tomlinson, *Globalization and Culture* (Chicago, IL: University of Chicago Press, 1999), p. 29.
22. Certainly many of these activities are no longer restricted to the teen arena. Indeed, the events I highlight may be viewed as a form of media development in general. However, I believe that teen culture still represents the most aggressive locus for these media industry practices. If only in terms of degree, teen culture remains the site where many of the most original and sophisticated crossover and global-oriented activities have arisen.

# 7

# 'My Generation': Popular Music, Age and Influence in Teen Drama of the 1990s

## Kay Dickinson

[A] particular generation was identified with 'youth' [the baby boomers] and invested with a certain power by a broad range of social discourses. The rock formation transformed that identity into a resource of affective power, determined by one's ability to invest in and live within the terms of the formation itself. In this way, the changing configuration of youth has played a major role in constructing the historical existence of rock, just as rock has had a complex and changing relationship to the various configurations of youth.

Lawrence Grossberg [1]

Without popular music, the representation and self-definition of the category 'teenager' – from its inception up until the present day – would be almost unrecognisable. Similarly, although popular music is stylistically diverse, one desire held dear by most of its proponents is to appear synonymous with youth, or at least youthfulness. How this interdependence might be fleshed out politically, what it might have to do with people who are far from under twenty, how 'youth' and 'youthfulness' are defined in the first place and how television figures in this mélange is the complex arrangement which this chapter seeks to survey.

### Music on (Youth) Television

Television has played a significant role in the intertwining of youth and music, although, in many instances, television has been considered meddlesome, even insensitive.[2] However, such a criticism should not overshadow the diverse range of popular music programming which has evolved on our TV screens over the last forty years or so. There are music (video) stations (like MTV), magazine programmes (like *Planet Pop*), documentaries and docusoaps (*Making the Band*), competitions (*Pop Stars*) and 'live' format shows (*Top of the Pops*), all of which seek to draw upon music's centrality within the teen sensibility (although this does not mean that the fans of either the shows or the music are necessarily actual teenagers). Programmes like these have already received the attention of scholars, most notably, Simon Frith,[3] John Mundy[4] and Karen Lury,[5] all of whom concentrate on non-fiction formats. Instead of travelling in the same direction, I want to set my sights on a less scrutinised interaction between music and television – how music operates within teen dramas. In such a short chapter, I only have space for three short extracts from two programmes. However, that such brief instances (often ten seconds or so at most) should bear the analytical fruit they do says much about the social, economic, industrial and semantic importance of music on television.

My first and last case studies are taken from *My So-Called Life* and both selections illustrate ways in which music can fortify a narrative theme by entering the storyline. In between, I shall explore the non-diegetic pop soundtrack to *Dawson's Creek*, elucidating how it functions simultaneously as a desirable commodity, a cultural compass and an extremely marshalled marker of 'youth'.

In both of these shows (as is the case with most programmes that employ compilation soundtracks), the implications of the music arrive in a coherent, pre-formed shape (which, in turn, may develop in response to the televisual context). Unlike, say, the specially composed score, the songs we hear on teen TV shows have usually held a prior place in the world and have already established a set of definitions for themselves. Consequently, such music *has* to be dealt with in reference to its extra-textual life; it may even be of more importance to teens than the shows which have chosen to adopt it. A television drama plays upon these strengths, using them to drive its own momentum, but the power exchange is two-way. Both TV and music offer each other contexts through which we can place ourselves: one may inform us of something the other cannot sufficiently articulate, or might add a dynamic contrapuntal flourish by saying something completely in opposition to the other's train of thought. Similarly, both music and TV stand for a set of multiple and ever-changing social practices and lifestyles which mean that their union has distinct economic and political repercussions. How might these positions cohere effectively, how might they clash and prove incompatible?

To start out with, as I have already hinted in the first sentence of this section, certain types of music have borne an animosity towards television. It is common practice – especially within youth subcultures – to deride 'cool' performers for having 'sold out' if they appear on television. Karen Lury's *British Youth Television* outlines the careful balance that makes up a successful music television show: the music is often treated with a straightforward sincerity while the presenter exudes an ironic, devil-may-care attitude towards the encasing format of television. Throughout its history, television has often been called upon to act as a passifier for music's more decadent and unpredictable proclivities. This reasoning depends upon a widespread understanding of television as public, mass and family-oriented entertainment and, likewise, upon popular music as niche-marketed and often more marginal – an equivalence which holds less and less weight within the contemporary media industries. However, the instances where this logic has taken hold have proven to be potent, even mythic moments in television history: Ed Sullivan persuasively argued to his audience that Elvis was a Nice (White) Young Man and Bill Grundy's interaction with the Sex Pistols proved that punk was just too rebellious for the square confines of television. Such stories allow us to believe – if we let ourselves be convinced so easily – that TV is safe and popular music is unpredictable, TV respects family values and popular music is more likely to sleep with its groupies and shrug off a barrage of paternity suits. TV sits in the patrolled environment of the home, while music often functions in much more illicit spaces. Although this set of oppositions is far too simplistic (and indeed, the reverse is often true – something to which my examples will bear witness), such cultural connotations place music in a strong position to function as narrative shorthand for a fancy-free, daring and irresponsible way of life – all the elements which are consistently attributed to and supposedly prized by 'youth'.

What needs to be acknowledged, however, is that these subversive resonances are largely constructed to bolster specific hegemonic positions and, moreover, industrial and political shifts may have occurred since these moments of music on television took place. This does not necessarily undermine the cultural propositions that 'music' or 'the musician' stand for, it just situates them somewhere different. We are now living in a time when teenagers have always had music videos, MTV and compilation soundtracks for films (and, increasingly, television shows). Unlike their older siblings, they will not be able to remember the inception of these relationships between the music and the moving image industries and, perhaps, will find it difficult to understand why certain types of music might have shied away from television for so long. Music is not an outsider to television any more, although it may often still play this role when needed (as we shall see). It is also now perhaps less likely to maintain the hypocritical posture of appearing to keep big business at arm's length, or to make somewhat tenuous assertions about its authenticity and refusal to 'sell out' (claims which commercial television itself rarely bothers to countenance in its own self-definition). Like television, popular music has, by and large, *always* been steered by large corporations (if not in production, then at least in distribution, licensing and so on) and its claims to the contrary are a fabricated but powerful collective fantasy which television readily draws upon. Perhaps because of the shakiness of this idealistic proposition, perhaps because of the increased horizontal integration of the entertainment industries (something I will explore in more detail shortly), television is now less and less likely to treat music apologetically, to play down its own worth in the presence of something supposedly much less sullied by the corrupting hands of big business capitalism. Unlike Lury's programme examples from the 1980s and early 1990s (such as *The Word* and *Rapido*), *My So-Called Life* and *Dawson's Creek* (which follow these shows by only a few years) are almost entirely sincere about their narrative themes and their use of music.[6] Although there are plenty of cynical and barbed musical genres that appeal to teens (from hip hop to goth and nu-metal), these two shows steer clear of them for the most part in order to invest themselves in a very distinct, earnest and regulated representation of adolescence through music.

### Bringing Music into the Storyline

In Episode 17 of *My So-Called Life*, a song is used not only to describe or evoke teenage tastes, but also (as it so often does in such drama series) to suggest that adolescents *choose* to play music in order to enhance or explain their moods. The show opens with a nightwear-clad Angela (our protagonist) lip synching and dancing freely around her bedroom to the Violent Femmes' 'Blister in the Sun', bouncing with the joy of being 'so over [ex-boyfriend] Jordan Catalano' (or so she thinks . . .). The music captures her disposition and she/the show's producers have selected the song to specifically co-ordinate with what she is going through – to underscore her mood. This example condenses a key quality which we ascribe to music: that it is one of the closest art forms to our emotional core, that, although music is usually a mass medium, it can speak about our most intimate and unique experiences. Certainly the frequent vagueness of popular music's lyrics (more of which later) and the use of first- and ambiguous second-person address might offer easy opportunities for individuals to interpret songs in their own ways. This special usage of music is something built up over a long and historically specific time-frame and such an attribution of worth perhaps explains why music has often been thought of as incompatible with television. How, after all, can such a public medium as TV evoke the intensely private and direct responses that music does for so many of us?

Although this argument does not hold up at all well (television has deeply personal resonances for many, and music is a communal activity in all manner of spheres), it does offer some clues about how music has been culturally inscribed. It is in no way coincidental that we should adorn music with these qualities and deny them to other media; in fact this indulgence stems from practices that have been maintained consistently for over two hundred years. In many ways, the musician (especially the rock musician) continues to play out the archetype not only of the wandering minstrel, but also of the more recent conception of the Romantic artist who is bohemian, unconventional and astutely at odds with mainstream society. Tracing the roots of this public persona would take at least an entire book,[7] but, unfortunately, there is space here to outline only a few of its principal features. Turmoils of the self are perennial topics of musical discussion, as are struggles against tangible and intangible forces which work to limit one's freedom[8] (bear in mind that these are prime preoccupations for a majority of adolescents too). Musicians following the rock tradition set themselves up as oppositional – if not in terms of how the music is produced and distributed (and this is often brushed under the carpet), then at least in their songs' thematic preoccupations. Unlike producers working for television, music is more often than not portrayed as the expression of some kind of outsider, but an outsider who speaks an understandable language, who voices concerns many of us share about 'the inside' and who, most importantly, celebrates marginality.

Interestingly, the official *Dawson's Creek* soundtrack website (www.dawsonscreekmusic.com) offers a particularly concise encapsulation of this phenomenon in its jokey page entitled 'what if Joey [a character on the show] were a rock star??' Although it only contains a paragraph of text and one photo, this page draws out a number of classic Romantic tropes such as Joey's poor family background and her self-determination battling against the odds. The accompanying image depicts Joey with a pained facial expression and wild flowing hair, both of which display appropriate artistic anguish and abandon.[9] The webpage works as pastiche precisely because these ideas are so deeply ingrained in us, even by our teenage years. However, the fact that this is an official website is also telling in the way that it connects commerce, adolescence and the artistic self. Although music is created by 'artists' (an idea to which even these consciously comical descriptions of Joey allude), it is also usually a product functioning within a competitive marketplace (something in which the website plays an integral role). In addition, this commercial configuration of music is increasingly global and horizontally integrated with strategic, if not corporate, links to the world of television. What I want to explore next is this interrelationship between music and TV, and how a soundtrack is so much more than merely something which shapes our understanding of on-screen drama.

*Dawson's Creek* is typical of the contemporary arrangement of music on teen TV. Its episodes are littered with tiny snatches of music – mostly of an 'indie rock' or 'new folk' persuasion. Like a whole host of such programmes, *Dawson's Creek* uses music as a sonic equivalent of the establishing shot. In fact, music is mostly likely to be heard in such shows either during establishing shots or across segues between scenes where it is used to smooth over the change in location or theme. Here the music provides (at least) two kinds of suturing: it distracts us from the editing process by bleeding over visual cuts (as sound/music often does) and, more importantly, it provides points of recognition and, hopefully, identification for a certain type of viewer – one who might relate to this music and think of it as an authentic expression of teen culture. As such, the music induces an appropriate (albeit rather loose) ambience and, from time to time, the narrative draws upon a song's lyrics to rather heavy-handedly reiterate a narrative theme (for example using Chickenpox's 'Pretty Face' in the episode called 'Beauty Contest'). Beyond this, however, these songs set some extremely complex machinery in place, something which has ensured the show's soundtrack high sales and chart positions,[10] and which Valerie Wee also explores in the previous chapter.

### Selling the Package: The Politics of the Teen TV Soundtrack

TV series like *Dawson's Creek* have acted not only as spaces which provide music with free airplay,[11] but also as ways of presenting a package which is simultaneously (as I've already suggested) tied in with a specific and highly appealing lifestyle, aesthetic and hegemony. The popularity of *Dawson's Creek* soundtracks could be attributed to viewers hearing the music on the show and liking it, or to a much less precise affiliation with the show, one which encourages its audience to follow up on all its leads, some of which include buying a music-related commodity (and, in this case, the purchase is far from an end point). In these instances, the music and the television series are working in tandem, drawing in audiences using their own talents, but ultimately working together.

This connection is made all the more explicit by the official soundtrack website where surfers can click onto links which will take them to the featured artists' homepages and where all manner of cross-promotions abound. If the show has drawn you to the music, then the website will helpfully assist you in identifying and locating the commodity for which you are searching. This is by no means a benignly indulgent favour on the part of Columbia Tristar Television, who are responsible for *Dawson's Creek*. The company is a fraction of a much larger concern, the Sony group who, through their many different branches, produce and distribute commodities on film, television, VHS and DVD formats; sell related merchandise; manufacture all manner of entertainment hardware; and, of particular value to this argument, run Sony Music. Columbia TriStar even distributes a number of films directed by Dawson's convenient idol, Steven Spielberg.

Although the show uses a large amount of music (at least six tracks per show) – many of which are licensed from other companies – what gets selected to be released on the official soundtracks (which are sold through Columbia Music, also owned by Sony) is revealing. The *Songs of Dawson's Creek Volume 2* album, for example, contains tracks by a number of Columbia's own roster (Jessica Simpson, evan and jaron, Train, Wheatus, Shawn Colvin, Lara Fabian, Five for Fighting and Peter Yorn) as well as by performers under contract to Sony's other labels Epic (Nine Days) and Sony Music (Michal). This leaves only four tracks which are not directly controlled by the Sony group. However, of those four, two (The Jayhawks' 'I'm Gonna Make You Love Me' and Mary Beth Maziarz's 'Daydream Believer') are cover versions. 'Daydream Believer''s publishing rights (not its version rights) belong to Untold Story Music, a subsidiary of Sony, and Sony own the rights to the original Diana Ross version of 'I'm Gonna Make You Love Me', which, by association, brings this older rendition into the consciousness of any listener who might be familiar with it when they hear this newer interpretation.

This one album, then, relays the extent to which the music and TV industries are interwoven and how the current situation shapes their modes of creativity. Evidently, in this formation, popular music cannot be conceived of as a more critical and rebellious form of expression which is reluctantly pinioned by the devious and always-already corrupt clutches of television. In fact, both forms of artistic production work in complicated but often united and similarly motivated ways, all of which inevitably help fashion available teenage identities. Following through on a variety of purchase-related strands, teenagers shape themselves through their increasingly independent buying power, whether that involves the interactive sociability of leaving comments on the show's official website's message board, or trying to alienate peers because they don't own certain desirable (perhaps television or music-related) consumer items.

However, to note that corporate systems are integral to, perhaps even the extent of, how adolescents present themselves and are interpellated is of little relevance unless some time is taken to untangle how this is achieved and what sorts of results are likely. Simply noting how global corporations control the media is not a sufficient objective to any enquiry. What I have been discussing is not a matter of television programmes foisting political stances on gullible teenagers. It is a subtle and extremely volatile balance of creating and rephrasing specific aesthetic gestures about 'youth', most of which have a certain lineage which I will explore more fully in a moment. First, though, it is necessary to home in on the specific contexts and connotations of the music which makes up the *Dawson's Creek* soundtrack. This will enable an understanding of the sorts of messages the chosen songs bear with them into the contemporary environment (messages whose meanings cannot have escaped the music supervisors of the shows). What significant moments in the past can such music be traced back to and who (or what) might it politically support in its contemporary context?

Of all the musical genres that the *Dawson's Creek* soundtrack could have chosen to draw upon, the two recurrent ones are indie rock (the tracks by, for example, Ben Folds Five, Eels, Wheatus and Weezer) and folk (Beth Orton, Dido, Eddi Reader, Heidi Berry, Jewel). Interestingly, both these idioms are the preserve of a mainly white majority. Just as tellingly, folk is a style which came to cultural prominence in the 1960s and indie finds its roots in the guitar bands of that era too. The implications of this provide rich food for thought and I will delve into this presently, but first it is worth investigating which types of music *don't* gain airplay as part of *Dawson's Creek*'s massive effort to showcase popular music.

As is typical on US shows, there is a glaring under-representation of non-English language material and, even more disturbingly, African-American performers, despite the fact that extremely prestigious and profitable artists such as Beyonce Knowles, The Fugees and Nas are at present signed to Columbia. When African-American artists *are* heard, their contributions provide quirky, mainly lyrical commentary rather than evoking 'teenage cool'. It is almost as if there were no place for African diaspora music within how *Dawson's Creek* defines adolescence, despite the central role such music has played in the historical inscription of the teenager from 1950s' rock 'n' roll onwards. Moreover, the African-American presence is again offset by the fact that the chosen tracks are performed by 'classic' artists like Louis Armstrong, Ella Fitzgerald, the Weathergirls and the Temptations, rather than by celebrities who are currently popular with the teen market. This marginalisation has enormous repercussions for the politics of representation, which I have no doubt are immediately apparent to the reader.

However, there are also other groups who have been sidelined. Despite huge sales to adolescent audiences, Marilyn Manson has only featured once and dance music (beyond Moby and the Chemical Brothers), goth, hip hop and nu-metal have been conspicuously missing from the show, were it in any way trying to replicate the tastes of the suburban (white) youth it chooses to depict and attract. What these absences seem to suggest is that the series is desperate to ignore the more illicit, destructive or subcultural tendencies of what is popular amongst the teenage demographic. In this sense, the *Dawson's Creek* soundtrack cannot be considered a mere mirror of adolescent sensibility, but instead a shaper of it, and one whose motivations are definitely and, in many cases, worryingly politicised.[12]

This becomes even more apparent when we break down precisely what *does* make it onto the show. Of all the featured artists, many of them are, in varying degrees, declared Christians making music with a Christian agenda (a list would include Jessica Simpson, the Newsboys, the Elms, Sixpence None the Richer, Tait, Switchfoot, Beanbag, Sarah Masen and Say-So).[13] Surprisingly, many of these musicians are on labels like Sparrow, Chordant and Forefront who are affiliated not to Sony, but to the EMI Group. These less evidently corporate-motivated inclusions can be read in two ways. First, they work on the level of a more abstract, less mercenary promotion of Christianity and its values. Second, the inclusion of these songs could be derived from a much more localised dilemma. *Dawson's Creek*'s country of origin – America – contains within it a forceful economic entity, the Christian moral majority. Within this group, there are factions who are often vociferous in their condemnation of shows with liberal attitudes towards sex and sexuality, and people who are keen lobbyists against and boycotters of culture which they see as morally corrupting.[14] *Dawson's Creek*'s use of soundtrack, then, is almost like *The Ed Sullivan Show* in reverse, with the music trying to soothe a concerned Christian demographic into thinking that the challenging themes of the TV show[15] are, in fact, 'safe'. Although I would not wish to suggest that all Americans are fundamentalist Christians who will *en masse* withdraw their support and money if sufficiently ired, Christianity, or at least Christian *values*, provide an enormous succour to many parents who are anxious about the influence of the media on their children.

Parents commonly feel anxious as their children pass into adolescence: a moral/political agenda is much more difficult to enforce as children become more independent and mobile and as even their spaces in the home become less governable. While a good American parent will try their best to give their offspring televisions and stereos for their bedrooms, this then leads them into a position of having much less say in what their children listen to and watch. Just as worryingly for parents, many forms of popular music are anti-family (or at least non-family) in their themes and proposed lifestyles. Here the proximity of certain Christian values (as expressed through religious rock) to those currently held by a particular embodiment of the 'traditional American family' could help ease the minds of parents who have an increasing (and often very measured) lack of influence over their children. In many senses, then, the use of music in these shows acts as a moral teacher or a watchful guardian maintaining parental values, whether these be the localised ethics of many actual parents, or the capitalist interests and related value systems of a parent generation who are now in control of the means of production. Likewise, these ideas are not just conveyed through lyrical messages, but also through the types of music that are drawn upon and the age of many of the chosen examples.

## Whose Generation?: The Use of Non-contemporary Music

I have not pointed this fact out yet, but it may well have dawned on the reader that much of the music in *Dawson's Creek* and *My So-Called Life* has more than a slight whiff of age to it. 'Blister in the Sun', a somewhat obscure 1983 track, is an odd choice of pertinent song for Angela, a teenager in the mid-1990s. And, earlier on in Episode 14 of *My So-Called Life*, Rayanne is requested to perform the Ramones' 'I Wanna Be Sedated' when she joins Jordan's band, the Frozen Embryos. Again, this seems somewhat awry considering that many of the viewers of *My So-Called Life* would barely have been born when the song was released in 1978. The preoccupation of these shows with a musical period spanning from the 1960s to the early 1980s is significant because it covers the exact time period when the presumed viewers' parents and the programme-makers would have been more actively engaged in youth culture. Less blatant, but still oddly plangent is the presence on the *Dawson's Creek* soundtrack of adult-oriented rock performers like Bruce Springsteen, Bryan Adams, Chris Isaak, Curtis Stigers and the Corrs – artists who continue to be musically absorbed in musical idioms established during the period when the baby-boomer generation were teenagers. The appearance of Bryan Adams's nostalgic 'Summer of '69' on *Dawson's Creek* speaks volumes and does little to convince us, as the official website wishes to, of the soundtrack's agenda of '[bringing] together fresh new talent, a hip young sensibility'.[16]

As I have already pointed out, even the contemporary indie rock and 1960s-affiliated folk of *Dawson's Creek* brings to mind music which was popularised by the baby boomers in *their* youth, and the connection to this era is enforced by the presence of 'first time rounders' like Joan Baez and Joni Mitchell on the soundtrack. In addition, *Dawson's Creek*'s incidental music is based around arpeggiating folk guitars and its theme songs (by

Jann Arden for Series One and, subsequently, by Paula Cole) are played on instruments typical of 1960s' folk, like acoustic guitars and penny whistles, by musicians who typify the singer-songwriter ideal of a specific type of 1960s' youth culture.

This conglomeration of musical meanings is initially a bizarre one. After all, while many teens try to act the adult (in terms of expected liberties, having their opinions respected and so on), their desires very rarely have anything to do with replicating the tastes and practices of their parents. Here we might be witnessing a knowing acknowledgement that the target audience for both *My So-Called Life* and *Dawson's Creek* stretches way past the teenage years and (deliberately?) taps into lucrative older markets (a tendency which Matt Hills' and Clare Birchall's chapters explore in more detail). Surely this use of music is not the result of a blind spot, an inability of writers and producers – who, in many other ways, prove themselves to be astute analysts of what adolescents do with their leisure time – to think past their own teenage music affiliations? What becomes clearer and clearer is that these shows are created for teenagers by adults who have an inevitable investment and location of themselves in the finished product. At the very least, this is an adult culture interfering in an opportunity for youth to develop in a manner distinct from its parents; a grown-up voice droning on about how things were better in its day, be these 'things' a Christian value system or the rawness of the Ramones' output. Yet these (arguably misjudged) selections are not wholly attributable to adults 'forgetting what it's like to be young'. There is also a sense that these interventions are tinged by adult survival instincts and a desire to strategically shape future generations in particular ways. These ambitions can be expressed potently through popular/rock music because it not only proclaims itself to be 'young', but it also has a history which overlaps with the baby-boomer and post-baby-boomer teenage period. Its 'youth' is contemporary, but adults can simultaneously claim its past (and, by various cunning sleights of hand, its present) as 'their own'.

Popular music as we now know it (and particularly in the forms that these shows promote) is no longer new youth music as it was in the 1950s and 1960s. While the parents of baby boomers may have been outraged by what their children were listening to, may have run from the room screaming, these children, many of them now parents themselves, are more likely to recognise the languages of rock music, maybe even buy it themselves. Styles may warp, may come and go, but much of the underlying ethos remains the same and is far from alien to the average parent. Yet if many of the modes of expression have a historical congruity, how is contemporary youth supposed to express its anger, revulsion and difference from the preceding generation? What does it mean to use 'their' language to express hostility towards 'them'?

Evidently we are taught languages in our social contexts and there is always going to be a large element of continuity. Likewise, there are definite consistencies in the youth experience, solid factors about the shift from childhood to adulthood which might prompt the recurrence of certain preoccupations. However, there is a significant distinction between the baby boomers' relationship to adolescence and that of *their* parents: on a much grander scale, they have refused to 'grow up' in the terms laid down by the generations before them. As Lawrence Grossberg argues in *We Gotta Get Out of This Place*:

> Youth today is caught in the contradiction between those who experience the powerlessness of their age (adolescents and college students) and the generations of baby boomers who have attached the category of youth to their life trajectory, in part by redefining it as an attitude ('You're only as old as you feel'). For the baby boomers, youth is something to be held on to by cultural and physical effort.[17]

Steven Spielberg, Dawson's hero, is a prime example of a baby boomer not 'growing up' in the traditional sense, although, and this is the crucial point, he is definitely adult in his capitalist savvy. Similarly, record labels are often controlled by men like David Geffen (who started Geffen) and Richard Branson (of Virgin) who have the wilful irresponsibility or playfulness that we usually attribute to youth. Such figures present a public image of being 'down with the kids', but it is perhaps more astute to question how these men and women are, in fact, simply inscribing their own understanding of youth upon a succession of age groups. Their authority, financial clout and ability to shape popular culture (with the help of many like-minded and similarly aged employees and clients) might have a lot of say in how the category of youth is asked to function in line with the protection of their own values and interests. Where these baby boomers might differ from their immediate predecessors is in their sheathing of this understandable political urge with a mask of irresponsibility. They assume a conviction that they are 'staying up to date' when, in actual fact, it may be that they are actually setting the pace to suit themselves.

These themes seep into a subplot of Episode 14 of *My So-Called Life* whose narrative rings out with discussions of how rock music moulds teenage interactions. The main storyline presents Rayanne's progress as a new member of the Frozen Embryos and as a recovering alcoholic in parallel with Angela's inability to cope with her split from Jordan. Intertwined with these diegetic threads, however, are numerous instances which not only debate the role of parenthood, but also tightly weave it into an understanding of music culture. Angela has a 'normal' (and relatively 'square') family: she finds it difficult to discuss her problems with Patty, her mother, who, because of this breakdown in communication, has taken to secretly listening in on Angela's phone conversations. On the other hand, Rayanne's mother, Amber, has a distinct hippiness to her: she wears floaty clothing, allows Rayanne to skip school and, significantly, has had an encounter with Bob Dylan (albeit only serving him a sandwich). Near the beginning of the episode, Rayanne seems increasingly frustrated with her mother's lackadaisical style of parenting. A concerned and busy-bodyish Patty rings Amber to admonish her for her child-rearing methods. And yet Rayanne and Amber are represented as having a bond which Angela and Patty lack, something that is played out in two important scenes which draw upon musical scenarios. The first places Amber and Rayanne singing 'I Wanna Be Sedated' in harmony together in front of a mirror; the second sees a distraught, post-gig Rayanne returning not to the streets and alcohol (as her friend Rickie and Patty suspect), but back home to Amber. The implication here is that Amber 'understands' Rayanne, understands her explicitly through reference to youth culture. However, the image of adolescent tastes which *My So-Called Life* projects in this episode is not one created by, or uniquely for Rayanne's generation; rather, it hinges upon the music of *Amber*'s younger days and, as a good parent, Amber is willing to share such things with her daughter. The show's conclusion sees Patty (who is faultily 'uncool' in that she would never have known the lyrics to a Ramones song) realising the strengths of Amber's 1960s-based bohemian liberalism. There is an overwhelming championing of specific residual baby-boomer beliefs in this episode which are cleverly knitted into not only contemporary teen culture, but also into the construction of (what *My So-Called Life* presents as) appropriate family values.

In subtle instances such as this one, baby boomers (like most dominant social groups) strive to create future citizens not unlike themselves who will either perpetuate the current system, or improve it according to established underlying principles. This endeavour to maintain cultural supremacy is executed in all manner of ways, including through the regimentation of the music which gets the most circulation. Moreover, a conspicuous element of such music – particularly the nostalgic kind played on *Dawson's Creek* – is that it is more tailored to the baby boomers' contemporary positions within capitalism than it is towards any past convictions or a possibly more naive youthful spirit. While the soundtrack to *Dawson's Creek* contains many a folk-style song, the lyrics are strangely devoid of the leftist politics which marked out the work of, for example, Bob Dylan (a performer who is markedly absent from the show). The lyrics' intentions are distinctly vaguer in these more recent incarnations and, as a consequence, their lack of semantic precision offers itself up to the potential of appropriation.

The huge melodic upwards leaps which characterise folk singing, for example, provide a thread of continuity from the 1960s to now, but it is all too easy (without the surrounding political clarity of lyrics) to re-frame what these musical trajectories mean. While in the past (and indeed now) such vocal swoops suggest a sense of carefree abandon, they could equally be read as aspirational, as striving for higher (perhaps material, rather than social) things. Moreover, many of the words we hear seem compliant with a Protestant work ethic which promotes enterprise, achievement and self-determination (and here we arrive back at the junction where religion, social formation, music and parenting meet). Distanced from the more left-wing history of folk music, many of the titles on the *Dawson's Creek* play-list seem oddly like chapters from a self-help manual designed to promote one's success in the office environment (for example, Abra Moore's 'Taking Chances', Amanda Marshall's 'Give up Giving in', The Barenaked Ladies' 'Who Needs Sleep?', Dag Juhlin's 'I Can't Try Hard Enough', Karen Blake's 'Why Walk When You Can Fly' and Susanna Hoffs' 'All I Want'). Admittedly, many of the writers of these songs would be appalled by such interpretations, but, within the context of the show, such lyrics are definitely hazy enough to be commandeered for these ends. Likewise, the words to Paula Cole's theme song,[18] 'I don't wanna wait for our lives to be over/I wanna know right now', may well reflect a liberal sense of freedom or a youthful exuberance and capriciousness, but their purpose is ambiguous and easily co-opted. After all, such an urgent demand could be something a boss would shout at you.

In pointing this out, I am not trying to argue that *Dawson's Creek* is a nefarious show which tries to brainwash its viewers into willingly signing up for the capitalist lifestyle (at least, no more than any other cultural product). This is not a chapter about the devious and secretly corrupting nature of such programmes – to be that it would have to have faith in the notion of a free, pre-capitalist concept of adolescence. I do not believe that there are spaces independent of such hegemonies (let alone ones to which music, but not television has access) precisely because there is no teen expression which is not mediated by an adult force of some description. In the mid- to late 1990s when *Dawson's Creek* and *My So-Called Life* first aired, there was a trend in America for Woodstock revivalism (again, a music culture-derived association), from wearing tie-dye to listening to new folk artists like Jewel. The fashion was not forced upon reluctant teenagers, but presented to them as a cultural option – one which, for various complicated reasons, they selected. Perhaps their choice was motivated by the ever-present aesthetic force of baby boomers who are merely looking after their own interests. Perhaps it was a group of equally cynical adolescents preparing themselves to join the current power structure by imbibing some of its more palatable value systems. Or, I suppose, it may just have been a kind of attractive idealism repackaged, as usual, in a profit-making format.

Youth, music and television are, as I have been arguing, inextricably tied up in financial exchange and how we define labour and professionalism. In addition, music both shapes the political and emotional registers of our teenage years and also, later on, strategically reconstitutes a 'youth' for us to look back on retrospectively. This makes music simultaneously a valuable cross-generational product and a means of control – something which both benefits and encourages a certain form of baby boomer-governed existence. In this sense, the role music plays socially (including televisually) is a pertinent reflection of how adolescence is often experienced: compromises and infringements by adults are utterly inevitable.

## Notes

1. L. Grossberg, *We Gotta Get Out of This Place: Popular Conservatism & Postmodern Culture* (London: Routledge, 1992).
2. As I shall go on to discuss later, fans and producers of music frequently criticise television for 'cashing in' on popular music's importance without the broadcasters truly understanding its messages or its worth.
3. S. Frith, A. Goodwin and L. Grossberg (eds), *Sound and Vision: The Music Video Reader* (London and New York: Routledge, 1993).
4. J. Mundy, *Popular Music on Screen: From Hollywood Musical to Music Video* (Manchester: Manchester University Press, 1999).
5. K. Lury, *British Youth Television: Cynicism and Enchantment* (Oxford: Oxford University Press, 2001).
6. However, the 'ironic distance' Lury attributes to these programmes' presenters is still maintained on such British shows as *Planet Pop* and even *Top of the Pops*.
7. See, for example, J. Toynbee, *Making Popular Music: Musicians, Creativity and Institutions* (London: Edward Arnold, 2000).
8. Such interpretations are easily elicited from many pop lyrics and are also perpetuated by significant bodies of critical and fan discourse.
9. Episode 14 of *My So-Called Life* provides a more extended exploration of this trope – one which, unfortunately, I have little space to describe in detail here. The plot centres around

Rayanne's desire to join Jordan's band. Of all the characters on the show, Rayanne is the most rebellious, outlandish, confident and outspoken and, as such, she comes closest to the ideal of both the rock musician and the troubled teenager in her demeanour – not least because she is a recovering alcoholic. The bias against women in such (rock-based) musical posturing is also tackled with delicate wit in this episode and any reader interested in this topic is recommended to read more sustained analyses of this problem in books such as M. Bayton, *Frock Rock* (Oxford: Oxford University Press, 1999) and S. Whiteley, *Women and Popular Music: Sexuality, Identity and Subjectivity* (London: Routledge, 2000). Interestingly, Rayanne's first gig is extremely unsuccessful: she misses her entry cues, is unable to find her voice and struggles to stay in tune, before quickly fleeing the stage altogether and running off into the night. This denouement makes it clear that, although Rayanne has a rock (or, rather, a punk rock) attitude, she lacks the requisite skill and training (and, perhaps, gender) to succeed as a live performer. In this sense, then, the episode unravels the Romantic rock myth somewhat by emphasising that, along with its spontaneity and expressiveness, rock performance is also an expertise and a profession.

10. According to www.dawsonscreekmusic.com, 'the first *Songs from Dawson's Creek* entered the Billboard 200 album chart at #7, tying the record set by *Songs from Ally McBeal* for the highest debut chart position for a television soundtrack . . . [it] was certified double gold in the UK (it was the #1 album in Ireland for five weeks and spent 12 weeks in the Top 10), triple platinum in Australia (where it spent 18 weeks in the Top 3)'.
11. In fact, if the television company does not have the rights to the music, it will have to pay for them.
12. If this is perhaps a diegetic suggestion that the main characters in *Dawson's Creek* listen to such songs, then their musical tastes clearly cohere with their idiosyncratic early maturity. In this sense, the characters' involvement with music traditionally associated with an older demographic matches their glaringly intelligent and articulate dialogue – a feature which both Matt Hills and Clare Birchall discuss more fully in their chapters.
13. My thanks goes to Rayford Guins who first alerted me to this fact.
14. For examples of web-based Christian arguments against *Dawson's Creek*, it is worth visiting www.cpyu.org and www.almenconi.com.
15. For instance, the show's sensitive and non-judgmental handling of homosexuality which Glyn Davis explores more fully in his chapter in this book.
16. See www.dawsonscreekmusic.com.
17. L. Grossberg, *We Gotta Get Out of This Place: Popular Conservatism and Postmodern Culture* (London: Routledge, 1992), p. 183.
18. 'I Don't Want to Wait'.

# 8

## Total Request Live and the Creation of Virtual Community

### Richard K. Olsen

'MTV, more than other television, may be said to be *about* consumption. It evokes a kind of hypnotic trance in which the spectator is suspended in a state of unsatisfied desire but forever under the illusion of *imminent* satisfaction through some kind of purchase.'[1]

MTV is big. It is a member of the culture-producing conglomerate Viacom that includes Showtime, CBS, UPN, Blockbuster Video (rentals and sales), Paramount, TV Land and Nickelodeon. MTV itself is made up of several divisions including MTV2, VH-1 (Video Hits One) and CMT (Country Music Television). MTV has also expanded internationally. Beginning with MTV Europe in 1987, it added MTV-Brazil (1990), MTV-Asia (1991/1995), MTV-Japan (1992) and others. While such growth may be viewed as crass cultural imperialism, in most cases, it has been tempered by a desire to allow indigenous artists to have a forum.[2] Still, the 1992 *MTV Music Awards* show, for example, featured predominantly US/Western artists and was broadcast in 139 countries. And MTV-Asia operates with a quota of only 20 per cent Asian artists.[3]

This chapter examines a programme within American MTV that grew to become the channel's most popular daily show: *Total Request Live* (*TRL*). At its peak, *TRL* drew well over one million viewers, making it one of the most popular shows ever in its timeslot in the entire history of television.[4] The question that drives this essay is: What specific features of *TRL* contribute to its tremendous popularity among teens?

In answering this question, I begin with a brief overview of the history of MTV as it relates to the development of *TRL*. Next I offer more specific analysis of *TRL*, highlighting three sources of control that help to explain the success of *TRL* among American teens.

### Where Did TRL Come from?

Shuker has argued that 'the nature of meaning in cultural products and practices must be located within the dynamic interrelationship of the production context, the texts and their creators, and the audience'.[5] My brief history of the station addresses some of his concerns. MTV is a commercial venture and so the commodification of music, artists and various facets of popular culture within its programming is evident and expected.

However, MTV is not monolithic and is riven with numerous contradictions. For example, MTV has offered responsible discussions of sexuality while also offering a soap-opera-style show called *Undressed*, which celebrates unsafe sex and sexual experimentation. It created the *MTV Unplugged* concert series that allowed artists – some of whom were dismissed by critics – to showcase their talent with acoustic instruments and minimal staging. Yet it also brought Beavis and Butthead into the world and the show *Jackass*, which features home video of mostly adolescent white males doing incredibly dumb, dangerous and often grotesque stunts such as jumping into cesspools of human waste. Some groups have criticised MTV for being too risqué in its content, and others for being too conservative by censoring video content. None of these critiques are mutually exclusive with a text as large and complex as MTV.

Two factors have influenced MTV's significant changes in programming. The first is adaptation to the medium of television. MTV began as 'radio on TV'. The videos were strung together by video jockeys (VJs) and MTV had its own radio-style promotional contests. While this format provided initial success, ratings soon flattened. MTV began to seek out attractive formats that could adapt to the unique logic of TV as a medium.[6] In 1983 MTV experimented with *Basement Tapes*, a monthly competition among unknown bar bands who sent in a tape with their best video. Viewers then called a 900 number (free to call) to vote for their favourites. The contest lasted six months and resulted in a winner getting a contract from a record company. One broadcast netted 81,000 phone calls and hinted at viewers' desire to vote about their taste in music.[7]

The second issue driving their changes is significantly more complex. Not only does the brain trust of MTV have the challenge of keeping music visually interesting, but they also have the continual challenge of positioning themselves as 'cutting edge' and 'new' to appeal to subsequent generations of teens. MTV has had difficulty relying on past successes because it has to be 'our MTV' as defined by 12–18-year-olds. Consequently, MTV is, in some ways, a slave to the very audience it often seems to control.[8]

In the interaction of the above factors, there has been a general migration from music videos as the mainstay of MTV programming towards what might be called 'lifestyle' and popular culture programming. The *MTV Movie Awards* show (debut, 1992) is indicative of this shift. Many of the MTV shows popularised in the 1990s have little or no musical content, other than soundtracking that might be typical of any contemporary TV show. *House of Style* (debut, 1989), *Real World* (debut, 1992), *Road Rules* (debut, 1995) and *Celebrity Death Match* (debut, 1998) are examples.

How does this inform our understanding of *TRL*? First, some of the guests on *TRL* also reflect MTV's shift from music to a broader pop culture focus. While its once popular network predecessor, *American Bandstand*, limited its studio guests to musical artists, *TRL* has opened its doors to film and TV personalities such as actor Jim Carrey, and contestants/performers on shows like *American Idol* (a talent contest show). Second, now that MTV programming has diversified, a show that actually plays videos stands out as unique. Thus *TRL* is popular not only because of its fairly novel format (discussed below), but because seeing top videos takes on added significance.

## The Popular Host and Unique Format of *TRL*

Carson Daly, MTV's most popular VJ, is the host of *TRL* and clearly sees other American media figures as role models. Included on his list of influences are *American Bandstand* legend Dick Clark, top-forty radio DJ Casey Kasem, game show host Bob Barker and talk show icon Johnny Carson. He admires them for their longevity as well as their skill, or as he puts it: 'Guys who keep workin' their asses off forever'.[9]

The star myth constructed around Carson Daly implies an apparent effortlessness and nonchalance. He has stated in several interviews that his early reflections on his vocation had him considering either Catholic priesthood or professional golf – quite a range. Jimmy Kimmel, a long-time friend and LA disc jockey, who later went on to his own successful career hosting *The Man Show*, invited Daly to intern at an LA radio station. He was clearly gifted and soon partnered a show with Kimmel. This provided the exposure necessary to his getting picked up by MTV.[10]

Daly has become savvy at managing his career. With the help of his stepfather working as his financial manager, he has secured additional TV and radio opportunities, hosted pageants such as *Miss Teen USA* and risen to a position as executive producer of *TRL*. He will also help in developing new shows for MTV and CBS and has a record label within Sony music.[11] While he comes across as laidback, his career goals are lofty: 'I think one day there might be a big, giant building that says "Carson" on it, with a magazine there, a record company and a production company for late-night TV and movies. But I'm in no rush.'[12] Daly as host, then, is the perfect reflection of *TRL*: seemingly informal and haphazard yet harbouring strategic commercial ambitions.

Two specific features of the format of *TRL* are worth discussing. First, *TRL* is live and it has adopted sophisticated ways of integrating shots of screaming teens lined up outside the studio and having audience members participate in the introduction of videos. This live characteristic contributes to the perception of the show as 'real'. There is the potential to view *TRL* as genuine simply because it seems 'unscripted' and 'unrehearsed' in the literal sense of those terms. However, that does not mean that *TRL* is without templates and clear outcomes in mind. And while an individual *TRL* episode is 'unrehearsed', there is a repetitive form that provides clear predictions about expected behaviours and content.[13] In addition, there is ample anecdotal evidence that suggests that producers direct *TRL* fans regarding what to do and say and when to do and say it.

Second, *TRL* incorporates audience involvement in evaluating musical content. The focus of *TRL* is to play the top ten videos as voted on by *TRL* viewers. Through phone and website voting a list is compiled and the most voted for videos are played (in part) on *TRL*. A key to success on the show is getting on it the first time. As Edwards notes: 'The *TRL* viewers tend to vote for what they see, which means that once a song gets into the Top Ten, it's hard to dislodge it.'[14]

## Analysing the Key Characteristics of *TRL*

Analysis in this section will focus on seven characteristics of *TRL* that emphasise interactivity, a unique form of discourse and consumption.

## My TRL: TRL as Interactive Multi-mediated Community

TRL presents itself as a ritualised community that viewers can participate in.[15] Viewer participation is possible largely due to advances in communication technology. A greater portability of cameras, for instance, has significantly shaped the presentation of the TRL community back to itself. Multiple cameras allow for greater shot diversity: interior, exterior, on location, close-ups and 'shout-outs'. 'Shout-outs' are opportunities for TRL fans to express their preferences for artists and videos, and make other statements of solidarity through video inserts of fans at the show and email messages from viewers that scroll across the bottom of the TV screen. These email shout-outs are taken from the MTV.com website, thus providing a seemingly seamless integration of cyber, televised and live community. During the show, video and email shout-outs and the occasional 'live line' phone conversation enhance the sense of real community involved in the programme.

The TRL website is far more than a cyber-kiosk for posting emails. One of MTV's site developers noted: 'TRL has been an incredible leader in convergence entertainment programming, from online voting to interactive chats with artists on TRL.'[16] The MTV site averages almost three million separate visitors a month. The TRL site includes voting options, new video releases, celebrity mailboxes, fan-of-the-week profiles, back-stage photos and a variety of other mediated experiences that suggest 'community' is taking place.

Closely connected to the idea of a mediated community is the interactive technology that makes it possible. The typical feedback loop between any given audience member and the mass media is indirect at best. Yet TRL has convinced its viewers that they can make a difference. Voting for the videos TRL will play can be done by phone or Internet. Since 'ballot stuffing' is easier to do on the Internet than by jammed phone lines, the phone-in votes are 'weighted' more heavily in the final tallies.[17] Since its debut on 18 September 1998, the key to TRL's success has been the ability of fans to vote for the videos they want to make it into the countdown. In a recent TRL broadcast, the guest host commented on a song vaulting four spots up the countdown to number three: 'Way to step it up fans.' Such commentary clearly suggests a direct interaction between fan behaviour and TRL content. The bridge between TRL's website and the TV programme also provides a unique perception of interactivity. TRL devotees can email a star, or email the TRL staff. They can subscribe to the TRL newsletter, check the message board or enter into the chat room.

While some aspects of interaction on TRL are not unique, the integration of so many opportunities and the centrality of the voting along with TRL's unprecedented popularity do make TRL an exclusive teen-culture phenomenon.

## Behind the Scenes: TRL as Back-stage

Carson Daly, TRL's host, comments: 'It feels like it's my house and people just kind of stop in and the viewers are my neighbors. Jim Carrey comes by, I take a bullhorn out my front door and go "Hey guys, Jim's here!" and they all come over.'[18]

TRL positions the show as 'back-stage'. Daly dresses very informally and the dress code for the audience, while filtered, is not strict or formal. It is not, of course, literally back-stage, but rather a carefully crafted set made to feel back-stage. The set has remained fairly small, though the show could support much larger audiences. The bench seating is fairly informal looking and there is no elevated stage or real 'performance space'. Celebrity guests must stand when visiting – there is no official space for them in this 'back-stage stage'. Such physical arrangements are only the first step in creating the back-stage feel of *TRL*.

*TRL* also presents itself as back-stage rather than on-stage by focusing on the paramusical issues between videos. For instance, during a September 2002 broadcast, two topics of what might be called 'family business' between musical groups represented in the day's video countdown were discussed. The first was a minor falling out between three hip-hop groups, B2K, TG4 and 3LW. One fan attempted to clarify the issue: 'I guess one of the members of B2K, Kiely, had a beef with one of the guys or somethin' happened, I don't know, but I guess they hate 3LW. Who knows?'[19] Obviously I have not included this quote for its clarity! Rather, it is indicative of the focus *TRL* places on getting beyond the public performances and personae and 'being real'. Whether or not the feud was real or a publicity stunt was not an issue: it was framed as real. Later in the broadcast, there was a phone call from members of B2K to try and 'clear everything up that was said and tell everyone what is really going on'. They then offered a clearly unrehearsed response about how 3LW 'posted our picture and wrote bad things under it. Plus, they said that we go with TG-4, which is not true. TG-4 is in our camp, but not our girlfriends.' The phone call was also indicative of the idealised interactivity between fans and artists that can take place within the back-stage scene of *TRL*. This issue is addressed later within the discussion of therapeutic discourse.

The videos provide a focus for the show. But the ground or context is the perception of getting back-stage to something authentic. Later in the broadcast referenced above, a 'news anchor' briefed the audience on the Tupac and Notorious B.I.G. feud, which many commentators and fans think led to the murder of Tupac. This discussion is framed as an 'only on *TRL*' experience that reinforces *TRL* as a unique place for insiders.

## What Do You Guys Wanna Do?: Host Positioned as Subordinate

Daly summarised his role on the show: '*TRL* is like a big family. I don't know what I am to that family. I don't think I'm the father. I'm more like Alice on *The Brady Bunch*. When anybody has a problem – Cindy, Sam the butcher, anybody – they go to Alice.'[20] This is clearly the way MTV and Daly want to be perceived: '*TRL* is your show; I'm just facilitating it.' Daly's dress is casual – almost to the point of seeming unprepared. He is fidgety and seems very eager to comfort and validate others. Yet, Daly is also clearly in control. As one critic put it: 'Daly has the sane, pleasant demeanor of a doctor who makes friends with his patients without even going so far as to remove his surgical gloves during the handshake.'[21]

The overall structure of the show and other production choices smoothly position Daly as subordinate. For instance, since fans vote the videos on, he is seen as bringing the viewers what they ordered, like a waiter. In addition, the live lines, shout-outs and live interviews are done in a style that almost makes them seem like interruptions. It is almost as if Daly is saying 'Hey, I was going to do X, but Britney just dropped in, so I'll do X some other time.' His ability to manage perceptions is not lost on MTV brass. MTV executive vice-president Dave Sirulnick compares Carson Daly to Johnny Carson: 'Johnny could sit down with comedians, actors and sports stars. He treated everybody equally, but you knew he was on top. We tell Carson that he is in control, whether it's Madonna or a new act, and he's learned to embrace that.'[22]

Another production decision that helps to position the audience as in control is that all the traditionally important people stand. 'Even big names – Madonna, Janet Jackson, Jim Carrey – when they visit *TRL*, they stand on the platform like everybody else and meet their makers.'[23] Traditionally, standing while others are sitting would put those seated in a subordinate position. However, as David Bordwell notes, we should take each text on its own terms. In this case, standing is the subordinate role, much in the way a waiter or waitress is subordinate to seated patrons.[24]

### Watch Closely . . . Now Cheer: Consumption of the Self on *TRL*

Consumption on *TRL* is a three-course meal. The first course is, obviously, the music product presented in the videos. While it is true that *TRL* viewers vote to construct the day's Top Ten, there are hegemonic forces at work to constrict the choices. As mentioned above, what gets played tends to stay on the list. Consequently, a very strategic feature of *TRL* is the video debut segment. New videos by marketable performers, such as boy band *NSYNC's Justin Timberlake, actually debut on *TRL*. This gives the video/artist/product a significant promotional boost since it is likely to make the *TRL* countdown because it has been seen on *TRL*. Such debuts bring brief discussion of reactions to the new video. However, there is no numerical or empirical rating award – no modernity here! Rather, a subjective reaction by a fan is read from an email. In the case of the Timberlake debut, the female fan's reaction is mildly negative and some hushed boos result from her deviant response. The guest host asks 'Anybody else want to admit to that?' and then moves on. This exchange exhibits many of the therapeutic characteristics discussed below. There is a sense of group therapy going on as the video is processed. And within that context some modelled behaviour regarding consumption: the negative reaction is met with resistance since it violates the role of satisfied consumer.

The second layer of consumption is consumption of the self. Since MTV has broadened its focus beyond musical artists to teen-lifestyle programming, *TRL* becomes a dynamic synthesis of both topics. Teen behaviour is consumed along with the videos. To get in the *TRL* studio audience, one must be selected, so *TRL* can filter the teen 'look'. To get on camera outside the studio requires the look plus the act. One must exhibit proper fan(atic) behaviour: cheer for the video/artist, MTV, friends back home, *TRL*. The crafting and selling of the teen experience back to teens is a central tenet of MTV and the station spends significant time and money doing this.[25]

The third layer is perhaps the most indicative of the self-sustaining power of MTV: the consumption of consumption. *American Bandstand* showed teens dancing to music and inspired teens to dance to music. Certainly, there was a form of consumption in operation. However, the music was, in a sense, the ground and the teens were the figure. In *TRL*, the teens are far more passive – frenetic cheering aside – as we watch them watch videos. *TRL* is centrally concerned with teens consuming MTV and legitimates teens as consumers: they vote for the chance to consume a music video product, then the studio fans cheer after getting the chance to consume the product created by the voting, and the TV fans watch them cheer.

This meta-consumption also manifests itself within the shout-outs and other features of *TRL*. Two email shout-outs during an Eminem video are illustrative: 'I love Eminem and this video. He's just so hot and so is this video. Keep voting for him on the countdown! Bye, y'all!' and 'Eminem's new video is off the hook! He's just so HOT! I listen to his CD every day after school and I'm his number one fan. I love you Em!' Danielle from New York and Jennifer from Ohio have performed admirably as MTV consumers, and *TRL* fans have watched them do so.

## 'I Love You Carson!' Parasocial Dynamics of *TRL*

Conway and Rubin argue that many media consumers develop a parasocial relationship with media figures and characters.[26] By parasocial they mean that the mediated (mostly one-way) presentation of a celebrity persona is processed by some viewers as a two-way interaction approximating face-to-face conversation because of the inner dialogue and identification that may take place during the viewing. Carson Daly certainly engenders that kind of relationship with his fans. This is to be expected with a host in Daly's position. Goodwin argues that 'The VJs represent the ordinary, and the rock stars in the video clips represent the glamorous'.[27] Daly seems to intentionally pursue this identification: 'I'm trying really, really hard to let everybody know that I am just a normal person that loves music.'[28]

A significant implication of viewing the relationships that hold together the fans, Daly and the celebrity guests on *TRL* as parasocial is that the viewers are more likely to conclude that they are meeting the person rather than the persona of Daly and his celebrity guests. Consistent with the idea that *TRL* is a back-stage place is the idea that Daly and the stars who 'drop by' are not performing. They are not operating out of their on-stage persona, but their back-stage/off-stage being. This perception feeds neatly into the idea of *TRL* as real community. Yet the celebrities and Daly are enacting a type of performance. As noted in the remark above, the surgical gloves have not been removed. Yet, this parasocial dynamic fosters two key sources of control within *TRL*: therapeutic discourse and manufactured consent.

## How Does Being on *TRL* Make You Feel?: *TRL* as Therapeutic Experience

Through the elements discussed above, *TRL* provides a nurturing environment for what Dana Cloud, among others, have referred to as 'rhetorics of therapy'. For her, the therapeutic 'refers to a set of political and cultural discourses that have adopted psychotherapy's lexicon – the conservative language of healing, coping, adaptation, and the restoration of a previously existing order – but in the context of sociopolitical conflict'.[29] The implications of this pervasive form of discourse are that people may view many external political and social events as extensions of their personal lives and are encouraged to cope with them privately rather than engaging in civic or social changes. Here is one clear example of this from *TRL*.

Daly takes a live line call from a tentative girl named Christina from Massachusetts. She lacks the usual excitement of *TRL* callers. 'Everything alright in your life? Can I help you in, like, 20 seconds to make things better?' Daly asks. He then suggests she needs to consume some Korn. Korn are a rap-metal band and he is positive cranking their music through her headphones will help her through what's troubling her. She then asks if she can give a shout-out to her science class since they were certain she would not get through. The audience snickers but Daly affirms her: 'You made it, didn't you. And you know what, Christina? They're playing with their Bunsen burners right now but you're on *TRL*.'[30]

In this exchange we see some important aspects of therapeutic discourse on *TRL*. First, topics often confined to the interpersonal or therapeutic setting are addressed on *TRL*. And second, *TRL* as a unique site/space as well as the music itself are presented as therapeutic. Much of this may come from Daly's own experience with music:

> Music saved my life. I know that for a fact. My dad died when I was five. Quinn [his brother] was eight. Quinn had a hard time with the loss, but it didn't really hit me till later. I was thirteen or fourteen, and all of a sudden I was like, 'What happened to my dad?' That's when my faith really kicked in, and that's when the music kicked in. Now, when I get to turn people on to music that brings me through, like P.O.D. or Papa Roach, it's like a perfect circle. It's complete.[31]

In another interview he admits that he enjoys defending boy bands from their critics: 'It's shallow to think that a certain genre of music is the only road to heaven.'[32] His easy synthesis of music and theology – which Cloud notes was the precursor to therapy – clearly defines music as a cure for what ails you, as well as a key to personal development and expression.

The third aspect is that music therapy can be linked to consumption. Daly's advice to the troubled caller to play Korn was therapeutic *and* an example of consumption. The consumption is framed as a necessary coping strategy: 'Feeling a bit disconnected? Consume something.' And while Daly might lose one viewer to some headphones if she follows his advice, it's worth the risk. In the process he has reinforced the idea that consuming music and music television is good, even helpful, and should be an important part of being a teen.

The discourse of *TRL* is clearly informed by this larger trend toward therapeutic rhetoric. Cloud's work critiques manifestations of this discourse within the political arena, news coverage and major social movements. She notes that therapeutic rhetoric functions hegemonically to personalise and privatise issues that might be better understood as public or systematised injustices.[33] *TRL* puts a unique spin on this by publicising the private rather than privatising the public. However, it is still a hegemonic move that makes *TRL* seem like a private experience rather than a highly profitable programme that advances many corporate interests. For instance, the group therapy session that followed the Timberlake video debut directed discussion away from the policy of debuting highly commercial artists on *TRL*.

A key outlet for therapeutic discourse is the shout-out. The very moniker is reminiscent of the early forms of anger management and self-discovery through primal screaming. Shout-outs are typically effusive streams of subjective perceptions and feelings about an artist, a song, and the mood they create for the listener or how the music helps them cope. For example: 'I love the song because it relates so close to my life'; 'Every time I hear the song I think of my best friend who just moved away.'[34] Most of the video shout-outs offer statements of affection for the viewers' actual friends – reinforcing a feeling of community.

The fans are not the only ones engaging in typically private or therapeutic acts. When A. J. McLean of the Backstreet Boys entered rehabilitation for depression and alcohol abuse, the rest of the band made the announcement during an MTV news segment on *TRL*. 'When you're trying to help someone who has a serious illness, they have to help themselves first before they can really receive help. They've gotta really want it', said band mate Brian Littrell. 'He came to us yesterday and for the first time I heard him say "Guys, I have a problem and I need to get help." We figured this was the best for him. It's all about him being healthy.'[35] Kevin Richardson, another band member, reminded the *TRL* faithful 'We want to be honest with our fans. He's getting help. He's going to be better.'

This example demonstrates the extent to which *TRL* has constructed itself as a therapeutic site. Typically private issues are openly discussed and addressed in ways that draw from the lexicon of contemporary therapy. Because of this, fans are expected to be accepting, empathic consumers of such messages, and Daly himself models this acceptance. Consistent with contemporary practices of psychotherapy, he offers little more than unconditional affirmations regarding various music selections and fan or artist self-disclosures. Daly simply attempts to facilitate self-discovery and acceptance.

## I Want Our MTV: Manufactured Consent on *TRL*

*American Bandstand* was hailed as the first show in America primarily for teens, featuring teens. It was a 'show for us' from a teen perspective. *TRL* is presented slightly differently. Because viewers vote for most of the content, it is not a show 'for us', but 'our show' within a cable station for us.

Stanley Deetz, building on arguments from Foucault, asserts that organisations can exert various forms of control over their members. He suggests that the most empowering form of organisational control is allowing each stakeholder in a decision to fully participate in that outcome. The most problematic form of control is consent, which can be manufactured. His concern is that this manufactured consent (a term he borrows from Burawoy and Chomsky) seems like it is participatory but is actually covertly structured in favour of dominant interest groups. Thus, other members of the organisation are unaware that they are participating in their own subjugation – or are vaguely aware but participate anyway since how or what to resist is unclear.[36] While Deetz is writing in the context of organisational communication, his insights on the concept of manufactured consent aptly summarise how many of the features of *TRL* addressed in this chapter work as a whole to facilitate consumption. There are two central strategies used by MTV and *TRL* to generate consent.

First, MTV makes the highly intentional production of *TRL* seem unintentional and natural. A subtle example of this filtered reality is Daly's informal wardrobe. He dresses very informally and gives the impression that he is unintentional in his choice of clothing. Yet, the reality is quite different. Manufacturers, in hopes that he'll wear their clothes on the air, send him lots of clothes. He and the producers sort through them and he makes the call on what he will wear on the air.

Shout-outs are an even more dramatic example. The content of shout-outs is highly selected, filtered and planned. They are not typically live, but are taped and then inserted. If an attempt at taping a shout-out doesn't 'work', it doesn't air. This absence goes undetected by viewers. Only conformity is shown in the broadcast. Yet the inserts seem like an empowering gesture by fans.

Emails are even more filtered. There are roughly ten to twenty email messages broadcast within each *TRL* episode, a very small percentage of the total email *TRL* receives. The gatekeepers can clearly filter such messages to set the agenda on many of the themes addressed above: *TRL* as community, music as therapy and teens as consumers. This filtering is reinforced as *TRL* fans begin to alter their behaviours and implicitly learn how to look, act and speak during a 'proper' shout-out, including knowing how to write an email that is more likely to get on the air. Manufactured consent assumes its full effect when those who do not directly benefit from dominant interests internalise the standards that suit those interests.

The second strategy used to manufacture consent is one of false empowerment. *TRL* positions itself as a bottom-up phenomenon directly reflecting the tastes and sensibilities of American teens. The reality is quite different. I have already discussed how the structural limitations in the voting process privilege the incumbent videos. Add to that the act of debuting only a very limited number of videos on *TRL* and one can see that the choices *perceived* to be available to most *TRL* viewers are limited indeed. Specific discourse patterns on *TRL* also serve to reinforce this false sense of empowerment. Take, for example, the apparent manifestation of 'fan power' when voting between the various midriff-baring sirens currently seducing the camera on MTV. Britney Spears, Christina Aguilera and Shakira (and this week's wannabe) are remarkably similar products, even if they are moderately diverse as musical artists. Consequently, major corporate interests are served regardless of who is selected for the *TRL* countdown. Yet fans are told they are making a difference and exercising their power by voting. They are led to believe they are participating in the process of shaping music when they are simply role-modelling the consumption of mainstream music product for other teens, which serves the interests of music corporations and established artists.

## Conclusion

*TRL* can seem like it is a very tolerant community: musical diversity may also give rise to cultural diversity. As Daly has stated: 'I don't think that five years ago you could have had Stone Temple Pilots and Coolio on the same show.'[37] MTV has been criticised in the past for its exclusive and – later on – segregated programming. *TRL* has, within the confines of pop music, transcended such limitations. Black and white artists from a variety of strains within pop music are shown to peacefully co-exist.

However, this tolerance may be achieved at the expense of any coherent logic or sensibility beyond the pleasure principle. Alan Light of *Spin* magazine has said: 'On *TRL* the operative word is instant gratification. It's about an immediate, one-dimensional response. This stuff is all very simple – and the music that is more grown-up or sophisticated has been pushed aside.'[38] Such a hedonistic logic when applied to musical preferences is perhaps acceptable. Such sensibilities applied beyond the boundaries of a taste community, however, could prove problematic. How does one develop a hierarchy of values, critical thinking or a mature reasoning process if the training ground has focused almost exclusively on across-the-board acceptance and consumption as pleasure, if not therapy?

Another potential concern is that *TRL* is a virtual community built on parasocial interaction. Yet the presence of interactive dimensions within the *TRL* broadcast and the MTV website heighten the perception that it is a real community. *TRL* is not a real community. However, it is not unreal because it is virtual or mediated: indeed, Fernback has noted that cyberspace has become a repository for cultural memory and a new arena for participation in public life.[39] Rather, *TRL* lacks many of the more complex benefits of a community because it is so heavily geared towards consumption and its interactivity is ruled by this prerogative. Some teens are savvy enough to recognise this. Others are not. A humorous anecdote offered by Daly is illustrative of the fact that many teens think *TRL* is real life, unplugged if you will. At the end of a *TRL* broadcast, but before the cameras were turned off, Daly removed the earpiece that keeps him in constant but unheard contact with *TRL* producers. A viewer saw him remove the earpiece and, thinking it was a hearing aid, wrote him an email congratulating him on overcoming his disability.[40]

*TRL* contains several specific features that promote consumption, and is essentially a show about teens consuming pop music and music television. This consumption is presented as desirable, even therapeutic. While the music videos provide a visual focus for the gathering, the reasons to gather, the shout-outs and live audience behaviours ultimately celebrate consumption. Consequently, what feels like a virtual community to many teens is, in reality, a highly intentional orchestration of perceptions packaged as *Total Request Live*.

## Notes

1. E. Ann Kaplan, *Rocking Around the Clock: Music Television, Postmodernism, and Consumer Culture*, (London: Methuen, 1987), p. 12.
2. Robert Hanke, 'You Quiero Mi MTV!: Making Music Television for Latin America', in Thomas Swiss, John Sloop and Andrew Herman (eds), *Mapping the Beat: Popular Music and Contemporary Theory* (Malden, MA: Blackwell, 1998), pp. 219–45.
3. Roy Shuker, *Understanding Popular Music* (London: Routledge, 2001, 2nd edn), p. 189.
4. Lorraine Calvacca, 'Total Request Live', *Advertising Age*, vol. 71, no. 27, 26 June 2000 (retrieved 14 November 2002 from Ebscohost Masterfile Premiere).
5. Shuker, *Understanding Popular Music*, p. 214.
6. Barry Brummett, *Rhetorical Dimensions of Popular Culture* (Tuscaloosa: University of Alabama, 1991).
7. R. Denisoff, *Inside MTV* (New Brunswick, NJ: Transaction Books, 1988), p. 105.
8. Dana Cloud, *Control and Consolation in American Culture and Politics: Rhetorics of Therapy* (Thousand Oaks, CA: Sage, 1998).

9. Rob Sheffield, 'Carson Daly', *Rolling Stone*, issue 849, 14 September 2000 (retrieved 14 November 2002 from Ebscohost Masterfile Premiere).
10. Jason Lynch and Cynthia Wang, 'The Daly Planet: Neither Rabid Fans Nor Rocky Romances Faze MVP Veejay Carson Daly', *People Weekly*, vol. 53, no. 21, 29 May 2000 (electronic version).
11. Joel Stein, 'Daly Is Going Nightly', *Time*, vol. 159, no. 2, 14 January 2000 (retrieved 14 November 2002 from Ebscohost Masterfile Premiere).
12. Lynch and Wang, 'The Daly Planet'.
13. Paul Monaco, *Understanding Society, Culture, and Television* (Westport, CT: Praeger, 1998), pp. 23 ff.
14. Gavin Edwards, 'The New American Bandstand: A Day in the Life of *Total Request Live*, the Epicenter of Pop', *Rolling Stone*, issue 834, 17 February 2000 (retrieved 14 November 2002 from Ebscohost Masterfile Premiere).
15. J. Cary, *Communication and Culture: Essays in Media and Society* (Boston, MA: Unwin Hyman, 1989).
16. MTV.com Announces.
17. Edwards, 'The New American Bandstand'.
18. Lynch and Wang, 'The Daly Planet'.
19. *TRL*, 10 September 2002.
20. Sheffield, 'Carson Daly'.
21. 'Picks and Pans: Tube', *People*, vol. 55, no. 17, 30 April 2001 (retrieved 14 November 2002 from Ebscohost Masterfile Premiere).
22. Lynch and Wang, 'The Daly Planet'.
23. Sheffield, 'Carson Daly'.
24. David Bordwell, *Making Meaning: Inference and Rhetoric in the Interpretation of Cinema* (London: Harvard University Press, 1989).
25. Barak Goodman and Rachel Dretzin (producers), *Merchants of Cool* (Boston: PBS Video, 2001).
26. J. Conway and A. Rubin, 'Psychological Predictors of Television', *Communication Research*, no. 18, 1991, pp. 443–63.
27. Andrew Goodwin, *Dancing in the Distraction Factory: Music Television and Popular Culture* (Minneapolis: University of Minnesota, 1992), p. 141.
28. Edwards, 'The New American Bandstand'.
29. Cloud, *Control and Consolation*, p. xvii.
30. Eric Messinger, 'You Know, Mom, He's Sorta Like – What's That Guy's Name? – Dick Clark', *New York Times Magazine*, vol. 149, no. 51346, 2 April 2000, p. 36.
31. Sheffield, 'Carson Daly'.
32. Edwards, 'The New American Bandstand'.
33. Cloud, *Control and Consolation*, p. 158.
34. *TRL*, 10 September 2002.
35. 'Backstreet Boy McLean Is in Rehab', *Associated Press Online*, 9 July 2001 (retrieved 14 November 2002 from Ebscohost Newspaper Source).
36. Stanley Deetz, *Democracy in an Age of Corporate Colonization : Developments in*

*Communication and the Politics of Everyday Life* (Albany, NY: SUNY, 1992).
37. David Bauder, 'Teens Tune in to MTV's *Total Request Live*', *Akron Beacon Journal*, 15 October 1999 (retrieved 14 November 2002 from Ebscohost Newspaper Source), p. 4.
38. Messinger, 'You Know, Mom', p. 38.
39. Jan Fernback, 'The Individual within the Collective: Virtual Ideology and the Realization of Collective Principles', in Steven G. Jones, ed., *Virtual Culture: Identity and Communication in Cybersociety* (London: Sage, 1997), pp. 36–54.
40. Edwards, 'The New *American Bandstand*'.

# Part III

## Identity

# 9

# 'Saying It Out Loud': Revealing Television's Queer Teens

## Glyn Davis

### 'But, um, you're gay, right?'

Dreams serve as a repetitive diegetic trope in the final episode of the short-lived, much-praised teen series *My So-Called Life*; at several points of sisterly confession in the narrative, female characters reveal the truth about their mind's unconscious night-time fabulations to other females. Central character Angela Chase dreams of yelling at her ex, Jordan, while her mother Patty dreams of Princess Di and an old boyfriend, Tony. Delia Fisher, former date of Angela's neighbour Brian Krakow, confesses that she had a dream (although 'it wasn't, you know, that type of dream') about Angela's queer Hispanic pal Rickie Vasquez, a character identified by Edwin J. Bernard as 'the first regularly appearing gay teen . . . in a prime time American television series'.[1] As the contents of our dreams often obliquely refract our lived experiences, it is no surprise that the contents of these dreams subsequently spill over into the 'real' lives of the show's characters. The dreams also become intertwined with the wishes and aspirations of several male characters in the programme: Angela's father Graham's ambition of starting a restaurant; Brian's long-burning desire for Angela; Rickie's wish to be straight.

This final episode of the only series of *My So-Called Life* seems to suggest that women are better at revealing the truth of their dreams to each other than men are (with some fudging; Patty doesn't tell her kids the erotic content of her dream). However, a late scene is crucial in complicating this schema, and in partially teasing apart the notions of 'truth' and 'dreams'. A number of high-school students – including Angela, Rickie and Delia – are preparing publicity and ticket distribution for the school play at the home of one of their teachers, Mr Katimsky. Earlier in the episode, Rickie had discovered Delia's attraction to him, and told Brian 'how much easier my life would be, if I could just like her back'. At Katimsky's, Rickie reveals to Angela that a love letter she received from Jordan was actually penned by Brian, and, as the group move to leave for pizza, Rickie takes Delia aside for a chat.

> RICKIE: Uh, Delia? Maybe we should, uh, go somewhere sometime?
> DELIA: Okay. [. . .] . . . but, um, you're gay, right?
> RICKIE: Well, I, you know, I, I . . .

DELIA: Oh, I'm sorry, I didn't . . .
RICKIE: No, it, it, it's okay.
DELIA: That came out so rude.
RICKIE: No, uh, see I, I try not to, um, no, I, I don't like, uh – [throws down the pencil he was holding] Yeah, I'm gay. I just don't usually say it like that.
DELIA: How do you usually say it?
RICKIE: I don't usually say it. I mean, I've actually never said it out loud.
DELIA: Wow. I feel kind of honoured. [. . .] I guess I'm just sort of in the mood to have a crush on somebody where it can't hurt too much.
RICKIE: Be my guest. Uh, Delia, if I were attracted to girls, I'd be attracted to you. [He takes her hand, and they exit the frame].

This sequence – including Rickie's revelation to Angela about the letter – posits the queer character as someone who lets the truth slip, a nexus of legitimacy and candour. Although he is coaxed into coming out by (white, straight) Delia – an utterance thus produced through a somewhat troubling racialised power dynamic – she admits to knowingly prefer an impossible, fantastic crush, in contrast to Rickie's surrender to the truth. Rickie's confession, in fact, shuts off the possibility of him attaining his dream, his 'chance of being straight', as the final line of the scene rather mournfully and poignantly attests. Indeed, in an episode filled with individuals telling lies and half-truths, and preferring to believe the fantastical, Rickie's coming out serves as a moment of perspicacity, direct honesty and clarity. Of course, it is pertinent that Delia explicitly names Rickie's sexuality before he does; in effect, she points out to Rickie what *we* know as well as she does. With his subtly camp eye rolls and hand gestures, single gold earring, penchant for eyeliner, soft voice and preference for hanging out in the girls' toilets, Rickie was always fairly clearly coded as queer. That we, the audience, knew of Rickie's orientation before he named it, places us with Delia as knowing subject; in fact, this is merely another manifestation of *My So-Called Life*'s female address (at the start of the episode under discussion, for instance, Angela's confessional voiceover is telling *us*, as putative female viewers, about her dream of Jordan). Delia is merely one of several female characters in the programme that seem to know Rickie's orientation even though it remains uncategorised or unnamed by him. This even applies to Danielle, Angela's younger sister, who nonchalantly tells their mother (in an earlier episode) that Rickie is 'probably bi', underlining the notion of heightened female sensitivity to matters of sexuality that Delia and Rickie's conversation suggests.

Rickie's final substantial scene in *My So-Called Life*, then, is centred around his coming out, which would seem to suggest such a confession as a potential narrative end point (in the eyes of television executives, at least).[2] But should it not have been a beginning? Further, what does the language used by Rickie in this sequence serve to reveal and obscure, figuratively and ideologically? This chapter will examine teen television's representation of queer adolescents, focusing in particular on those portrayed in several series. The coming-out scene in *My So-Called Life* described in detail above brings into play several key elements worthy of exploration, which will be used to structure the material that follows. First, is it possible to depict overt homosexuality in television drama as anything other than a revelation, an issue? Second, what are we to make of the overdetermined narrative emphasis placed on coming-out scenes, what do they imply, and how are they structured? Finally, what are the political ramifications of depicting queer teen desires on TV? Evidently, these issues overlap with each other; however, for reasons of clarity they will here be somewhat artificially separated.

## Queers against Television, Teens against Television

Before we can begin to consider the place of queer teens on television, it is necessary to identify a more fundamental problematic. A number of theorists have argued that television as a medium has developed in such a manner that its institutionalised form is antipathetic or inimical to queerness. As Anna McCarthy has written in relation to the ABC sitcom *Ellen*, 'same-sex desire plays a deeply agonistic role in the unfolding of temporal structures associated with television's modes of (auto)historiography – the media event, the television schedule, the season run, the final episode'. In addition, she goes on to identify 'the problem that queerness poses for television's representational politics: the difficulty of making same-sex desire uneventful, serial, everyday'.[3] That is, it is not solely that television's (hetero)structural form is, however covertly, hostile to queerness, but that the formats adopted by television programmes and the matters they address – in particular, the quotidian, the repetitive – struggle to integrate depictions of homosexuality.

In this regard, the comments of two writers analysing specific US television series are instructive. In an examination of *LA Law*, Rosanne Kennedy identifies the way in which the programme reduces queer sexual relationships to moral/political concerns, despite featuring a queer character (C. J. Lamb, played by Amanda Donohoe): '*LA Law* achieves potential points for representing gay and lesbian issues without, however, doing anything to revolutionize, or even create a space for, the visual representation of gay, lesbian or queer sexuality on mainstream television.'[4] In other words, when queerness appears as a diegetic element within a mainstream narrative context, its implications may be discussed, but it cannot actually be shown or normalised. A similar point is made by Dennis Allen, in an article on *Melrose Place*: 'in the heterosexual imaginary that dominates the show', he writes, 'the revelation of homosexuality is the *only* story that can be told about it. . . . [P]recisely because homosexuality is not assumed but is itself the secret that produces narrative complication, the disclosure of homosexuality is continually substituted for any possible narrative, romantic or otherwise, predicated on such a sexuality.'[5] That is, coming out over and over again is all that Matt, the gay character on *Melrose Place*, can do.[6] Allen goes on to extend his analysis to other television shows, observing an identical dynamic at play in programmes such as the sitcoms *Roseanne* and *Friends*, and the teen series *Beverly Hills 90210*.

The discontent and frustration voiced by these writers is palpable; expecting and demanding some sort of satisfactory queer representation from the medium and its schedules, they find both wanting. The problem is, of course, that even though queer characters now appear on television in notable numbers, they are absorbed into the heterosexuality of the medium and its representations. In relation to television, that is, queers always have to find a place in a heterosexual structure and system. As Larry Gross notes, '[g]ay and lesbian characters have become familiar visitors and even regulars on several sitcoms and dramatic programmes but they are still odd men and women out in a straight world'.[7] This means that only certain types of queers get represented, and only certain issues are addressed by the programmes in which they appear. Queer sexual activity, for instance, is minimal, in contrast to extensive, occasionally graphic, heterosexual coupling. On the whole, drama series individualise the struggle of characters like Rickie Vasquez; any wider examinations of systematic social and cultural homophobia, of institutionalised inequalities and differentials of power are beyond the representational regimes of the programmes, the networks and the medium. This is part and parcel of what I would like to call the general 'liberal conservatism' of television's representations of queerness. If the teen series has the potential to tell us things about queer teens, it will only tell us certain things, and not others.

However, to adhere to this condemnation of television is perhaps unfairly pessimistic, underestimating the potential of the medium. Lurking beneath the surface of many academic commentaries on television programmes, especially those shows which attempt to represent minorities 'fairly' (whatever that may mean), there seems to lie a deep-rooted wariness about popular media forms, wide audience catchments and the potentially damaging effects of the mainstream breaking down any group's cohesive and insulating 'community' walls. As Marshment and Hallam identify, '[t]his may be partly a suspicion of success itself, and partly a suspicion shared by many that the forms and contexts of popular culture are intrinsically hostile to the possibility of radical messages'. Through a close reading of the BBC television adaptation of Jeanette Winterson's novel *Oranges Are Not the Only Fruit*, the duo argue, on the contrary, that realist drama 'is certainly able to convey challenges to the dominant ideology'.[8] Indeed, surely some of the concerns raised above by McCarthy, Kennedy and Allen are difficult to maintain following the production of a number of television series which have featured gay core characters – *Tales of the City*, *Queer as Folk*, *Six Feet under*, *Dawson's Creek* – all of which have had openly gay personnel working on them, and which have attained critical adulation and solid, appreciative audiences.

What is intriguing in light of the concerns raised above about the thorny, troublesome intersection of queerness and television is the way in which these comments echo similar insights proffered by Karen Lury about the intersection between 'youth' and television. As she states:

> Generations of youth are often seen by observers (and are frequently articulated as such by young spokespeople themselves), as being opposed to a dominant or mainstream culture (to, perhaps, 'everybody else'), which, more often than not, is identified with its presentation through the compromised medium of television . . . television and youth are naturally, and diametrically, opposed social and theoretical constructs.

This argument seems to postulate a position for 'youth', in relation to television, which could be seen as analogous to that of queers; that is, as outside the mainstream, not wishing to be compromised by the representational regime of the popular medium.

Indeed, in Lury's subsequent claim that 'television. . . . may even be seen as contaminating in its attempts to approach or represent the supposedly authentic pleasures and activities of the young people themselves',[9] we can identify a mistrust regarding the mainstream depiction of a specific cultural identity similar to that noted by Marshment and Hallam. Theoretically, then, this makes the queer teen spectator doubly distanced from television and its representations.

Part of the problem here relates to *who* has the power to represent specific groups. Dramas made for a youth audience, and which represent adolescent experience, are (almost exclusively) produced by adults, and for major corporations. This is a concern that has been noted in this book's Introduction, as well as by such authors as Jon Lewis and Henry A. Giroux.[10] More specifically, Ben Gove, writing about the representation of queer adolescents in film, theatre and television, has pointed out that 'adult framings of pre-adult sexuality always involve an uneasy use of discursive power, for the adult show of interest immediately implicates the framer in what she/he frames'.[11] And yet, teenagers *do* take pleasure in the commodities and culture marketed to them, despite its production by adults, and adolescent adulation for specific television programmes can be emphatic and heavily invested. Perhaps the distrust of television evinced by critical commentators on adolescence such as Gove and Giroux once again serves to underestimate the potential of the medium. Indeed, the teen series seems to embody great promise for bringing to the screen lives, desires and issues that are often ignored, stymied or cursorily treated by television (and other media). One key element here is longevity: the sheer length of a long-running series allows for the development of characterisation, and substantive narrative depth and complexity; further, particular issues and storylines can breathe and develop in some detail and at a slow (and thus potentially more realistic) pace.[12] The teen series, then, offers great potential for the representation of teen lives and desires, including those of queer teens. In the subsequent sections of this essay, the forms of, and limitations imposed upon, queer teen characterisation – especially those that circulate around the all-important coming-out scene – will be discussed in detail.

### 'I've Never Been So Sure': Coming out, Language and Epistemology

Coming out as gay, declaring one's queer identity, occupies a pivotal position in the teen series' narrativisation of queer adolescent subjectivity. This makes sense: what is usually captured in these sequences is the *first* experienced instance of coming out, a self-conscious taking-on of a new, specific identity (and thus the one that is potentially emotionally most resonant for the character and/or for the programme's audience). Whereas, in previous decades, homosexuality *per se* was used by television series as a 'problem', the contemporary teen series (and other television series) now often depict coming out as the major problem for queer individuals to overcome.[13] The passage of information coded in the language used becomes a moral and ethical issue: who is responsible for the telling, and who has a right to know? I wish to argue that, at first glance, coming-out scenes in teen series seem to reinforce the act as an individualised one, and as an exultant liberationist confession of one's essential(ised) identity. However, in addition, they enact a complicated enunciation of queerness, in which, despite privileging a liberal paradigm, a range of different models of homosexuality are brought into play. The most notable tension evinced is one between essentialism and the constructionist notion of the performativity of speech; that is, between language as a tool used to reveal an essential pre- or super-linguistic truth, and speech acts as the very iterative creator of truth, repetitively producing (an always partial and somewhat elusive, semiotically slippery) factuality.

To take a specific example: mid-way through the fourth series of *Party of Five*, Sarah's sex-shy boyfriend Elliot takes a shine to Sarah's ex, Bailey, asking him, in a scene whose dialogue could have been lifted from a gay porn movie, 'Where do you work out?' That Elliot's interest in Bailey might be due to an undisclosed ardour is signalled to Bailey by a peripheral female infant character (the daughter of Bailey's current girlfriend, Annie), playing with two 'Ken' dolls as though they were the two teen boys kissing. (Once again, this suggests, as in *My So-Called Life*, that there is a female sensitivity to issues of sexuality that men lack.) Later, while the two boys train together, Bailey tries to assess whether Elliot is gay through thinly veiled questions about Elliot's aesthetic taste in musicals, opera, sport and interior decoration. Elliot, misreading Bailey's probing as sexual interest, subsequently turns up at the restaurant at which Bailey works. The two sit down to talk at a table for two, as if on a romantic date: a fire roars in the background, lighting their faces; the table is decorated with a single rose in a vase; quiet jazz piano plays in the background.

> ELLIOT: . . . I know what you were hinting around at, OK, and I want you to know that I am, like, so relieved.
> BAILEY: Relieved?
> ELLIOT: Yeah, 'cause, I think, er, I think maybe I am too.
> BAILEY: You think 'maybe you are too' what?
> ELLIOT: Well, you know, gay, like you. Man, OK, I said it. Er, it's like, you've been so great, Bai, this has been, you've made this so much easier for me, and, I mean, I thought Sarah was going to be it, you know, prove to me that I wasn't, [Bailey fingers his collar, which is suddenly too tight] and then, then you come along, and it just felt, it was different, you know, like I got that vibe and it just seemed right, or something, and now it's like, I am sure, in fact, I've never been more sure about anything in my life . . .
> BAILEY: Look, Elliot, it's totally cool that you're, [*sotto voce*] *you're gay*. I, I have no opinion about that, um, but I think that maybe you got the wrong – I, I *know* that you *definitely* got the wrong idea this morning because *I'm not*. I was just, I'm, I'm sorry, but I was just trying to find out if you were.
> ELLIOT [emotionally shattered]: Oh. Oh, man. Well, then maybe we should, er – Maybe I should – I'm gonna go. [He gets up and leaves; Bailey rests his face in his hands].

Elliot's lengthy monologue tumbles pell-mell from his mouth; his barely contained euphoria at having found another gay teen (or so he thinks) to talk to, combined with nerves, fractures his language, such that snatches of phrases stumble over each other. He tells Bailey that he has come to knowledge – 'I've never been more sure' – and yet that knowledge is based on a fundamental misunderstanding: that Bailey is also gay. Bailey, despite having guessed that Elliot is gay, seems thrown by their conversation; this is perhaps because Bailey realises that his own behaviour (gym activities with another man, probing questions about *Cats*) could be read as queer. His statement about himself shifts from an unstable, uncertain 'I think' to the more concrete, overly emphatic assertion, 'I *know* that you *definitely* got the wrong idea'. And yet this attempt at stability is ineffective as the partial, almost affective, queering that Bailey experiences bleeds into subsequent scenes. When Bailey reveals to Sarah that he knows why Elliot dumped her – 'He never told you?' – she replies: 'Told me what? Wait a minute. Bailey, Bailey, you guys didn't – Oh, oh, well, that's, that's humiliating, that you guys—.' The vocal ellipsis here is, of course, 'talked'; but Sarah's unmarked linguistic elisions suggest that Bailey could easily have come to his knowledge through other, physical, routes. That Elliot revealed his true nature to Bailey is suddenly open to transposition onto fucking; speech becomes a sexualised act.

In an attempt to downplay the intimation that Bailey might be gay, ensuing scenes depict Bailey and Sarah, then Sarah and Elliot, discussing the moral and ethical issues circulating around coming out as queer. Sarah tells Elliot that 'You made me feel like there was something wrong with me' and Elliot replies (in an echo of Rickie's melancholy yearning for heterosexuality) 'I thought you were like my salvation or something. I thought . . . if I could just love this woman, then it will make it all go away.' By the end of the episode, Elliot and Sarah are reconciled as friends, watching *Oliver!* and ogling the lycra-clad ass of a man rollerblading past them on the street. But whereas Elliot's coming out could have led to subsequent narrativisation as a substantial character within the programme, his declaration (like that of Rickie) actually acted as a narrative end-point: he never reappeared in the programme.[14]

Elliot's disclosure seemed to upset the epistemological basis of Bailey and Sarah's comfy heterosexuality; perhaps this is why he was written out of the programme. His revelation of his sexual orientation makes for a fascinating comparison with that of Jack McPhee, who came out in Season Two of *Dawson's Creek*. Over two episodes, Jack struggled to a painful self-recognition; this storyline evinced a sophisticated understanding of the power of language in facilitating the formulation and construction of queer identity. In the first episode, following a suggestion by friend Dawson to write by 'listen[ing] to yourself', Jack produces a poem that he is subsequently forced to read aloud in class. His verse seems to imply gay feelings, although he breaks down trying to deliver it: his writing may reveal (in a somewhat opaque fashion) his 'true' nature, but Jack stammers, cracks and fails to vocalise the words. The written word, then, 'speaks' the truth, but spoken language fails to provide an adequate resource for enunciating or revealing.

Subsequently, the rest of the episode's narrative focuses on the words of Jack's social group – girlfriend Joey's rapid-fire delivery, telling Jack, repressively, 'do me a favour? No more poems'; sister-in-therapy Andie's revelation that she would be disappointed if her brother was gay; and Dawson's banal Oprah-like homilies, to just 'be honest'. This focus serves to point out, first, how the speech of some individuals can structure the silence of others, and second, how the proliferation of different forms of contemporary discourse (including different types of therapy-speak) can produce a confusing social and cultural terrain for the queer teen, in which the closet may be the safest place to which to retreat.

At one point, words literally and concretely surround Jack as his poem is photocopied by an unidentified school bully, and stuck all over the school walls. In addition, the word 'FAG' is daubed in red paint on Jack's closet-like locker; Joey's show of support for Jack is to kiss him up against the locker in full view of the school crowd. Everybody at school (including the school *itself*), it seems, is talking about Jack, but he cannot find the appropriate words to talk about himself.

## Evaluating the Teen Series' Queer Teens

It is extremely tempting to offer evaluations of each queer teen character that has appeared in a teen series (and there are such a small number that it would be perfectly possible to do so).[15] And yet to judge individual portrayals as 'positive' or 'negative' is a complex, contradictory effort, and often a personal one which, in recent years, has been subject to much criticism. Authors such as Ellis Hanson, B. Ruby Rich and Clare Whatling have argued that it is possible, and acceptable, for queer audience members to take pleasure in the representation of queer villains in films such as *Basic Instinct*.[16] As these critics note, what constitute positive representations, which audience they are being produced for and why that audience should even want them are all contentious issues. And yet this particular polemical analysis does not seem to apply to child and adolescent audiences. Indeed, what *they* watch – and are allowed to enjoy – remains carefully policed and much debated. It tends to be assumed, for instance, that children are susceptible to television imagery in a way that adults are not. And if the media can influence people's opinions regarding social and cultural groups, directly and/or cumulatively, then the educative potential that lies behind the representation of queer individuals cannot be ignored. As Diane Waldman has stated, despite all the problems associated with the positive images debate, '[w]e certainly should . . . applaud "positive images" when they do appear: that these media images *do* serve to shape children's attitudes, behaviours, and expectations is undeniable'.[17]

Perhaps this is why almost all televisual representations of queer teens are remarkably 'positive': their potential as role models or transmitters of politicised messages seems to have been recognised by liberal drama writers, series producers and television executives. It is possible to detect here the Reithian 'public service broadcasting' notion that television can serve as an educative tool to improve and inform its audiences.[18] Actor Kerr Smith (Jack on *Dawson's Creek*) has stated that 'you can't be flippant about a gay teenager whose every next move is being scrutinised by millions of gay teenagers'.[19] Indeed, what is significant about the representation of queer teens on television is that they *may* provide representational examples to audiences who are unable to learn about homosexuality from more traditional sources of education. A range of educators and journalists have written in recent years about the lack of 'queer curriculum' in schools in Britain and America, and the impact that this can have on queer youth attending these institutions. As Gerald Unks has written, '[t]he absence from the curriculum of valid information about homosexuality cuts both ways; heterosexual students are given no reasons not to hate homosexuals, while homosexual students are given no reason not to hate themselves'.[20] However, the introduction of homosexuality into the school curriculum in any field (except nominal nods in sex education classes) is unlikely to happen for some time. Many parents continue to fear their children being taught about homosexuality; some teachers, unsurprisingly (given the social attitude towards queerness), do not want to be seen as associated with it in case of homophobic reprisals from students and/or parents; and this state of affairs is often supported by government policy forbidding the 'promotion' of homosexuality to school children.[21] 'Given this critical state of affairs,' writes Ben Gove, 'popular representations and debates hold an especially intense significance as informal methods of sex education, and as self-validation, for gay and lesbian youths.'[22]

Television, then, is obviously a major resource for queer youth and, for that reason, televised representations of queer characters are meticulously scrutinised by concerned adult commentators. One focus of the analyses of these critics in relation to the representation of queer teens – and this is connected to the desire to portray 'positive images' – is the need to avoid stereotyping. This debate is one that has been well rehearsed elsewhere.[23] A further concern for adult critics is presented by those teen series that complicate their representation of adolescent queerness by conflating it with other variables. For instance, the relationship between Willow and her girlfriend Tara in *Buffy*, although on the surface a solid and interesting (if slightly mawkish) depiction of lesbianism, is made seriously troubling because the show connects the girls' sexuality to their status as witches. As Harry Benshoff has noted, '[t]he linkage of homosexuals and witchcraft within popular understanding has a long and tangled history';[24] Willow and Tara's embodiment of both, no matter how rounded their characters, is problematic.[25] As a second example, the representation of Rickie's race in *My So-Called Life* is worth commenting on. Arguably, by having a working-class, Hispanic, gay man as the main queer character in the show (middle-class gay men only turn up later on in the series, in the form of Mr Katimsky and his partner), homosexuality can be seen to be predominately a concern of less socially empowered and/or non-WASP cultural groups, thus marking queerness as 'other' to a presumed WASP majority. Rickie is accepted by his white friends but not his own family; the latter – as representatives of Hispanics as an ethnic group, although they remain virtually unseen – are demonised as judgmental, in favour of the understanding white folk.

Despite these criticisms, however, there are favourable evaluations to be made of the queer teens that appear in teen series. Jack, Willow, and Alex in the British show *As If* are all long-running, central characters in their respective series. All three programmes, while recognising the 'difference' of these individuals' sexuality, attempt to make their queer characters ordinary, and their lives as everyday as those of their friends (and thus contradict the arguments put forward by Allen, Kennedy and McCarthy raised earlier). As Kerr Smith has stated, '[t]he biggest thing we're trying to get across to people is that Jack is a normal kid'.[26] In addition, Rickie, despite the short-lived nature of the series in which he appeared, and the complications noted above which are posed by his race, can be seen to have troubled the whiteness of TV's queerness – as Gross notes, 'television's queers are as white-washed as their straight counterparts'.[27] (Indeed, Rickie could be seen as a bold challenge to predominant stereotypes of [straight] Hispanic machismo.) If, to a slightly more jaded adult audience, the teen series' representations of queer adolescents can seem somewhat 'worthy', it is feasible that, with an increased number of queer teens depicted from the current handful, there would be room for more variability in characterisation.

## Dreaming of the Queen: Queering the Teen Series

Quite apart from the literal, concrete representation of queer teenagers in the teen series, it is arguable that the genre has an implicit appeal to queer audiences, especially gay male viewers. The dominant register of the form, as Rachel Moseley and Miranda J. Banks have argued, is a melodramatic one,[28] and melodrama (a genre which is routinely critically derided) is often culturally associated with women and gay men.[29] It is thus perhaps unsurprising that many of the concerns that the queer and female teen characters in the teen series express serve as echoes of those of melodramatic narratives perhaps familiar to audiences of the 'women's films' of the 1940s and 1950s. For instance, finding one's place in society, experiencing true love, and resisting/accepting stereotyping are repeated motifs; and in teen series, as much as 'golden era' women's pictures, lead characters are often trying to find the easiest route to 'being happy with their lot'.

In addition to appeals to generic staples, the teen series offers alternative sources of pleasure to the gay male spectator. A number of specific teen series regularly present the spectacle of male flesh for their audiences' delectation. The men displayed are often conventionally 'pretty', and the scenes of exposure often have little narrational motivation (in a reversal of filmic logic, this rarely happens with female characters). Notably, however, the men that disrobe are rarely the gay teen characters.[30] Male characters are often filmed in bed, working out, stepping out of showers, and (this is a ridiculously repetitive trope) wounded and in need of medical attention. In *Buffy*, Angel and Riley seemed to shed their shirts at least once an episode; *Angel* often offers David Boreanaz's pierced and scarred flesh up for viewing, in a manner reminiscent of imagery of Saint Sebastian; and *Roswell High*'s Max and Kyle both regularly bare their muscular torsos.[31] In *Smallville*, Clark Kent, played by former model Tom Welling, is often clothed in T-shirts one size too small for him, his biceps bulging under tight white cotton, and in one episode an exploding truck literally blows his shirt off him. James Wolcott has referred to Welling as 'a dreamy boy toy', 'dewy enough to leave droplets on the screen'; early publicity shots for the series, he claims, made Welling 'look like trade'.[32] It would seem that the writers of the show are aware of their queer audience: the friendship between Clark and Lex is a fairly evidently homoeroticised one. Wolcott draws attention to the first episode of the programme, in which more wounding of teenage male flesh occurs:

> Lex discovers Clark strung up like a scarecrow in a wheat field, a blood-red *S* painted across his bare chest. The Crucifixion pose taps into the Superman-as-Messiah myth, maintaining continuity with the original, but its staging and lighting make it also a classic tableau of homoerotica... Lex's fixation on Clark/Superboy always had a jilted-lover quality, a spurned fury, to which the comic-book writers seemed oblivious...[33]

These queer pleasures – hovering somewhere between being inherent in the text and constructed by the active viewer – complement the overt representation of queer teens in the teen series. In fact, for those critics who believe that television and queerness are fundamentally antipathetic to one another, these queer readings are seen as the saving grace of television's fractious relationship with homosexuality. As Anna McCarthy concludes in her analysis of *Ellen*, 'queer network television appears more readily through practices of reading the television past, like camp, or the familiar "between-the-lines" stance of the queer reader than through official moments . . .'[34] And yet, as I hope this chapter has demonstrated, television's overt representation of queer adolescents contributes to filling a representational void produced by evasive school curricula; and, contrary to what several (rather defensive) theorists have argued, the depictions of queer characters offered by a number of teen series suggest that television is capable of making queerness 'ordinary', serial, mundane. Further, although seemingly adhering to a liberal political stance, such depictions in fact interact with, and bring into circulation, a range of different models of identity, without ever advocating one as definitive.

Of course, queer audiences always want more, dream of more, from television. For me, at least, the final episode of *My So-Called Life* was both enormously satisfying and a tremendous letdown. Rickie's coming out may have narratively shut down the possibility of *his* reaching his dream (of heterosexuality). However, as a key scene in the final episode of the series, it paradoxically opened up extra-diegetic avenues for spectatorial dreaming and fantasy: of the realms of possibility for television's queer teens, of what never happened or got to happen in *My So-Called Life*, of what may still be to come in other series.

## Notes

1. Edwin J. Bernard, 'Wilson Cruz – Life After *Life*', interview conducted May 1996, archived online at www.mscl.com/encyclopaedia/media/show_media.phtml?layout=low&id=105, accessed 29 July 2002.
2. Accounts of why *My So-Called Life* was axed vary. Bernard (ibid.) points to the show's low ratings, and to the fact that 'Claire Danes [who played Angela] . . . wanted a movie career'. One ABC executive suggested that the series 'turned off a lot of teens' because '[i]t was too real' (Jeff Bader, quoted in 'TV Shows and Schools', *Minneapolis Star Tribune*, January 1997, archived at www.mscl.com/encyclopaedia/media/show_media.phtml?layout= low&id=57, accessed 7 July 2002). Justin Quirk also notes that the dominant register of *My So-Called Life* affected its longevity: 'This dark tone meant the show was dogged with problems before it was even broadcast. Despite it coming from producers with a proven track record ..., ABC sat on the show for almost a year before broadcasting it' (Quirk, 'When Youthful TV Was Truthful', *Guardian*, The Guide, Saturday 23 November 2002, p. 13).
3. Anna McCarthy, '*Ellen*: Making Queer Television History', *GLQ*, vol. 7, no. 4 (2001), pp. 597, 609. In relation to the latter point, it is also worth noting Joy V. Fuqua's comment that 'it is the representation of the "everyday" in relation to gay characters which causes the difficulty for soap opera' ('"There's a Queer in My Soap!" The Homophobia/AIDS Storyline of *One Life to Live*', in Robert C. Allen (ed.), *To Be Continued: Soap Operas around the World* (London and New York: Routledge, 1995), pp. 208–9).
4. Rosanne Kennedy, 'The Gorgeous Lesbian in *LA Law*: The Present Absence?', in Diane

Hamer and Belinda Budge, eds, *The Good, the Bad and the Gorgeous: Popular Culture's Romance with Lesbianism* (London and San Francisco: Pandora, 1994), p. 139. See also Sasha Torres, 'Television/Feminism: *HeartBeat* and Prime Time Lesbianism', in Henry Abelove, Michele Aina Barale and David M. Halperin (eds), *The Lesbian and Gay Studies Reader* (London and New York: Routledge, 1993), pp. 176–85.

5. Dennis W. Allen, 'Homosexuality and Narrative', *Modern Fiction Studies*, vol. 41, no. 3–4 (Fall–Winter 1995), pp. 610–11.

6. Intriguingly, Kerr Smith (who plays Jack McPhee in *Dawson's Creek*) has contrasted *Creek* with the limited representational strategies of *Melrose Place*: 'Kevin [Williamson, *Creek*'s gay creator] said to me, "What do you think about making Jack's character gay?" And I said, "OK, but it can't be like *Melrose Place* where there's a gay guy on the show, he hugs or kisses a guy every episode and that's it. It's a weak story." I wanted to tell a story about a 16-year-old kid who's struggling with his sexuality, he comes out of the closet, and then he has to deal with the repercussions of that' (Simon Button, 'Up the Creek', *Attitude*, July 2000 (issue 75), p. 57). Kerr Smith may be overestimating the amount of kissing that took place on *Melrose Place*: see Larry Gross, *Up from Invisibility: Lesbians, Gay Men and the Media in America* (New York: Columbia University Press, 2001), p. 91.

7. Gross, *Up from Invisibility*, p. 257.

8. Margaret Marshment and Julia Hallam, 'From String of Knots to Orange Box: Lesbianism on Prime Time', in Hamer and Budge, *The Good, the Bad and the Gorgeous*, pp. 143, 146.

9. Karen Lury, *British Youth Television: Cynicism and Enchantment* (Oxford: Clarendon Press, 2001), pp. 12–14.

10. Jon Lewis, *The Road to Romance and Ruin: Teen Film and Youth Culture* (London: Routledge, 1991); Henry A. Giroux, *Stealing Innocence: Corporate Culture's War on Children* (Basingstoke and New York: Palgrave, 2000).

11. Ben Gove, 'Framing Gay Youth', *Screen*, vol 37, no. 2 (Summer 1996), p. 177.

12. Winnie Holzman on *My So-Called Life*: 'I wrote it originally as a half hour [programme], and after I finished I went to [the producers] and said: "This needs to be an hour show." They agreed and I went back and at that point was able to add the complexity and fullness to the pilot that you can bring to hour drama. Because you have time to explore character and to really pay moments off' ('Ask . . . Winnie Holzman', interview conducted by Viewers for Quality Television, 20 March 1995, archived online at http://www.mscl.com/encyclopaedia/media/show_media.phtml?layout=low&id=68, accessed 31 July 2002).

13. An overview of criticisms of the stereotypical coming-out scenario has been offered by Robert McRuer: 'theorists have critiqued coming-out stories for their emphasis on the discovery of an individual and essential gay identity, unmarked by other categories of identity, such as race or class' ('Boys' Own Stories and New Spellings of My Name: Coming Out and Other Myths of Queer Positionality', in Carol Siegel and Ann Kibbey, eds, *Eroticism and Containment: Notes from the Flood Plain* (New York and London: New York University Press, 1994), p. 261. Indeed, coming-out stories in teen series are – with the exception of Rickie in *My So-Called Life* – predominately white, middle class and individualised. Never is there any consideration of the fact that some teens may not be able to come out due to their race or class background. And rarely is there recognition of a wider, politicised queer community to

which the queer teen could affiliate themselves; this is especially ridiculous in the case of *Party of Five*, which is set in San Francisco.

14. On television's 'use [of] marginal characters to introduce taboo social issues', see Fuqua, '"There's a Queer in My Soup!"', pp. 200–1 (quote from p. 201). It is also worth noting that Elliot's storyline is seen mostly through the heterosexual eyes of Sarah and Bailey; for commentary on how queer characters' narratives in mainstream media are structured through straight surrogates, see Larry Gross, 'Out of the Mainstream: Sexual Minorities and the Mass Media', in Ellen Seiter, Hans Barchers, Gabriele Kreutzner and Eva-Maria Warth, eds, *Remote Control: Television, Audiences, and Cultural Power* (London and New York: Routledge, 1991), pp. 130–49.
15. In addition to the teen series mentioned in this essay, it is worth noting that queer teens have also appeared in soaps: in Britain, in *Brookside*, *Emmerdale*, *Crossroads* and *Hollyoaks*; in Australia, in *Breakers*; and in America, in *One Life to Live* and *All My Children*. Queer teens have also featured in British series and miniseries targeted at an adult audience: *Tinsel Town* and *Queer as Folk* (the latter has been remade for an American audience, in a substantially altered form, by cable channel Showtime).
16. See: Ellis Hanson, 'Introduction: Out Takes', in Hanson (ed.), *OutTakes: Essays on Queer Theory and Film* (Durham, NC and London: Duke University Press, 1999), pp. 1–19; B. Ruby Rich, 'New Queer Cinema', *Sight and Sound*, vol. 2, no. 5 (September 1992), pp. 30–5; Clare Whatling, *Screen Dreams: Fantasising Lesbians in Film* (Manchester and New York: Manchester University Press, 1997), esp. pp. 79–115.
17. Diane Waldman, 'There's More to a Positive Image than Meets the Eye', in Patricia Erens (ed.), *Issues in Feminist Film Criticism* (Bloomington and Indianapolis: Indiana University Press, 1990), p. 18.
18. Lord John Reith was the first director of the British Broadcasting Corporation (BBC): he believed wholeheartedly (if somewhat paternalistically) in the potential of television to educate, as well as morally and spiritually 'improve', its audiences.
19. Button, 'Up the Creek', p. 57.
20. Gerald Unks, 'Thinking about the Gay Teen', in Unks (ed.), *The Gay Teen: Educational Practice and Theory for Lesbian, Gay, and Bisexual Adolescents* (New York and London: Routledge, 1995), p. 5. For more on supporting queer kids, providing safe spaces and constructing a queer curriculum, see Jonathan Keane, 'The Young and the Restless', *Pink Paper*, 9 January 1998, pp. 9–10; and Robert E. Owens, *Queer Kids: The Challenges and Promise for Lesbian, Gay and Bisexual Youth* (New York: Harrington Park Press, 1998).
21. In the United Kingdom, the Thatcher era saw the introduction of 'Clause 28', a piece of legislation which explicitly forbids the 'promotion' of homosexuality in schools; although later erased in Scotland, the Clause still has effect in the rest of the UK. To date, no one has been prosecuted in relation to the legislation. In contrast to Britain, in America sodomy is still illegal in eighteen states; further, America has a much larger (and more vocal) religious population. For comments on teachers' fears of dealing with gay issues, and an analysis of psychiatry's construction of queer children, see Eve Kosofsky Sedgwick, 'How to Bring Your Kids up Gay', in Michael Warner (ed.), *Fear of a Queer Planet: Queer Politics and Social Theory* (Minneapolis: University of Minnesota Press, 1993), pp. 69–81.

22. Ben Gove, 'Framing Gay Youth', p. 179.
23. For discussion of lesbian and gay stereotypes, see Richard Dyer, *The Matter of Images: Essays on Representations* (London and New York: Routledge, 1993). For an analysis of the stereotypical characterisations at work in teen series' depictions of queer adolescents, see Gross, *Up from Invisibility*, esp. p. 176.
24. Harry Benshoff, *Monsters in the Closet: Homosexuality and the Horror Film* (Manchester and New York: Manchester University Press, 1997), p. 103.
25. In season six of *Buffy the Vampire Slayer* – yet to be aired on British terrestrial television, and thus unseen at the time of writing this essay – Tara is murdered, and Willow goes on a vengeful rampage. For a politicised evaluation of this representational strategy, see 'The Death of Tara, the Fall of Willow, and the Dead/Evil Lesbian Cliché FAQ', www.abooth.demon.co.uk/lesbiancliche.htm/, accessed 7 August 2002.
26. Button, 'Up the Creek', p. 59.
27. Gross, *Up from Invisibility*, p. 256.
28. Rachel Moseley, 'The Teen Series', in Glen Creeber (ed.), *The Television Genre Book* (London: BFI, 2001), p. 42 and Miranda J. Banks in this volume.
29. In an episode of *Will and Grace*, Will sadly tells Grace of how he always wanted a cowboy-themed birthday cake as a child, but never got one. 'Oh Will,' says Grace, 'that's so *Party of Five*.'
30. Jack's buff body was covered up following his coming out; earlier, when he was dating Joey, one storyline had her painting him in the nude.
31. In episode 7 of the British version of *Queer as Folk*, Vince is given a video for his thirtieth birthday by camp pal Alexander: 'You'll never guess, it's every episode of *Saved by the Bell* with Zack taking his shirt off, I've been four years taping that' (Russell T. Davies, *Queer as Folk: The Scripts* (London: Channel 4 Books/Macmillan, 1999), p. 177. As an additional intertext, it is worth noting that Jason Behr (Max Evans in *Roswell High*) played a gay teen in the TV movie *Rites of Passage*.
32. James Wolcott, 'It's a Bird, It's a Plane . . . It's the *Zeitgeist!*', *Vanity Fair*, March 2002, p. 59.
33. Ibid. The cast are clearly aware of the erotically charged relationship between Clark and Lex, too. In an article on the programme in *Rolling Stone* magazine, Erik Hedegaard recounts an incident of Michael Rosenbaum (Lex) and Tom Welling rehearsing a scene: '"Don't you remember anything about the accident?" Rosenbaum asks Welling. "I remember pulling you out," says Welling. "That's all." "You sure you don't remember anything?" asks Rosenbaum. He pauses. He lifts an eyebrow. Finally, displaying his own intuitive feel for the *zeitgeist*, he says, "My ass was sore afterward. You sure you didn't give me a superfuck?"' ('Tall Tales from Smallville', *Rolling Stone*, issue 892, 28 March 2002, p. 44). The eroticised relationship between the two male characters has also led to the production of a slew of slash fiction, art and video material.
34. McCarthy, '*Ellen*', p. 615.

# 10

# Dormant Dormitory Friendships: Race and Gender in *Felicity*

## Sharon Ross

### Introduction

Female friendships have long been a topic within popular cultural representations in the United States. Many female friendships within television have been presented as secondary aspects of narratives concerning the nuclear family or the ensemble-cast workplace. However, shifts in US culture and society have increasingly testified to the cultural and economic viability of television shows focused on female friendships. Scholars have taken note of this trend and its relationship with the rise of niche marketing's attempt to appeal to the highly lucrative female audience – be it teen, young adult or adult.[1]

The television network with a literal corner on the female teen and young adult market is the growing Warner Brothers (WB). Some of WB's most critically acclaimed and lucrative shows, however, do 'more' than feature young females in their narratives: they feature, specifically, white females. *Felicity* in particular is glaringly and paradoxically white. One of its lead characters is African-American, yet the storylines and structure of the show effectively downgrade her status as a lead character, and also completely ignore the issue of her 'race'. The purpose of this essay is to explore the representation of this (African-American) character, Elena, in terms of her function in the show as a friend and classmate of the primary lead (white) character, Felicity. The show's shifts between melodrama and romantic comedy function in part to marginalise Elena within the series in comparison with Felicity's other (white) female friends. What does Elena's marginalisation and the colour-blind approach of *Felicity* suggest about how Hollywood perceives female friendships in a multicultural country?

Some scholars argue that television's increasing use of niche marketing strategies is reinforced by television melodramas in particular, because of melodrama's focus on the world of the private individual. Lynne Joyrich argues that television melodramas aimed at women leave the spectator at the mercy of the story in a way that reinforces female political passivity in society.[2] Other feminist scholars working within psychoanalytic film theory or British cultural studies have evaluated similar texts and their audiences more optimistically.[3] Both approaches to studying media, however, have been criticised for a tendency to overlook specificities of race, ethnicity and class.

Part of what drives these academic exclusions are the overwhelmingly white landscapes of film and television – particularly when considering narratives that focus on females and/or female friendships. In Karen Hollinger's examination of contemporary female friendship films, she notes that popular films from the 1970s onwards have seldom focused on women of colour, and that interracial female friendships remain underdeveloped.[4] The majority of female friendship films instead have focused on identity formation and shared intimacy within a self-contained, melodramatic, white world. While *Felicity*'s colour-blind and often melodramatic approach to storytelling does work to set up a self-contained diegetic world of whiteness, this show also expands that world to include social issues. Notably, however, issues related to race receive scant attention in comparison with the many other social issues that *Felicity*'s use of melodrama allows in; the colour-blind world of the show only opens up so much.

This discrepancy is not new in texts featuring female friendships. Julie D'Acci's research on *Cagney and Lacey*, for example, revealed that this show increasingly de-emphasised social connections between gender and race across its run.[5] Exactly ten years after *Cagney and Lacey* ended as a series, *Felicity*'s continuation of this pattern is troubling, given that one of the female friendships the show 'features' is interracial. The show's colour-blind approach to storytelling has left the interracial friendship in the show vastly underdeveloped, while the intraracial ones flourish. As a feminist scholar and college teacher, it is distressing to me that this pattern of racial erasure and marginalisation is present in a critically acclaimed and popular show set in an urban college and marketed to a college-aged female audience. While I applaud the show's attention to issues concerning gender, class and sexual orientation, I am disheartened to see that attention to these areas of life seems to happen at the expense of addressing race. The marginalisation of race as a topic or identity factor worthy of address reveals, at the very least, models for interracial friendships that are sorely unhealthy and naive.

## Melodrama versus Comedy

One of the primary ways in which *Felicity* marginalises Elena is through generic segregation. Elena, for much of the series, serves as a genre-oriented counterpoint to Felicity and her white friends (Julie, and when Julie leaves, Megan). When the white female characters' stories are melodramatic in nature, Elena's are comic and vice versa. It is only in the second half of the series that Elena is situated in the same generic mode as the other females (serial melodrama). However, in the final season, this equality falls apart as Elena gradually receives less screen time. Key moments in Elena's trajectory as a character demonstrate how genre works to marginalise this character and her race. I will examine how Elena's placement within comedy excludes her from the melodramatic (important) world of the other women in the show and how her gradual melodramatic inclusion does not then remedy the marginalisation (when logically it should).

When *Felicity* first started, it was immersed in melodramatic situations that serve as the formation of Felicity's bond with Julie. The pilot episode details Felicity's decision to go to New York University instead of Stanford, where she had been accepted in a pre-med programme (preparatory classes for a degree in medicine). The catalyst for this decision is Ben, a good-looking athlete from Felicity's high school whom she has had a crush on for the past four years. Felicity follows Ben to New York and is dismayed when she sees Ben kissing another girl. Felicity then meets Julie in class and the two begin their friendship when Julie tries to cheer up Felicity. However, not knowing Felicity's true feelings, Julie becomes romantic with Ben, setting up numerous episodes to come, in which the primary stumbling block to the two females' friendship is competition over Ben.

Thus, a boy threatens Felicity and Julie's friendship; as the series continues, however, the friendship is strengthened as they learn to overcome this obstacle. In addition, by the second episode, Julie's own melodramatic narrative is revealed: she has come to New York because this is where her birth mother lives, and she hopes to find her. (Julie is adopted.) Therefore, Felicity and Julie are framed within strategies typical to serial melodrama. Their stories focus on female intimacy, the obstacles of heterosexual romance to this intimacy and other college-oriented soap operatic plotlines (such as date rape, sexual relationships and planning their careers).

A discrepancy evident early on in the series is the reliance on the character of Elena for comic relief. Elena becomes marginalised by narratives that do not permit her entrance to the melodramatic world of Felicity and Julie – a veritable segregation within the diegesis of the show. This same segregation makes the friendship between Felicity and Elena shallower than that between Felicity and Julie. While Felicity and Julie are featured talking – a lot – Felicity and Elena are shown arguing over comical misunderstandings and events that situate their friendship as secondary within the melodramatic world of the show. Also, because Elena's stories are comic rather than melodramatic, her stories are also non-serial in nature. In other words, comic situations do not have the *importance* of melodramatic ones and therefore do not require further development. Felicity and Julie's stories last for seasons and intertwine in standard soap operatic fashion, developing fully; Elena's, however, generally last for one episode and rarely connect with other characters' plots.

As the Felicity and Julie friendship continues to grow, Felicity and Elena bond on a strictly competitive level. In the first full episode that includes Elena, her function is to lecture Felicity about the potential problems of a romantic relationship with their resident advisor (another boy, Noel). When Felicity wins a lottery for a refrigerator in her dorm room, Elena accuses her of sleeping with Noel to get it, and this misperception serves as a source of comic relief from the 'heavier' story involving Julie, Felicity and Ben. This pattern continues for some time: Elena is comically 'bitchy' and her friendship with Felicity is tested largely by this bitchiness; Julie is empathetic and her friendship with Felicity is challenged and strengthened by their mutual interest in Ben. The relationship between Felicity and Elena is represented spottily, overshadowed by the issue-oriented melodramas of Felicity and Julie.

There are moments when it would be easy to bring Elena into the melodramatic fold. Elena meets a young black man (Blair) at a Halloween party and is anxious about dating him. The narrative, however, does not take this relationship seriously; Elena's romantic dilemma is positioned as comically misguided due to Elena's harsh attitude towards a man who is presented as desirable in every way. Whereas Julie's and Felicity's situations with men are melodramatically inflected and presented as worthy of serious discussions, Elena's story situations are the site of many jokes. For example, after Elena sleeps with Blair the first night she meets him, she corners Felicity in the elevator to demand her help. Elena explains to Felicity that she has sex with most men because: 'Men have needs; I have needs. Sex happens, and then I usually squash it dead' – a statement that greatly amuses Felicity. In another episode, Elena asks for Felicity's help when Blair gives Elena a gift – a headband that she mistakes for a skirt and wears around the dorm, reiterating her purpose as a comic foil. Another particularly disturbing example of Elena's exclusion from melodrama occurs when Julie is date raped: while Julie and Felicity grapple with this melodramatic event, Elena 'grapples' with having to house an annoying prospective student.

While the comedy of Elena's romance with Blair is, in my opinion, highly enjoyable and empathetically presented, this comedic designation does not allow for much serious bonding between Felicity and Elena. Further, this placement of a black character within the realm of comedy speaks to a long and problematic history within the United States of restricting black actors to comic roles. Countless television scholars have noted the entrenched pattern within US television of black characters being clustered in situation comedies; Children NOW's most recent study reveals that this pattern still holds.[6]

While I do not mean to argue that situation comedies are an inherently problematic genre for black people, the over-reliance on this genre as a space for black characters and their stories speaks to a continued cultural relegation of the black community to the realm of the 'non-serious'. Within the USA, the majority of such 'black' shows appear on one network (UPN), further segregating black characters from white ones. Sitcoms such as *Moesha* and its spin-off *The Parkers* have featured interracial, black-to-white friendships, but in a strictly non-dramatic venue. US 'dramedies' (hour-long series that cross between drama and comedy) like *The Gilmore Girls* and *Ally McBeal* have incorporated interracial friendships with little attention to race. These patterns make the appearance of a black character such as Elena in a *drama* even more important – and even more disheartening given her comedic plotlines.

## Visual Isolation

The visual strategies typically associated with serial melodrama also serve to marginalise Elena within the series. Just as Elena's comedic functions keep her separated from the melodramatic incidents in the series, the *visual* dynamics of the show also isolate her in the early seasons of *Felicity*. In many episodes Elena appears on the edge of or in the background of the frame, *watching* (rather than interacting with) the melodramatic action of others. Often Elena literally passes through or past melodramatic scenes involving other characters. These patterns are in keeping with Elena's comic position within the series. Melodrama operates with a visual language of close-ups and shot-reverse-shots that focuses viewer attention on characters' emotional reactions to melodramatic revelations; because Elena has little of melodramatic importance to divulge or be privy to, there is little point in using such editing and framing strategies with her.

A 'recap' montage in the final episode of the series demonstrates this pattern quite well. Felicity is telling an outsider about her friends and each friend has a flashback montage to 'explain' who they are. Elena's montage features comic moments of Elena acting out physically: Elena punching a boyfriend who cheated on her; Elena telling a boy she could 'kick his ass'; Elena tackling Felicity to practice self-defence. As Tania Modleski and Yvonne Tasker have noted, it is not uncommon for popular culture to represent black women as 'inherently' physical and aggressive; US culture has a long history of viewing non-white women as 'closer to nature' and therefore less civilised than white women.[7]

One clip in this montage represents a melodramatic moment – when Elena's boyfriend Tracy proposes to her in the third season. Thus, eventually Elena did receive melodramatic storylines in the show. However, the development of this pattern poses a new set of problems in regards to her marginalisation as a black character. To begin with, when the show first gives Elena access to the melodramatic realm in which Felicity and Julie live, Felicity as a character is switched to being framed as a romantic *comedic* heroine. Thus, at a time when Elena could connect with Felicity, Felicity has become comic and therefore melodramatically unavailable. In addition, Elena's melodramas for some time are non-serial in nature. Her problems are therefore only superficially discussed – wrapped up in one or several disjointed episodes. Two particular melodramatic stories demonstrate this point, and reveal how race becomes a major obstacle for the writers of the show when they attempt to address it within these scanty melodramatic structures.

Elena's first full melodrama emerges when Felicity sees Blair (Elena's boyfriend) kiss a young black woman in the school library. In a single episode, as Felicity's comedic relationships begin to solidify, Elena loses Blair to her best (black) friend from home (Tara) when the two have an affair. While this situation serves to bring Elena more fully into the melodramatic fold, it also disconcertingly represents racial dynamics of friendship that remain uncommented upon. As Felicity struggles with the dilemma of whether or not she should tell Elena what she has seen, race never becomes an issue worthy of exploration. In fact, the only time that race is briefly mentioned is when Felicity tells Blair that she saw him – and he replies to her that just because she saw a 'brother' does not mean it was him. (This inclusion of race is immediately demonstrated to be inappropriate, for Blair *was* cheating on Elena.)

This melodramatic storyline for Elena also draws upon stereotypical representations of black heterosexual men defining their masculinity via sexual prowess, and, as bell hooks notes, 'internecine gender conflict between black women and men strengthens white supremacist capitalist patriarchy'.[8] This melodramatic event also presents the lack of viability of the *intra*racial friendship between Elena and her old friend (effectively shutting down an opportunity for the show to present a strong black female friendship and a strong black heterosexual romance). On the surface of the show, this dilemma allows Elena to be presented as having romantic problems – 'just like' Felicity and Julie. However, this romantic problem is *not* just like the other ones presented; by this point in the series, the shift to romantic comedy has worked to stabilise the relationship between Felicity and Noel, and the relationship between Ben and Julie is getting stronger, leaving the black relationship as the solely dysfunctional (and soon non-existent) one. In addition, even though this is ostensibly Elena's story, the visual point-of-view shots in this episode are almost entirely Felicity's (she *sees* the cheating, she *watches* Elena interact with Tara and Blair, she goes with Elena to be an *eyewitness* to the continued cheating).

Another melodramatic storyline involves Elena having an affair with her and Felicity's professor. Without Felicity knowing, Elena begins to have an affair with the (white male) professor when she becomes his 'assistant'. At one point, he raises her grades immediately after she sleeps with him. Elena decides, regardless, to continue the relationship. While it makes sense that Elena would keep this affair a secret, it is somewhat ironic that, just before the affair began, she gave a small speech about how Felicity is her best friend and she is 'one with' her. Yet, when Felicity and her other friends decide to travel across the country for the summer, Elena is too busy keeping her secret to participate in such plans. This very important story-line of the affair (from a social issues perspective) is overshadowed by the impending trip that everyone else is planning: the travel plans fall apart when jealousies between Felicity and Julie arise. Visually, this melodramatic tension (and Elena's displacement from it) is symbolised when Felicity's roommate rips up a group photograph of everyone and tapes it back in the wrong order. Felicity notes in a voiceover (as the camera scans the photo) that she and Julie are next to the 'wrong' men – and the camera stops panning just when it would have revealed where Elena literally fits into the picture.

## Generic Equity and Erasure

These patterns with Elena continue until the third season. Even when Elena finally meets a decent man, the relationship is again played to comic effect against a backdrop of Felicity and Julie continuing their melodramatic escapades. Elena's boyfriend, Tracy, is a black pre-med student who is a devout Christian; in spite of this relationship's focus on the social issue of abstinence/premarital sex, this issue is contained by a comic emphasis on Elena's sexual desires being frustrated by Tracy's religion. However, in the third season, Julie leaves college and Megan (Felicity's quirky Wiccan gothic-punk white roommate) moves to a more prominent role in the series; concurrently, the writers begin developing more melodramatic storylines for Elena in relation to Tracy.

The major melodramatic development for Elena occurs when her relationship with Tracy is threatened and eventually destroyed after she has an affair with Tracy's (white) lab partner. In an almost two-season-long storyline, Elena grapples with losing Tracy several times over. Suddenly, scenes emerge in which the camera shoots Elena in close-up and two-shots and scenes feature Elena in discussions with Felicity where Elena is not off to the side or in the background visually. In addition, with Megan in the melodramatic picture, things begin to even out between the characters. (It is also evident that Elena's earlier marginalisation was therefore not about having 'too many' women to focus on melodramatically.) Felicity deals with Ben and then his alcoholic father. Gay rights come up when Felicity and Ben's boss, a partnered gay man, asks Felicity to donate an egg for them to have a child. Megan deals with her boyfriend (Sean) getting testicular cancer and then rediscovering his Judaism. Through most of these serial events, Elena is privy to the necessary melodramatic discussions and debates, and appears in many more group scenes than she had for the past seasons.

For almost an entire season, then, Elena is *not* generically marginalised – either through plots or visual strategies. She becomes a part of the melodramatic world and receives multiple melodramatic serial storylines that further bind her to the world of the other characters in the show. The most prominent serial story involves Elena and Tracy breaking up, having sex, breaking up again *because* of the sex, getting back together and ultimately becoming engaged to marry. In short, Elena's romantic entanglements operate almost identically to Felicity's and Megan's. The writers even bring back the story of Elena's affair with the white professor and allow her to tell Felicity and discuss things with her as Elena faces having to appear before a disciplinary board. However, in the final (fourth) season of the show, Elena is quickly remarginalised with the departure of Tracy. Eventually Elena is literally erased from the series in the most extreme way: she progressively gets less screen time and near the end of the series she dies.

When it is time for Elena and Tracy's wedding, things go awry after Megan tells Elena that the only reason there is a wedding is so that Elena and Tracy can have sex. Felicity is of little emotional help to Elena; she has just had sex with Noel in a moment of weakness and has then broken up with Ben. With both Elena and Felicity in a melodramatic tizzy, but not talking to each other about why, everything falls apart when Elena and Tracy call off the wedding moments before it is to begin. Elena and Felicity are thus *mutually* heartbroken, and Megan comes out the winner when she proposes to Sean, and they get married instead of Elena and Tracy. At this point, then, the final season is primed to deliver full melodramatic storylines for all three women, but this never happens. Instead, Megan and Felicity continue to have full melodramatic stories, and Elena begins to disappear. Indeed, even within the wedding episode, signs of Elena's erased future emerge. Once Elena announces to those gathered for the wedding that it has been called off, she is literally reassigned to the sides of the frame and the backdrop of the group scenes while Megan and Sean marry. In fact, at the following reception, the viewer does not see Elena at all – the visuals focus on Megan and Sean and, of course, on Felicity and her multiple beaux.

As the show moves to its series finale, Megan and Felicity grapple with serial melodramatic stories. For Megan, her stories revolve around her newly married status and Felicity, of course, dominates the season as she copes with having slept with Noel and then Ben finding out. Elena, meanwhile, is reintroduced to life as a tertiary character. While she is there to advise Felicity during a pregnancy scare, the scripts largely foist Elena off on a mix of comical episodes with Javier (Felicity and Ben's gay boss) and her new boyfriend (Ben's white lab partner). In fact, Elena's new boyfriend gets more screen time and more melodramatic storylines than she does. Elena 'struggles' with annoying roommates who steal her clothes and then she worries about her new boyfriend's intelligence (thinking that she may be too smart to date him); in short, Elena 'struggles' with comic storylines once again. And by the time of graduation, Elena has largely gone missing.

This erasure makes it all the more intriguing that the one post-Tracy episode in which Elena gets considerable screen time features, of all things, race. 'Ben Don't Leave' features a secondary storyline in which Richard (an annoying coed who has been present throughout the series) asks Elena out on a fake date to impress a girl he likes. The girl in question is an environmentalist liberal, and Richard, who is white, thinks that bringing a black girl to a party will seem politically impressive. When he tells this to Elena, she is furious and punches him in the eye. Richard, however, is genuinely puzzled about why Elena is upset and why she calls him racist. 'You're not really black', he tells her (in what may be one of the more ironically insightful statements in the series about Elena's character). Richard explains his point of view: Elena has all white friends, she dates white men, etcetera. This, apparently, is 'not black'.

While Elena is able to explain to Richard why what he did was offensive, she begins to wonder if there is something to what he has said. She decides to go visit the African-American House on campus (a scene which the viewer is not privy to) – and that is the end of the subject. Unsurprisingly, this plot is overshadowed by Felicity's (Ben is almost killed in a car accident), but I find it admirable that (finally!) someone on the writing staff thought to address the longstanding 'whitening' of Elena in the series. However, this attention to race and Elena's blackness is an anomaly. The more predominant pattern for Elena as the series ends is the aforementioned erasure. This is most noticeable on a visual level. As earlier in the series, Elena increasingly is not on-screen when major events occur. Even when Felicity almost dies in a fire, Elena is not around. The ultimate erasure, though, arises when Elena as a character is unceremoniously killed off.

After graduation, Felicity moves to California to go to med school and Ben surprises her by moving there too. We find out where everyone else is in a voiceover by Felicity that accompanies visual shots of what her friends are doing after graduation – all of her friends, that is, except for Elena. A year passes (one episode) and suddenly, Elena is dead (in a car accident) and everyone is at her funeral. A greater erasure follows Elena's death, however, when the show takes a generic detour into science fiction. Felicity travels back in time from a spell Megan casts, and thus Elena is alive again. Yet, this makes little difference. Visually, Elena is present on-screen only slightly more than when she was dead.

When Felicity travels back in time, her actions cause everyone else's lives to unravel. However, Elena has little to do. We *hear* (from Megan) that Elena and Tracy still called off their wedding; we see Elena from time to time coaching Javier *comically* for his acting roles; and we see Elena *briefly* when she helps Javier after his coffee shop gets burgled. Megan, meanwhile, gets considerable melodramatic screen time because Felicity's history-altering antics lead to Sean breaking up with her because of his crush on Julie – who returns to receive almost more screen time in the series' finale than Elena has had for the entire season. Dead or alive, Elena is left out of the picture once again. Felicity does make it back to the future, with everyone alive and happy – including Elena, who somehow is alive. Apparently, while in the past, Felicity warned Elena so that she would not be in her car accident – scenes that never made it into the show's final episodes (leaving many viewers considerably confused and irritated). It seems that the poorly executed results of this time travel were not even worth taking the time to explain by refocusing some attention on Elena. I suppose we should be thankful that at least she was alive when the series ended its run.

## Conclusion

In *Black and White Women as Friends: Building Cross-Race Friendships*, Mary McCullough interviewed black and white women who were close friends. The women stated that issues of white guilt, black self-esteem and social taboos concerning their friendships had to be talked through and explored. It was further noted that these tensions tended to emerge very early on in interracial friendships – often in college.[9] The complete lack of such elements in the interracial female friendships presented in *Felicity* point to an element of disregard on the part of those behind the scenes of the series in terms of representing a full portrait of interracial friendships.

Elena's marginalisation also speaks to the problematic dimensions of niche marketing in the television industry. One of the easiest ways to break down the mass audience into discrete marketing groups is along the lines of gender and race or ethnicity, and the increase in such segmentation has sadly served to dissociate race and ethnicity from gender. In a manner, this reiterates the common claim of many black feminists that 'all the women are white and all the blacks are men'. If a show features gender issues, the 'woman' is white and if a show features racial issues, the 'black' is male; *black women* are literally left out of the picture. Given the fact that one of Felicity's defining personality traits is her propensity to over-analyse every situation she and her friends become immersed in, I must wonder how it is that this bright, friendly and analytical character has failed to note the fact that one of her closest friends is, in fact, black. Likewise, the character of Elena is hardly unaware of the political dimensions of gender in her own and her friends' lives, begging the question of how she remained unaware for so long of the racial dynamics at work in her college experiences.

*Felicity*'s narratives rebel against many hegemonic conceptions related to gender, class and sexual orientation, but hegemonic conceptions of race persist. The show works to support the valorisation of racial and ethnic pluralism – a pluralism that is a variation of 'separate but equal' disguised as multicultural diversity. This pluralism is also uniquely suited to the structures of niche marketing: a different show for each 'difference' that exists socially in the USA (at the very least). What women are being appealed to in the case of *Felicity*? As Annette Kuhn cautions scholars, what do we (or the television industry) mean when we say a show is 'aimed at a female audience?'[10] This type of question is, of course, unanswerable. However, when a 'woman's show' (especially one featuring a woman of colour) erases race and simultaneously markets itself as a realistic drama, *all* women are losing out.

## Notes

1. See, for example: Mica Nava, *Changing Cultures: Feminism, Youth and Consumerism* (London: Sage, 1992); Angela McRobbie, *Postmodernism and Popular Culture* (New York: Routledge, 1994); Elayne Rapping, *Media-tions: Forays into the Culture and Gender Wars* (Boston, MA: South End Press, 1994).
2. Lynne Joyrich, 'All that Television Allows: TV Melodrama, Postmodernism, and Consumer Culture', in Lynn Spigel and Denis Mann (eds), *Private Screenings: Television and the Female Consumer* (Minneapolis: University of Minnesota Press, 1992), pp. 227–52.
3. See, for example: Jackie Byars, 'Gazes/Voices/Power: Expanding Psychoanalysis for Feminist Film and Television Theory', in Deidre Pribram (ed.), *Female Spectators: Looking at Film and Television* (New York: Verso, 1988), pp. 110–31.

4. Karen Hollinger, *In the Company of Women: Contemporary Female Friendship Films* (Minneapolis: University of Minnesota Press, 1998).
5. Julie D'Acci, *Defining Women: Television and the Case of Cagney and Lacey* (Chapel Hill: University of North Carolina Press, 1994).
6. *Fall Colors 2001–02: Prime Time Diversity Report* (www.childrennow.org/pubs-media.htm, 2002).
7. Tania Modleski, 'Cinema and the Dark Continent: Race and Gender in Popular Film' in Katie Conboy, Nadia Medina and Sarah Stanbury (eds), *Writing on the Body: Female Embodiment and Feminist Theory* (New York: Columbia University Press, 1997, pp. 208–30; Yvonne Tasker, *Spectacular Bodies: Gender, Genre and the Action Cinema* (New York: Routledge, 1993).
8. bell hooks, *Black Looks: Race and Representation* (Boston, MA: South End Press, 1992), p. 102.
9. Mary McCullough, *Black and White Women as Friends: Building Cross-Race Friendships* (Cresskill, NJ: Hampton Press, Inc., 1998), pp. 160 and 169.
10. Annette Kuhn, 'Women's Genres', in John Caughie and Annette Kuhn, comp. Mandy Merck (eds), *The Sexual Subject: A* Screen *Reader in Sexuality* (New York: Routledge, 1992), pp. 301–11; esp. p. 303.

# 11

# 'We Don't Need No Education': Adolescents and the School in Contemporary Australian Teen TV

Kate Douglas and Kelly McWilliam

### Introduction: Teens, TV and the School in Australia

Television remains the number one leisure pursuit of Australian teenagers, yet teenagers occupy a number of complicated, sometimes contradictory, spaces on contemporary Australian television.[1] Non-fictional teen representations range from the routinely apocalyptic (such as the 'street kids' and 'drug addicts' of news media), to the conventionally 'beautiful' (on reality programmes such as *Search for a Supermodel* and *Popstars*). Alongside these images are a variety of fictional teen images dominated by those on soap operas such as *Home and Away* and *Neighbours*, programmes which have successfully targeted teen and young adult demographics for a number of years.[2] Since the mid-1990s, there has also been a (relatively unsuccessful) shift in Australia towards 'quality teen television drama' – programmes fundamentally for and about youth.[3]

In this chapter we focus on *Heartbreak High*, arguably the most significant Australian 'quality teen television drama' of the 1990s.[4] We explore how the programme's diegesis negotiates and maps identities for contemporary Australian teenagers. More specifically, we examine constructions of teenage identities in contemporary Australian 'quality teen television drama' via representations of 'the school' and 'post-school' options within the programme. We investigate how *Heartbreak High* has responded to (whether by conforming to, or exceeding) the available cultural spaces for narrating adolescent experiences, but also to the broader social relationship between adolescents and schools. How does this programme represent the accord and tension between teens and schools? Do these representations offer diverse or uniform outcomes for their teen characters in relation to educational and post-school options, and what are the implications for Australian teen identities more broadly? We overview *Heartbreak High* and its reception, but also make comparative references to other Australian programmes that feature teens prominently.

The school has traditionally occupied a marginal space in Australian television programmes that feature central teen characters. (This is intriguing, given that school is compulsory for Australian teens, up to the age of 15 or 16, depending on state law). In soaps such as *Neighbours* and *Home and Away*, the school is usually an extension of the fictional local community, but is rarely the central narrative site. The introduction of *Heartbreak*

*High* in 1994, a programme set in a school that featured culturally diverse teen characters, was widely celebrated as an exciting, original premise.[5] These two characteristics in particular promised to separate *Heartbreak High* from previous teen stereotypes – such as those of surfers, 'larrikins' and romance-obsessed girls – which until then had dominated representations of fictional TV teens.[6]

## Heartbreak High

*Heartbreak High* was a spin-off from a play and, later, a successful Australian film titled *The Heartbreak Kid* (1993). In its re-emergence as a teen TV programme, *Heartbreak High* retained a number of its characters (and actors) from the film, including popular lead actor Alex Dimitriades. *Heartbreak High* first aired on Channel 10 Australia amid a flurry of media interest, most of it celebratory.[7] As Sue Williams notes, it was promoted as 'the ultimate drama for schoolkids: tough, gritty, and an accurate reflection at last of young, vibrant, multicultural Australia'.[8] From its inception, *Heartbreak High* had more in common with overseas teen TV predecessors such as *Degrassi (Junior) High* (Canada) and *Grange Hill* (UK) than it did with the predominant representations of teens on Australian soaps. *Heartbreak High* focused on contemporary teen issues, anticipating an empathetic target audience, and was underscored with a chic soundtrack.[9]

Unfortunately, *Heartbreak High* struggled for ratings on Channel 10, a commercial station, which had ironically only recently refocused its programming on capturing the youth market.[10] Timeslot shuffling during 1994 and 1995 saw it lose its audience, until eventually it was dropped by Channel 10.[11] At one point, *Heartbreak High* was being produced only for overseas markets, until the ABC – a non-commercial public broadcaster – picked up the rights to the show in 1996 and began screening the series in January 1997.[12] *Heartbreak High* was an international success: its 210 episodes, over seven seasons, were sold to seventy countries including Britain, France, Germany, Indonesia, Israel and South Africa.[13] Most commentators agreed that there were significant changes between *Heartbreak High*'s seasons: the first two seasons (on Channel 10, in a forty-five-minute format) being the most diverse and innovative, and later seasons (on ABC, in a twenty-five-minute format) seeing *Heartbreak High* more closely resembling a *Home and Away*-like soap opera populated with 'conventionally Australian' characters (an issue we explore later).[14]

When it began, *Heartbreak High* was considered groundbreaking because, as Mark Gibson argues, it broke 'with the established formula for successful Australian audio-visual exports'.[15] Unlike previous Australian cultural products, particularly soaps, that depicted Australia's innocence, harmony and (usually) cultural homogeneity, as Gibson suggests, it became the first Australian television programme to have multiculturalism as a central theme. Elizabeth Lopez writes that *Heartbreak High* emerged at a time when Australian television's 'Anglo-centric casting' had been heavily criticised on many levels: '[a]ccording to one British commentator, our soaps might as well have been cast by Hitler. Schoolgrounds where more than half the students have a parent not born in Australia or the United Kingdom have been a fact of life for years.'[16] *Heartbreak High*, at least to some extent, can be read as a reaction to soaps such as *Neighbours* in which, as Alan McKee suggests 'Australia is white, middle-class and terribly, terribly young'.[17] In the first season, more than half of *Heartbreak High*'s key characters were non-Anglo – the two male leads, Nick Poulous (Alex Dimitriades) and Con Bordino (Salvatore Coco), were Greek and Italian respectively. This can largely be understood in terms of contemporaneous shifts in government policies. For instance, Pieter Aquilia notes that '[t]he producers' casting of Dimitriades in *The Heartbreak Kid* and *Heartbreak High* in the early 1990s coincided with a push by Actors' Equity and the Office of Multicultural Affairs to redress the under- and misrepresentation of non-Anglo-Australian character roles'.[18] School staff in the first and second seasons were also culturally diverse, and included a Lebanese (counsellor Yola Fatoush, played by Doris Younane), an African-American (English teacher Ronnie Brooks, played by Deni Gordon) and an Aboriginal teacher (Media Studies tutor Vic Morris, played by Ernie Dingo).

*Heartbreak High* is set in a fictional Sydney state high school, where students wear casual streetwear rather than school uniforms. All of the standard markers of 'rebellious youth' are evident: music in the corridors, student–teacher conflicts, a bully senior teacher, detention, graffiti and, more seriously, drug abuse, racism, violence, homophobia and poverty. In early seasons, the classroom is a consistent backdrop for the exploration of adolescent personal and social problems. For example, in a Season One episode, domineering teacher Southgate is leading a classroom science tutorial. The discussion topic is overpopulation, but quickly this becomes the catalyst for a debate on contraception and women's rights, and eventually the dramatic unveiling of student Rose Malouf's pregnancy. While other students spontaneously call out their answers, with Southgate enforcing control by asking for a quiet and ordered discussion, Rose is set apart as a hard-working, sensible student by raising her hand before speaking, and in her measured, thoughtful responses:

> ROSE: You're talking about planets and species, isn't this about whether a woman wants to have a child?
> SOUTHGATE: Yes! Good! One of the questions we should ask is whether selfish, personal decisions matter more than the good of the planet. [. . .]
> ROSE: I don't think anything is more important than the rights of the mother.
> SOUTHGATE: That doesn't sound very scientific, Rose. [. . .]
> ROSE: I'm going to have a baby. And I'm real sorry if I'm a threat to the planet.

Later in the same episode, the school corridors and staff room become sites for the discussion of Rose's pregnancy, among students and staff respectively. And, despite executive producer Ben Gannon's suggestion that the programme is not didactic, these various discussions work to represent a range of different positions on the broader issue of teenage pregnancy.[19] For example, students Katerina and Rivers debate whose fault it is when a teenage girl becomes pregnant:

> KATERINA: Poor Rose.
> RIVERS: Come on, if a girl gets herself knocked up she's to blame.
> KATERINA: Come off it – that's exactly the response I'd expect from someone like you.

Similarly, in a school office, Mr Malouf (Rose's father) attempts to consider Rose's options with her:

> ROSE (to her father, yelling): You can't make me have an abortion!
> MR MALOUF: Is this my smart, clever daughter talking – smart enough to get herself a good education, a future . . . and now?!
> ROSE: I'm not ashamed.
> MR MALOUF: This isn't something that happens to us.

These conversations – between Katerina and Rivers, and Rose and her father – function in a number of ways. Primarily, these conversations encourage a particular teen (sexual) citizenship, which is associated with institutional dialogue: not only between teen and family (presented as a crucial element of Rose's preparation for her child), but also between teen and school. When Rose announces her pregnancy the school functions as both mediator, between daughter and father, and as pseudo-family (with school peers representing siblings, and teachers representing pseudo-parents). On the one hand, Southgate becomes the disappointed, disciplinarian father: he presents a stern face to Rose in class, similar to the way Rose's real father reacts later in the programme, but also relays his shock and disappointment to other teachers in the staff room. On the other hand, counsellor Yola becomes the nurturing, supportive mother who encourages Rose to discuss her pregnancy with Mr Malouf, while telling Mr Malouf to be more empathetic to Rose. Here the school literally negotiates teen identity (teen as expectant mother) in relation not only to the school (Rose announces her pregnancy in class, to a teacher), but also to other institutions (primarily family, between Rose and Mr Malouf and, perhaps also, Rose and her baby).

In early seasons in particular, *Heartbreak High* also covers a range of relatively daring topics, including racism and homophobia (experienced by both students and teachers), interracial teenage romances, sexualities, drug abuse, self-supporting teens, students who financially support their families and school-related issues (such as selective versus state schools).[20] Almost all of the adolescent characters in the early series are sexually active, which allows the programme to cover such issues as condom-vending machines in high schools, the socialisation of sexuality and teenage pregnancy. In another episode – which screened shortly after the earlier episode that addressed Rose's pregnancy – viewers witnessed a discussion between school counsellor Yola and an unnamed young female student, who tells Yola she thinks she might have a sexually transmitted disease.

> YOLA: And why weren't you using protection?
> STUDENT: I don't know.
> YOLA (sternly): What do you mean you don't know? Did he force you?
> STUDENT: No, it's my fault.
> YOLA: No, no, there were two of you involved. I can't believe you had unprotected sex. I mean, that's pretty irresponsible don't you think?

In the next scene Yola confronts acting principal Southgate in the staff room on this issue:

> YOLA: We need to do some serious talking to these kids about safe sex.
> SOUTHGATE: They already have sex education.
> YOLA: It's not getting through.
> SOUTHGATE (annoyed): Good God, the government spends millions bombarding them with these messages.
> CHRISTINA: It's not sinking in.
> SOUTHGATE: If they're too dumb to not have got the message by now then they shouldn't be doing it in the first place [. . .] Are you going to teach them abstinence as well because that's the only guaranteed method against STDs and pregnancies? But then again that's not as trendy as letting them bonk on regardless.

As in the earlier episode where Rose announced her pregnancy, this dialogue (and two later examples from the same episode where students debate the subject and where the Parents and Friends Association has a meeting over the issue) represents a range of ideological positions on the eventual topic of condom-vending machines in high schools. The show's penultimate conclusion shows a victory for both the younger, more liberal teachers (Yola, Christina) and the students (represented by class captains Nick and Rose, who organised a student petition), when the Parents and Friends Association reluctantly agrees to supply the requested machines. This locates the school as a site for socially relevant debate, where active students can effect change. The issue is both problematised, when the episode concludes with Southgate dismissing the decision on the basis of new government regulations that do not allow condom-vending machines in schools, and potentially resolved, when teachers Yola and Christina arrange for the machines to be fitted in a local café near the school, which is popular with Hartley High students and staff.

These and similar issues are foregrounded in *Heartbreak High* (though always in the context of particular teen experiences and/or relationships). This largely breaks with the conventions of soaps such as *Neighbours* and *Home and Away*. While soap operas do depict similar issues, the narrative contexts tend to be very different. For instance, teen sex on soap operas occurs within long-term relationships and between mutually consenting, usually virginal teens (such as *Neighbours*'s Flick and Tad).[21] There also tend to be lengthy lead-up periods to the actual sex 'act', which is positioned as a pivotal event (consider *Neighbours*' Billy Kennedy and Anne Wilkinson's elaborate preparation for formal/prom night). Sex is rarely articulated directly – and certainly not by people outside the couple – but, rather, expressed indirectly through euphemisms and visual allusions. Indeed, as Stephen Crofts notes, *Neighbours*' teens are fundamentally 'unrebellious youth [. . .] they are often 15 going on 40, and their metamorphoses from schoolchildren to sexually aware young adults are handled with discretion'.[22] *Heartbreak High* teens, however, are rebellious and rarely discreet; *Heartbreak High* regularly discusses casual teen sex, promiscuity and STDs. Perhaps most significantly it depicts frank dialogue about all of these issues between a range of characters, from teens to teachers.

Heartbreak High, particularly in the early seasons, depicts more active, even 'taboo' sexualities – sexualities that exceed institutional discipline (medical, cultural, family or religious) – whereas the sexualities presented on soaps tend to be homogeneous and exist within boundaries of institutional control (monogamy, heterosexuality, patriarchy, usually leading to marriage and family). In some ways, the Heartbreak High teen sexualities that do exceed institutional control reinforce the institutional and ideological need for 'the school'. For example, the female student who suspected she had caught an STD became the catalyst for a school-based, then community-based, discussion about the need for condom-vending machines in high schools.

Interestingly, Australian teen TV programmes and soaps present queer sexualities in relatively similar ways.[23] While there have been only a small number of teen queer characters – usually minor characters who do not last beyond one or two episodes – regular queer characters tend to be adults.[24] For example, both Heartbreak High and Neighbours have had queer teachers – gay men in both instances – while Home and Away featured a lesbian writer. Both teachers, Graham Brown (Hugh Baldwin) of Heartbreak High and Andrew MacKenzie (Chris Uhlman) of Neighbours, were the focus of homophobic abuse from students and parents, and were impermanent additions to their respective programmes.[25] While adult queer identities are closely regulated – evidenced by the institutional prejudice the two teachers faced (from the students and community), and framed in terms of their potential 'queer risk' to the teens in their care (as teachers) – teen queer identities are less visible. Indeed, regular teen queer characters are rare. A recent Australian teen TV example is Basia Lem (Freya Stafford), a bisexual film-maker on the fictional programme Head Start. However, Basia only seemed romantically and/or sexually interested in Kyle Richter (Ryan Johnson), which perhaps suggests a certain 'tokenism' to her bisexuality.[26] In a general sense, queerness (largely represented by Graham) was effectively removed from Heartbreak High, like the more visible elements of multiculturalism, in a bid to increase ratings.

### Education and Nationality

According to Gibson, Heartbreak High differs in both style and content from existing Australian soaps, such as Neighbours and Home and Away. Gibson argues that as a result of its slickly paced rhythm and editing, Heartbreak High resembles a polished American-produced drama, while its subject matter seems reminiscent of gritty British-produced drama series.[27] Heartbreak High is characterised by its realist style – though the students are commonly attractive, they are not conventionally so by Australian television norms. Unlike American teen programmes such as Dawson's Creek, Heartbreak High's teens are often inarticulate, even aggressive, and frequently use colloquial, sometimes racist, language. For example, Peter Rivers in the first season of Heartbreak High refers to an Asian classmate as a 'slope' and to his white Anglo classmates as 'Aussies'.

These factors – combined with Heartbreak High's almost exclusive focus on youth from lower socio-economic backgrounds – promote the show as representative of, and relevant to, 'average' Australian teens. This is not to suggest that lower socio-economic groups are the economic average in Australia, but, rather, that this is one way Heartbreak High positions itself *against* the white, middle-class affluence of conventional soap opera suburbs.[28] Consequently, 'average' functions as a marker of difference from, for example, *Neighbours'* Erinsborough. In this way, *Heartbreak High* trades in a form of 'gritty' or 'radical' chic.

This is reinforced through *Heartbreak High*'s setting in Hartley High, a state school. This is consistent with both the majority of schools represented on Australian TV, and what the majority of Australian teens attend more generally. After all, approximately 75 per cent of Australian high-school students attend state high schools.[29] This construction of the 'average' school populated with 'everyday' teens, however, is complicated by depictions of state high schools as fundamentally limited. For instance, in *Heartbreak High* students commonly criticise the socio-educational shortcomings of Hartley High, and are represented as having to leave state schools in favour of 'good schools' (that is, selective or private schools). Criticisms of 'the school' reflect one way this programme effectively engages with contemporary social concerns regarding access and equity issues in education, such as state versus private school debates, or the relevance of contemporary education more generally. Consider the example of Jack Tran, whose good grades motivate his move to a selective school. However, selective schools are also implied to be pretentious (and consequently 'un-Australian'). For example, when Rose and Jack argue, Rose tells Jack to 'Go to hell . . . go back to your selective school', which is seemingly a serious indictment of his difference. Here the school is an explicit symbol of belonging (and, more broadly, teen identity): where the state school is a marker of 'average' or 'everyday' normality, private or selective schools are an indication of unacceptable difference.

The 'everydayness' of these state schools and teens also draws on popular myths and stereotypes of the ideal Australian – they are almost always honest (and have their honesty tested), hard working (though often 'larrikins'), unassuming, irreverent and, most importantly, unpretentious.[30] The use of Australian ideals in characterising both Hartley High and its students serves a number of purposes. First, it displaces other markers of difference, and locates *Heartbreak High* teens, particularly non-Anglo teens, as 'real Aussies'. Indeed, in some ways, it rewrites national character: in *Heartbreak High* the 'Aussie battler' – quintessentially white, male, heterosexual and adult – is rewritten as non-Anglo, non-gender-specific, non-sexuality-specific and adolescent.[31] This locates teen identities, especially non-Anglo teen identities, as nationally valuable. It also, in some ways, 'culturally exoticises' them by associating their cultural capital with their difference from Australian representational norms. Second, these 'ideal Australian' values function to frame potentially rebellious or antisocial student behaviour within the context of broader values and institutions. For instance, when Rose chooses to have her baby rather than abort it, it is framed not as irresponsible naivety (the surrounding episodes stress how much Rose has thought about, and understands the reality of, her decision), but rather as an example of her responsibility and morality. Rose chooses to have her baby to 'make right' her experience of not knowing her own mother. She tells Jack that all she needs is her father's support: 'If I have my family there, I can go back to school, get an education, get a career.' Jon Lewis argues, with reference to teen movies, that '[b]y and large, the teen film presides over the eventual discovery of viable and often traditional forms of authority . . . the restoration of the adult culture informed rather than radicalised by youth'.[32] This is apparent with Rose's decision: Rose's act reflects a desire for paternal authority (as she takes on her absent mother's role), but is also an inscription of dominant institutions (family, school, work). Here Rose's transgression from conventional teen girlhood represents her shift into a conventional adulthood, marked by 'appropriate' institutional dominance.

On *Heartbreak High*, such representations allow the programme to endorse its characters – including apparent transgressions, such as Rose's pregnancy – as good, 'everyday' citizens worthy of teen viewing. This foregrounds the school as a site of appropriate Australian citizenship, but equally draws attention to the marginalised place of (higher) education in adult citizenship on Australian TV. That is, education does not typically figure in post-school, teen TV identities. This highlights an interesting difference between Australian and American teen TV, given that most central characters on American teen TV in recent years have made the transition from high school to university. Consider the example of *Dawson's Creek*, where all but Pacey have gone to university (similar examples exist on *Buffy the Vampire Slayer* and *Beverly Hills 90210*). What might this suggest about Australian teen TV characters and their relation to 'real' Australian teens?

## School, Post-school – Teen TV and Adolescent Containment

Contemporary Australian youth-marketed programmes have a conspicuously ambivalent relationship with post-school education. In the early series of *Heartbreak High* students rarely express the desire to go to university. Students are more likely to follow creative pursuits – for example, many plotlines in the early series are devoted to Jodi's plans to be a singer and Con's entrepreneurial exploits. Another common strategy is that students 'fail' their Higher School Certificate or gain lower results than expected. In these instances students 'repeat' Year 12, as Katerina and boyfriend Charlie do (and, in fact, at least six other popular characters in later seasons).[33] This allows the programme to conveniently retain characters and their romance plot-line/s. This has also been the dilemma in American teen TV programmes such as *Beverly Hills 90210* and *Dawson's Creek*; producers of these programmes had to decide how to retain their popular cast and still allow them to 'grow up'.

In *Heartbreak High*, a relationship could be drawn between the lower socio-economic state school environment of Hartley High and the lack of a transition between school and university. As Elizabeth Lopez argues, '[t]he kids are working class – from broken or struggling homes – and are sceptical of the promises of formal education'.[34] Indeed, *Heartbreak High* students commonly find school incompatible with their 'real world' concerns (such as travel, gaining employment and income, or raising a family). Moreover, the theme of educational inequality present in the first two seasons of *Heartbreak High* mirrored the wider social concerns circulating in and around the Australian education system at the time. Nevertheless, considering the extent to which the programme challenged so many other limitations placed on youth from ethnic and lower socio-economic backgrounds, it is curious that access to tertiary education was not also challenged.

Furthermore, as *Heartbreak High* made its transition from its evening forty-five-minute format (Channel 10) to its afternoon twenty-five-minute format (ABC), the school became decreasingly important as a site for the exploration of teen issues – with family homes, the beach and cafés becoming recurring locales. Critics suggested that *Heartbreak High* 'sold out' to commercial interests, and consequently lost its two strengths: its commitment to multiculturalism, and realist explorations of the school and education.[35] According to Williams,

> scripts were changed, the confrontational aspects of the show were toned down in favour of more concentration on relationships, the violence was cut, the racism was phased out, but it still didn't rate well. [Valerie] Hardy [Channel 10's head of drama] believes perhaps kids weren't ready for the ethnicity of a show that, in stark contrast with soaps like *Neighbours* and *Home and Away*, included a Greek, an Italian, a Salvadorean, a Vietnamese and a Lebanese among its core cast.[36]

Aquilia notes that, '*Heartbreak High*'s poor ratings were blamed on the series being too multicultural for young audiences. The producers killed off Dimitriades' character in a boxing match, and his family was relocated to Greece in favour of a new Anglo-Australian cast.'[37]

The marginalisation of the classroom in favour of more generic/non-specific locations resulted in an obvious under-representation of the school, not only in comparison to the frequency of scenes in other community institutions (such as the 'Shark Pool' pool hall or local café), but also in relation to the amount of time 'real' teens spend at school. That is, while school scenes were shown infrequently, 'real' teens spend approximately 30 per cent of each weekday at school. This under-representation of the school can be partly understood in terms of the restrictions and conventions of television, but this does not adequately explain it. Schools are effectively marginalised as less important and/or less interesting than other settings or activities, or only function as interim spaces between other spaces of 'living' (family, work, social milieux).

Williams suggests that *Heartbreak High* was altered because it was 'too edgy', citing Australian academic Sue Howard whose study of teens' reactions to *Heartbreak High* revealed that they objected to its confrontational realism.[38] Whether it was the actual 'realism' of the show that was problematic for teen audiences, it is possible that such a promotional tactic may have backfired.[39] By promoting the show *as* 'realistic' and 'representative' of contemporary Australian teens, the producers of *Heartbreak High* may have unknowingly encouraged viewers to be especially critical of the show and its claims to 'realism'. The 'difference' of the show from existing fictional representations of teens was certainly compounded by the different ideologies of *Heartbreak High* in comparison to soap operas like *Neighbours* and *Home and Away*. Viewers were more familiar with the community and family-based settings of Australian soaps, which commonly depict students as early school leavers who are more focused on marriage and family than diverse career options.

Indeed, contemporary Australian soaps have a conspicuously ambivalent relationship with tertiary education. On *Home and Away* there have been at least thirteen marriages (including three weddings called off at the altar) and at least sixteen deaths, and almost every character in its fourteen-year history has been involved in a romantic plot. Yet few have progressed from school to university. Recent teens that have chosen against university study include Jack Wilson (Navy), Selina Cook/Roberts (married) and Sam Marshall (professional surfer). Some notable exceptions are Sally Fletcher and Steven Matheson, who both returned to Summer Bay with teaching qualifications after absences from the show.[40] (It is significant that there was little visibility of the university as a narrative site on the show.) Similarly, on *Neighbours*, most recent teen characters have chosen not to continue to university. Examples include Billy Kennedy (carpenter's apprentice), Paul McClain (football contract) and Amy Greenwood (flight attendant). Of the few *Neighbours*' teens that have attended university, most leave the show before completing their degrees, such as siblings Anne and Lance Wilkinson. Together, these programmes may reflect a broader educational cringe.[41]

It is significant to note, however, that these depictions of 'everyday' teens in Australian soaps and teen TV diverge from actual education statistics in Australia. In the 1990s, approximately 77 per cent of Australian youth finished Year 12.[42] Adrian Harvey-Beavis and Lyn Robinson note the increased community acceptance of school completion, where completing Year 12 has become the new norm. Their studies suggest that the majority of Australian students want to finish school and go to university.[43] (Predictably, students attending private schools, as well as students from higher socio-economic backgrounds have higher retention rates.) There are also an increasing number of Australian school-leavers proceeding to both TAFE and university.[44]

However, these teens form a minority in Australian teen TV. One possible explanation for this is that *Heartbreak High* may have been consciously rebelling against 'real' Australian educational norms. That said, this is not a convincing explanation given that this trend is consistent not only across the seven *Heartbreak High* series, but also across other representations of teens on TV (particularly on soaps such as *Neighbours* and *Home and Away*). Another possibility is that there are very few traditional narrative spaces available for post-school teens, outside of working or family-centred possibilities. That is, the status of post-school teens as 'not-quite-adults' is fundamentally ambiguous and narratively problematic: these teens are no longer at school, but not yet marked by conventional adult institutions such as employment and marriage (the two most common narrative possibilities for late teens and early adults on fictional television).

It is perhaps unsurprising, then, that within this context of representational ambivalence about school and post-school options for teens, a number of fictional Australian programmes have centred on vocational options for teens – or school-aged youth in career-related environments – such as *Raw FM* (ABC 1997–8), which focuses on a youth radio station; *Sweat* (Channel 10 1997–8), which centres on a sporting academy; and *Head Start* (ABC 2001), which follows the aspirations of young entrepreneurs funded by the 'Head Start' programme.[45] These teen TV shows devise 'options' for teens and young adults, which though enhancing the diversity of teen TV representations, further reinforce the move away from formal education for teens on TV. Each of these shows depicts teens' relationships with specific institutions (radio station, sporting academy, bank). Indeed, the vocational success of their teen characters often depends on how they negotiate an identity in terms of the relevant institution. Consequently, these programmes offer teens models of citizenship outside student/school relationships (and outside formal education more broadly). Collectively then, these programmes may begin to challenge the containment of teen identities in 'the school', which was such a feature of the early seasons of *Heartbreak High*.

## Conclusion

Though Australian youth were likely to be simultaneously gaining their fix of American and possibly British teen identities elsewhere, the Australian teen TV programme *Heartbreak High*, and other examples discussed in this chapter, are significant sites of fictional contestation of Australian school-based teen identities. These depictions have added to the broad range of cultural sites where teen issues are considered and charted, and identities challenged. *Heartbreak High* – the primary Australian teen TV programme to air in Australia in the 1990s – engaged with the issue of what it means to be a teenager and to have to go to school. Its (in many ways) realist representations have meant that this programme has, perhaps unavoidably as well as actively, engaged with some of the key issues affecting contemporary Australian schooling – for example, access to education, student empowerment and, as discussed in this chapter, retention rates and post-school options.

These television representations have been active in challenging stereotypical or uniform depictions of adolescents. Throughout the 1990s there were a range of students represented in *Heartbreak High*: teenagers with varying desires and goals. *Heartbreak High* – with its focus on both adolescent characters and the school, its depictions of a multicultural school and its open dialogue on sexually active teens, racism and homophobia – was clearly a reaction, at least to some extent, against previous fictional depictions of teens on Australian television. *Heartbreak High* was also significant for its insistence on representing the impact cultural background and social class have on students' educational outcomes.

However, much of the ground that was gained by this programme in terms of its empowered constructions of teen identities was problematised by its narrow and uncomplicated representations of teens within school and post-school activities. *Heartbreak High*, like Australian soaps, consistently evaded the complex tensions between adolescent and student identities, opting instead for uniform representations of, for example, early school leavers, school 'failures', low-skilled employment seekers and a minority of teen tertiary entrants. These trends are especially notable when considered within the context of actual school retention rates and tertiary participation in Australia.

We have sought to explain these representations, firstly, and perhaps most simply, as they function as symptoms of television formats. However, such an explanation proves ideologically unsatisfying for those interested in interrogating the discursive influences of cultural representations of teenagers. Instead, in this chapter, we have looked for explanations for these depictions within constructions of (appropriate) adolescence, its containment within citizenship (based around family, community and employment rather than education), and the appropriation of teenage characters into apposite adulthood. The ambivalence towards education reflected in *Heartbreak High* reflects a broader ambivalence towards the teens depicted in the programmes we have discussed, and towards teens across Australia.

## Notes

1. Graeme Turner and Stuart Cunningham (eds), *The Australian TV Book* (St Leonards: Allen and Unwin, 2000), p. 3.
2. Sally Stockbridge, 'The Strategies of Audience Capture: The Case of Network Ten', in Turner and Cunningham, *The Australian TV Book*, pp. 190–200. One of Australia's most popular soap operas, *Neighbours* both targets and rates most successfully with the 16–24 demographic.
3. We describe this as a 'relatively unsuccessful' shift because Australian 'quality teen television drama' continues to rate relatively poorly, with quality teen TV programmes such as *Raw FM* struggling to find audiences. We follow Rachel Moseley's definition of 'quality television drama' in 'The Teen Series', in Glen Creeber (ed.), *The Television Genre Book* (London: BFI, 2001), p. 42.
4. We consider *Heartbreak High* the most significant Australian example for a number of reasons. It was, for instance, one of the earliest examples of 'quality teen television drama' in Australia when it first aired in 1994. It was also one of the most popular, having aired on and off for approximately four years (significantly longer than other examples). It also received considerable media attention, some of which we discuss later in this chapter.
5. See Mark Gibson, *Heartbreak High* (Description): http://www.museum.tv (accessed 12 October 2002); Elizabeth Lopez, 'School's in', *The Age: Green Guide*, 24 February 1994, p. 1; Lisa Mitchell, '"Heartbreak" Goes to ABC', *The Age: Green Guide*, 31 October 1996, p. 12; Sue Williams, 'Heartbreak from on High', *The Australian*, 8 November 1995, p. 28; 'New Series Takes Edge off Heartbreak', *The Australian*, 3 February 1997, p. 12; 'Ratings Low, Heartache High', *The Australian*, 19 May 1995, p. 12; Mark Woods, 'Aussie's Legitimate Success', *Variety*, vol. 375, no. 4, 7 June 1999, p. 41; and 'O'Seas Sales Slip Stings Prod'n', *Variety*, vol. 374, no. 11, 3 May 1999, p. 52.
6. A 'larrikin' is an Australian (and New Zealand) colloquialism, which, according to the online *Macquarie Concise Dictionary*, refers to a 'mischievous young person': http://www.macquariedictionary.com.au/ (accessed 24 November 2002).
7. As Lisa Mitchell notes, Channel 10 was at this time also broadcasting *Beverly Hills 90210* ('"Heartbreak" Goes to ABC', p. 12).
8. Williams, 'Ratings Low, Heartache High', p. 12.
9. Ibid.
10. Stockbridge, 'The Strategies of Audience Capture', pp. 191–4.
11. According to executive producer Ben Gannon, the only reason that Channel 10 continued to broadcast the programme was 'clearly to satisfy the drama quota requirements' (Mitchell, '"Heartbreak" Goes to ABC', p. 12).
12. Ibid.
13. Gibson, *Heartbreak High*; Woods, 'Aussie's Legitimate Success', p. 41.
14. Pieter Aquilia, 'Wog Drama and "White Multiculturalists": The Role of Non Anglo-Australian Film and Television Drama in Shaping a National Identity', *Journal of Australian Studies*, vol. 67 (March 2001), p. 104–8; Holly Lyons, 'One from the Heart', *Sydney Morning Herald: The Guide*, 17 February 1997, p. 12; Mitchell, '"Heartbreak" Goes to ABC'; and Williams, 'Ratings Low, Heartache High'.

15. Gibson, *Heartbreak High*.
16. Lopez, 'School's in', p. 1.
17. Alan McKee, *Australian Television: A Genealogy of Great Moments* (Melbourne: Oxford University Press, 2001), p. 248.
18. Aquilia, 'Wog Drama', p. 105.
19. Mitchell, '"Heartbreak" Goes to ABC', p. 12.
20. Throughout this chapter, we use 'state school' as a synonymous shorthand for 'state high school'.
21. There are, of course, exceptions. Consider *Neighbours*'s Amy Greenwood's unexpected pregnancy to Damien, with whom she was having an affair during her relationship with boyfriend Lance Wilkinson.
22. Stephen Crofts, 'Global Neighbours', in Kate Bowles and Sue Turnbull (eds), *Tomorrow Never Knows: Soap on Australian Television* (Melbourne: AFI, 1994), p. 55.
23. We use 'queer' to refer to 'a range of nonstraight expression . . . [which] includes specifically . . . [gay,] lesbian, and bisexual expressions; but . . . also includes all other potential (and potentially unclassifiable) nonstraight positions' (Alexander Doty, *Making Things Perfectly Queer: Interpreting Mass Culture* (Minneapolis: University of Minnesota Press, 1993), p. xvi.
24. That said, the short-lived Australian teen TV programme *Sweat* did feature Heath Ledger as gay teen Snowy Bowles. See David Dale 'Out on a TV near You', *Sydney Morning Herald* online, 23 September 2001: http://www.smh.com.au/text/articles/2002/09/22/1032055034419.htm (accessed 27 November 2002).
25. Adult queer characters are more visible in fictional Australian drama series. For example, popular series *Water Rats* featured lesbian character Sergeant Helen Blakemore (Toni Scanlon), who was prominent throughout the show's six series. Other queer characters in popular Australian drama series include Dr Martin Dempsey (Damian Rice) in medical drama *GP*, Tony Hurst (Jake Blundell) of hospital drama *All Saints*, Wazza (David Walters) in police drama *Blue Heelers*, Dr Charlotte Beaumont (Tammy McIntosh) in *All Saints*, and barman Simon Trader (David Tredinnick) and actor Richie Blake (Spencer McLaren) in *The Secret Life of Us*. See ibid.
26. Inevitably, one of the obstacles to articulating queerness is timeslot regulations, and the accompanying public debates on what is and is not 'offensive'. Teen TV and soap programmes tend to be screened in the late afternoon to early evening timeslots (4–7.30 p.m.), which, on commercial free-to-air television, are regulated by 'General Classification'. That is, any programme aired on commercial channels during this time, 'must be very mild in impact and must not contain any matter likely to be unsuitable for children to watch without supervision' (Facts [Federation of Australian Commercial Television Stations], 'Commercial Television Industry Code of Practice', April 1999: http://www.aba.gov.au/tv/content/codes/commercial/pdfrtf/factscode1999.pdf (accessed 27 November 2002)). In other words, as David Dale notes, while 'soap *Home and Away* [. . .] has dealt with lesbian and gay relationships in recent months, . . . [because it is] showing at 7pm, it cannot use those words' (Dale, 'Out on a TV near You'). Consequently, programmes airing during these times can imply queer relationships, but cannot easily articulate them.
27. Gibson, *Heartbreak High*.

28. In 2001, the median Australian weekly family income was $800–$999 (Australian Bureau of Statistics, '2001 Census Basic Community Profile and Snapshot': http://www.abs.gov.au/ausstats/(accessed 24 November 2002)). This is almost double the Australian federal minimum wage, which is '$431.40 for a standard 38-hour week' (Australian Council of Trade Unions, 'The Minimum Wage in Australia': http://www.actu.asn.au/public/about/minimumwage.html [accessed 24 November 2002]). Consequently, the economic 'average' is not synonymous with those of lower socio-economic backgrounds.
29. Anthony Welch, *Australian Education: Reform or Crisis?* (St Leonards: Allen and Unwin, 1996), p. 132.
30. For a discussion of stereotypes of 'Australianness', see, for example, Andrew Pike and Ross Cooper, *Australian Film, 1900–1977: A Guide to Feature Film Production* (Melbourne: Oxford University Press, 1998) and Russel Ward, *The Australian Legend* (Melbourne: Oxford University Press, 1978).
31. An Aussie 'battler' is similar to an 'underdog', and is someone who is typically from a lower socio-economic background, 'who struggles continually and persistently against heavy odds' (online *Macquarie Concise Dictionary*: http://www.macquariedictionary.com.au/ [accessed 24 November 2002]).
32. Jon Lewis, *The Road to Romance and Ruin: Teen Films and Youth Culture* (New York: Routledge, 1992), p. 3.
33. The Higher School Certificate (or 'HSC') is the final, cumulative qualification for graduating Year 12 students in the state of New South Wales. It includes a list of all subjects studied at high school and the grades achieved. The results a student gets on their HSC define the post-secondary courses they can (or cannot) gain admission to at TAFE or university.
34. Lopez, 'School's in', p. 1.
35. Lyons, 'One from the Heart', p. 12; Williams, 'New Series Takes Edge off Heartbreak', p. 12.
36. Williams, 'New Series Takes Edge off Heartbreak', p. 12.
37. Aquilia, 'Wog Drama', p. 105.
38. Williams, 'Heartbreak from on High', p. 28.
39. Williams, 'Ratings Low, Heartache High', p. 12.
40. Steven, an original cast member and 'maths genius', returned to Summer Bay as a maths teacher after finding himself disgruntled with postgraduate study. He became a love interest for one of the Bay teens – Selina.
41. We use this term as a play on the phrase 'cultural cringe', which the online Australian *Macquarie Dictionary* defines as 'a feeling that one's country's culture is inferior to that of other countries': http://www.macnet.mq.edu.au:8008/anonymousEF56232614+3/-/macshowrecord/1/3 (accessed 12 October 2002).
42. Stephen Lamb, *Completing School in Australia: Trends in the 1990s*, ACER (1996), p. 1.
43. Adrian Harvey-Beavis and Lyn Robinson, *Views and Influences: Tertiary Education, Secondary Students and their Advisors*, ACER (2000), p. 13.
44. TAFE is an acronym for 'Technical and Further Education' and is Australia's version of UK Technical Colleges or Trade Schools.

45. Perhaps Australia's answer to the UK's *Press Gang* because of their common focus on (school-aged) teens engaged in group-based, vocational pursuits.

# 12

## Roswell High, Alien Chic and the In/Human

### Neil Badmington

These are the days of Alien Chic. At the beginning of the twenty-first century, Western culture positively glows with a love of all things extraterrestrial. What was once widely feared and hated[1] is now welcomed and desired. Television series such as *Taken*, films like *Mission to Mars* (Brian De Palma, 2000) and the work of the psychiatrist John E. Mack[2] all suggest that close encounters with beings from other worlds might actually be good for us, and that the real enemy is now more likely to be the American government. Meanwhile, shops are filled with alien key rings and T-shirts, badges and socks, stationery and inflatable sofas, snacks and baby clothes, jigsaw puzzles and guitar picks, doormats and bottles of mineral water, garden gnomes and, perhaps for the city-dweller, a large metal sign that reads 'Reserved Parking – Aliens Only'. Alien love appears to have invaded. And, as is so often the case, love leads to sex: when I asked a group of students to bring as many examples of 'alien love' as they could find to a seminar, one person drew attention to the Alien Love Doll, available from www.sextoy.com for a little over thirty dollars. 'Has open mouth and inflates by blowing in crotch', promises the company's website. As Jodi Dean puts it, referring to a visit to Roswell in 1997, 'You could buy alien *everything*.'[3]

A cultural critic looking only for easy answers might take this as a sign that humanism (which established an absolute and hierarchical distinction between the human and the inhuman) is well and truly a thing of the past. If 'we' now love aliens, the argument might run, if we welcome them into 'our' homes, a sense of an 'us' and a 'them' can no longer exist. I am not at all convinced by such an account, and in describing the present moment as one of 'Alien Chic', I am deliberately calling up a particular ghost.

In an essay first published in 1970, Tom Wolfe set out to expose 'the essential double-track mentality'[4] of what he named 'Radical Chic', the phenomenon that saw wealthy residents of New York's more privileged neighbourhoods throwing spectacular *soirées* for poor and oppressed revolutionaries. Behind this apparent liberalism, Wolfe detected a more conservative impulse. There was, he concluded, a sense in which the rich and powerful legitimised themselves as such in the very act of supporting 'worthy causes'. The presence of the Black Panthers in the Bernsteins' Manhattan penthouse, for instance, actually reinforced the traditional distinction between '*them* and *us*'.[5] The season of Radical Chic was simply that: a season, 'a trend, a fashion'[6] which offered the upper classes a touch of exoticism, seasoning, a glimpse of authentic 'Soul, as it were'.[7] Contrary to first appearances, little had really changed.

I think that the same applies to what I am calling Alien Chic.[8] It seems to me that the current celebration of extraterrestrials ends up, against all odds, reinforcing the principles of humanism. In short, 'we' love aliens from a distance. While they invade 'our' lives on a daily basis, 'we' love 'them', quite simply, as a 'them'. They are welcomed, celebrated, desired, but only ever *as aliens*. Their otherness remains, not least at the level of the signifier, which continues to mean, and to mean something substantially different from 'human'. Alien Chic, from this perspective, marks nothing new in the realm of power relations: an alien is still an alien.

This should not, however, be taken as proof of the inevitability of anthropocentrism, and I want to turn my attention to a contemporary example of Alien Chic, drawn from the realm of teen television, in an attempt to question the hegemony and heredity of humanism. What might the teenage condition have to contribute to an understanding of the posthuman condition (in which the opposition between the human and the inhuman is radically unstable)?[9] Could it even be that alien-ated youth opens up a space in which to rethink the relationship between the human and the inhuman?

*Roswell High* knows its moment.[10] It knows, moreover, that it knows its moment, for as it narrates the adventures of a group of teenage aliens doing their best to fit into a small community in New Mexico, it at once narrates the culture of Alien Chic. Roswell, of course, is the holy city of UFOlogy, the alleged site of an infamous flying saucer crash to which all true 'X-philes' must make a pilgrimage. And this is precisely where *Roswell High* begins, setting its pilot episode in a week in which the city is due to celebrate the close encounter of 1947. The opening scene takes place in the CrashDown Café – a diner, situated opposite the local UFO Center, where staff wearing extraterrestrial badges, aprons and headgear serve 'alien-themed greasy food' – and sees one of the waitresses asking her customers if they 'are here for the crash festival' (a spectacular event, complete with plummeting UFO, which forms the backdrop to the episode's climax). From the outset, that is to say, Alien Chic makes its presence felt, and the series goes on repeatedly and playfully to invoke the cultural phenomenon to which it owes its existence. Its roots are at once its routes.

But if *Roswell High* is a fine example of Alien Chic – if it thrives upon a conventional opposition between the human and the inhuman – I want to suggest that this is by no means the end of the story. The series, in fact, ceaselessly starves the humanism upon which it seems to feed, both calling forth and calling into question the belief in an absolute difference between the human and the alien. If such an opposition undoubtedly drives the narrative (without it, there would be no Alien Chic), it simultaneously leads to a drift away from the orbit of humanism. The familiar turns uncanny as humanism reveals itself to have been always already housing the alien of posthumanism. And teenagers are to blame for everything.

## I Was a Teenage Teenager; or Why Aliens Need (V)ISAs

What could be more predictable, more formulaic, than a teenage drama set in and around a high school?[11] If the archetypal (American) teenager is not to be found at the drive-in or the diner, he or she will surely be skulking at the back of the classroom, dodging the Hall Monitor, or, at the very least, inhaling illegal substances somewhere on the premises. For obvious reasons, most teenage fiction has something to say about the institution of education, and teenage identity, more often than not, is articulated in a struggle against the values posed and imposed by such a system. Within teenage culture, education is, quite simply, familiar to the point of invisibility. I want to suggest, however, that in *Roswell High*, its very obviousness – the name of the series is, after all, the name of a school[12] – actually has the strange effect of destabilising the opposition between the human and the inhuman. Education, it transpires, educes the possibility of posthumanism.

Although one of his books has made an appearance in *Melrose Place*, I do not know if the makers of *Roswell High* have ever read the work of Jean-François Lyotard. And Lyotard, if he were still alive, would probably not be a fan of the series.[13] In the opening pages of *The Inhuman*, however, he contemplates the relationship between education and the human in a way that raises an intriguing question about *Roswell High*:

> If humans are born humans, as cats are born cats (within a few hours), it would not be . . . I don't even say desirable, which is another question, but simply possible, to educate them. That children have to be educated is a circumstance which only proceeds from the fact that they are not completely led by nature, not programmed. The institutions which constitute culture supplement this native lack.[14]

Humans, that is to say, *become* human with time and encouragement. Left entirely to their own devices, they would probably never become human, probably never take up their places within the symbolic order. Culture may well be ordinary, as Raymond Williams insisted, but it is also what makes 'us' ordinary human beings.[15] In the absence of cultural institutions, 'we' would not be human. 'We' (if, that is, 'we' could still be called 'we') would remain inhuman, non-human, a-human, posthuman. 'Our' apparently natural state of being, of being *human*, is, it follows, anything but natural. It is, rather, a question of culture and the lead of education. 'Our' source lies not, as humanism proposes, in nature, but in culture. 'Our' origins are, in other words, profoundly non-original. Once upon a time, 'we' were aliens. The other is all that 'we' once were. 'We' are made; the 'we' is made.

If Lyotard's argument is considered alongside Althusser's insistence that the cultural institutions which function as Ideological State Apparatus must continually *re*state and *re*work their claims upon their subjects (and school, for Althusser, is the dominant ISA[16]), the line that humanism confidently draws between the human and the inhuman becomes even less certain. 'We' need to be kept in check, kept human; the inhuman is never too far away. Through its institutions – education, law, religion, morality, common sense – culture ceaselessly (re)makes humans (why else would 'we' need such entities in our adult lives?). And the presence of those very institutions in *Roswell High* testifies to the work that humanism must perform in order to maintain its hegemony. If school exists – and, moreover, exists as *a legal requirement* – 'we' cannot originally, naturally, eternally be the 'we' of humanism. There is, as Lyotard suggests, a 'native lack' with which to reckon and wrestle.

From this perspective, teenage rebellion is a rebellion against humanism. When *Roswell High*'s human characters refuse to take the edicts of education as a given, or engage in a game of trickery against the authorities, they are alien-ating themselves, turning away from the human. To challenge both school and law is to challenge the culture of humanism and the humanism of culture.[17] Max, Michael and Isabel might literally be aliens, but the actions of human characters like Liz and Maria also go some way towards the earning of such a label. The familiar theme of teenage alienation is, in other words, taken somewhat literally in *Roswell High*: human teenagers are (almost) as alien(ated) as the aliens they befriend.

Meanwhile, the aliens' desire to fit in is profoundly humanist in intent, for, unlike their human allies, the extraterrestrials *want* culture to pass for nature, in order that they can be viewed and treated as ordinary human beings. 'Everything has to be normal', says Max at one point, even if 'normal' has suddenly begun to look like a look, a host of conventions. The alien simulates the human; the human makes itself alien. The borders of humanism have been crossed. In a further twist, Michael's tendency to miss many of his classes is understood by his art teacher to be a symptom of *ordinary* teenage rebellion: his absence is neither unusual nor suspicious. The school has seen it all before, and even expects pupils to behave in such a manner (why else would records of attendance be kept?). One of the fundamental institutions of humanism, that is to say, actually predicts the possibility of posthumanism, caters for it, structures its rituals in accordance. Teenagers, it seems, would not be teenagers if they did not act a little inhuman, a little alien-ated, from time to time. The inhuman (alien) passes for human (teenager) by appearing inhuman (alien-ated truant), and the traditional opposition between the real and the simulated finds itself even deeper in crisis. Youthful rebellion, so often dismissed as nothing more than an unfortunate side-effect of growing up, turns out to pose a challenge to humanist discourse. For humanism, teenagers are nothing but trouble, and trouble, as Judith Butler has mischievously pointed out, need not always be seen in negative terms.[18]

## (Posthu)Manly Sports and Jobs for Life (But Not as We Know It)

If no teenage drama is complete without high school, no American high school is complete without sport. While sport certainly plays a compulsory part in British schooling – I have both physical and mental scars to prove it – a higher value appears to be placed upon such activities in the United States, where it often appears that there can be no education without physical education.[19] And, in keeping with tradition, the narrative of *Roswell High* sports a commitment to games. From the brief glimpse of the gymnasium provided in the opening episode, to Kyle's distinctive jacket and status as all-round 'jock' (he is identified as 'Student Athlete of the Month' at one point), sport is always part of the fabric of life at West Roswell High. While this is perfectly predictable, the ordinary has extraordinary implications. In sport, humanism meets its match.

As the first scene of the pilot episode makes clear, the aliens have powers and abilities that are noticeably different from those of their human classmates: with bare hands, Max miraculously heals Liz's life-threatening gunshot wound. It seems to me, however, that the institution of sport confirms the presence of people with differing powers and abilities *within the human race itself*. Without such variation, in fact, sport would not be possible, for if everyone possessed entirely equal talents, there could be no such thing as competition. While there are, of course, established rules to which all players must conform, there is, as Don DeLillo's *End Zone* makes clear, a differend[20] that divides, that *must* divide, team from team, competitor from competitor. At one point in the novel, for instance, the narrator outlines the metaphysics of (American) football: 'Each play must have a name. The naming of plays is important. All teams run the same plays. But each team uses *an entirely different system of naming*.'[21] In competition, at the very heart of sport, lies the untying of humanism's insistence upon an underlying likeness. Events such as the Olympic Games might be hailed as a global celebration of human achievement and spirit, but, from this perspective, they are at once the murmur of posthumanism. The medals and the trophies, the cheques and the champagne, all point to the fact that sport relies upon a fundamental *difference* between its players. Once again, in its entirely familiar *mise en scène*, *Roswell High* reveals that humanism's sacred sameness fails to qualify.

But sport is not the only ordinary feature of school life to imply that humans differ quite radically from each other in ability. An early episode is framed around the events of 'Futureweek', during which pupils are subjected to a series of personality tests and eventually informed, by Miss Topolsky, where their futures ideally lie: 'I want', she announces, 'to help you discover exactly what's right for you.' It seems to me, however, that the seemingly banal ritual of careers guidance further undermines humanism's faith in identity, simply because it acknowledges that human beings do quite different things with their lives. People, as Topolsky goes on to suggest, have different 'strengths'. This, in fact, makes the whole practice of careers guidance possible, for if everyone were exactly the same, there would be no need for such a system of advice. *Roswell High*, in fact, even shows, in precise detail, the variety of futures eventually offered to the pupils: writing, law enforcement, psychology, professional football, retail. No two people, however, have the same 'strengths'. If Futureweek is intended to 'discover exactly what's right' for each student, it follows that certain professions would be unsuitable. Difference is at work everywhere, both in the present and the future. The aliens' alterity might appear to lie in their extraordinary abilities, but Futureweek, like the equally familiar institution of sport, implies that there is no such thing as an ordinary, standard, essential, human ability. Aliens differ from humans, but humans differ from themselves.

I do not even think that the series ultimately permits the strange powers of the extraterrestrials to stand as a sign of absolute otherness. While the aliens are certainly above the laws of physics – Michael casually bends the bars that cover the window of the Sheriff's office; Isabel reheats food with a gentle wave of her hand – their powers are not without limits. In the episode entitled 'Leaving Normal', for instance, Liz's grandmother suffers a stroke shortly after arriving to visit her family. As her favourite relative lies on the verge of death, Liz asks Max to use his healing powers. But Max, it now transpires, cannot always defer death: 'Liz, when I saved you,' he explains, 'it was because you were shot. There was a bullet in you. Something was happening to you that wasn't supposed to happen. It was before your time. But I can't just heal people – I'm not God.' In this instance, there is little that he can do.[22] The grandmother's time, quite simply, has come, and after a final few moments with her granddaughter, she passes away. At the end of the day, the aliens' powers are no match for the oldest problem of them all. Death is undying.

'Leaving Normal' reveals, in fact, that certain humans share the extraterrestrials' miraculous abilities, for, upon her arrival at the hospital, Liz's grandmother is revived by electric shocks that are administered by a team of doctors. In certain cases, that is to say, humans can be brought back to life *by other humans*. Death does not always have to be the end. At times it can be tamed, overcome, deferred by human hands. What appears to be an exclusive trait of the alien is actually a quality shared by certain members of the human race. And if those qualities are mutual, the boundaries marked out by anthropocentrism have been breached. Medicine doctors humanism.

### I've Got UFO under My Skin

As Liz lies close to death on the floor of the CrashDown Café, Max's intervention affords him a strange insight into her innermost thoughts and memories. Her life, it might be said, flashes before his eyes. 'We can connect with people', he explains, apparently identifying another mark of the alien. But once again, it seems to me that *Roswell High* fails, through the tales that it actually tells, to make this characteristic a sign of absolute difference.

Like education, romance is a familiar feature in teenage fiction. And at the heart of *Roswell High* lies a love story. At the very beginning of the first series, Liz develops feelings for Max, but is already romantically involved with Kyle, the son of Sheriff Valenti. To make matters worse, she cannot be sure that Max is really interested in her: does he share her passion, or has he revealed his secret out of mere *com*passion?[23] In the meantime, Kyle has grown increasingly suspicious about the time that Liz has been spending in Max's company (it is at this point that the other members of the football squad, in a touching gesture of solidarity, assault Max in a darkened alley).

Liz discusses her dilemma with her grandmother, who suggests that 'if it isn't complicated, he probably isn't a soulmate'. 'Complicated', I think, is the perfect word to describe the intricate series of connections that *Roswell High* traces between its human characters. Love and friendship are seen to lie at the heart of everyday teenage life, affecting how people connect, disconnect and reconnect with each other. And these connections are as strange as they are complicated. Love, in particular, moves in mysterious ways. It cannot, as Liz comes to realise, be mastered or rationalised. 'The tough thing about following your heart', she says, shortly after leaving Kyle:

> is what people forget to mention, that sometimes your heart takes you places you shouldn't be, places that are as scary as they are exciting, and as dangerous as they are alluring. And sometimes your heart takes you places that can never lead to a happy ending. And that's not even the difficult part. The difficult part is when you follow your heart, you leave normal, you go into the unknown, and once you do, you can never go back.

Love is shrouded in mystery. In its distance and difference from what is 'normal', it is 'unknown'. Romance, however thrilling, however 'alluring', is never simple, predictable, measurable. 'It's complicated' is all that Liz will, or can, say to Kyle when bringing their relationship to an end.

Platonic friendship, meanwhile, is no less complex, no less alien to reason and common sense. Although the affair between Liz and Kyle is broken off early in the first series, there remains another man, besides Max, in her life. Alex Whitman has been a close friend to Liz for many years, but the episode entitled 'Blood Brother' sees this friendship thrown into crisis. When Max is injured in a car crash and taken to hospital, a routine blood test threatens to reveal his extraterrestrial origins. Realising that the sample must be intercepted and replaced with a test tube of human blood, Liz asks Alex to be a donor. Although this conveniently saves the day, Max urges Liz not to tell Alex the truth, and a tale about drug abuse is quickly concocted. But Alex is no fool, and soon realises that something else is at stake. He decides to confront Liz, arguing that a friend ought to be able to confide in another friend. Liz, however, insists that a *true* friend would respect silence and secrecy:

> LIZ: I need you to believe in me, even though I can't . . . I can't tell you what you want to know.
> ALEX: Because of Max.
> LIZ: No. Forget Max, Alex. This is between us. Look, I told you before that this was complicated. Well, maybe it's not. There is a right side and there is a wrong side, and if you choose the wrong side right now, Alex, something really terrible is going to happen to all of us. I am begging you, Alex, if five years of friendship have meant anything to you, please trust me. I swear to you, I am on the right side.

Although Alex is clearly upset by Liz's actions, he remains faithful, respects her silence and takes her side (without, of course, knowing what that side might be).[24]

How can this strange and powerful bond possibly be explained, rationalised, figured? Common sense, logic and reason would all surely compel Alex to refuse to help Liz without knowing why he is placing himself in a position of danger ('What I just did, I could get arrested for', he says, shortly after donating his blood), and yet he continues to stand by and support his friend. How, moreover, can Liz hope to honour her acquaintance with Alex when her involvement with Max pulls her in an entirely different direction? How can a friend lie to a friend at the request of another friend (and, adding insult to injury, actually admit to the deception)? Things are evidently, as Liz might put it, 'complicated', and *Roswell High*, tellingly, does not try to resolve matters. It has no answers. It shows the existence of connections between people, but does not (or cannot) explain the phenomenon. Such an approach marks, I think, yet another way in which the series troubles the opposition between the human and the alien: while the extraterrestrials have the ability to connect with people in mysterious ways, everyday human life involves the making of similarly mystifying connections with others.[25] Love and friendship are just as bizarre, just as inexplicable. However 'normal', they are utterly strange.

The dark secret at the heart of *Roswell High* is thus revealed: 'the other is in the same.'[26] What seems, at first glance, to be little more than a glossy example of Alien Chic turns out to be far more complicated, far more undecidable.[27] Alien Chic is certainly at work – aliens are celebrated *as aliens* – but it is at once reworked, worked over, worked-through (in the Freudian sense of the term[28]). The human is never quite at home with itself, and never without the alien. In the most familiar themes of teenage life – alienation, rebellion, love and friendship, uncertainty about the future – *Roswell High* unearths resources for a rethinking of the relationship between the human and the inhuman, between 'us' and 'them'. In its stories, the signifiers 'human' and 'alien' are rearticulated until the relationship between them is no longer one of absolute difference; this is what Jacques Derrida might call a tale of *différance* (with an 'a').[29] Neither the human nor the alien is ever entirely revealed in the plenitude of opposition; there is a repeated deferral, an endless retreat. Against all odds, an apparently harmless example of teen television offers a radical challenge to traditional ways of understanding who 'we' and 'our' others might be. Such undertakings, it transpires, are not confined to the realms of philosophy or cultural theory. Teen television can also play a part in the shaping of posthumanism, and offers, in this case, a glimpse of what lies beyond the humanist impasse of Alien Chic. And if, as Cary Wolfe puts it, 'no project is more overdue than the articulation of a post-humanist theoretical framework for a politics and ethics not grounded in the Enlightenment ideal of "Man"',[30] *Roswell High* has fallen to earth at the perfect moment.

## Notes

I should like to thank Clare Birchall for putting me in touch with the editors of this volume, Glyn Davis and Julia Thomas for kindly commenting on earlier drafts, and Richard Vine for classified information.

1. See, for instance, the many alien invasion movies of the 1950s. Notable examples include: *The Thing from Another World* (Christian Nyby, 1951), *The War of the Worlds* (Byron Haskin, 1953), *Invasion of the Body Snatchers* (Don Siegel, 1956) and *The Blob* (Irwin S. Yeaworth, 1958).
2. See John E. Mack, *Abduction: Human Encounters with Aliens* (New York: Scribners, 1994) and *Passport to the Cosmos: Human Transformation and Alien Encounters* (London: Thorsons, 2000).
3. Jodi Dean, *Aliens in America: Conspiracy Cultures from Outerspace to Cyberspace* (Ithaca, NY and London: Cornell University Press, 1998), p. 182.
4. Tom Wolfe, *Radical Chic and Mau-Mauing the Flak Catchers* (London: Cardinal, 1989), p. 86.
5. Ibid., p. 11. Emphasis in original.
6. Ibid., p. 31.
7. Ibid., p. 21.
8. I discuss the concept at greater length in my *Alien Chic: Posthumanism and the Other Within* (London and New York: Routledge, forthcoming 2004).
9. For an introduction to the concept of posthumanism, see Neil Badmington (ed), *Posthumanism* (Basingstoke and New York: Palgrave, 2000).
10. Although the series has always been known in the United States as *Roswell*, it was first transmitted in Britain under the title *Roswell High*.

11. My decision to focus on early episodes of *Roswell High* stems from the fact that, towards the end of the first season, the narrative became less 'teen' and far more science-fiction in character.
12. Well, almost. The fourth episode of the first season reveals that the school is actually called *West* Roswell High. See Keith Topping, *High Times: An Unofficial and Unauthorised Guide to Roswell* (London: Virgin, 2001), p. 25.
13. Commercial television, Lyotard once concluded, was not really tuned in to the demands of philosophy. See Jean-François Lyotard, *Political Writings*, trans. Bill Readings and Kevin Paul Geiman (Minneapolis: University of Minnesota Press, 1993), p. 91.
14. Jean-François Lyotard, *The Inhuman: Reflections on Time*, trans. Geoffrey Bennington and Rachel Bowlby (Cambridge: Polity Press, 1991), p. 3. Ellipsis in original.
15. Raymond Williams, *Resources of Hope: Culture, Democracy, Socialism* (London and New York: Verso, 1989), pp. 3–18.
16. Louis Althusser, *Lenin and Philosophy and Other Essays*, trans. Ben Brewster (New York: Monthly Review Press, 1971), pp. 156–7.
17. The link between posthumanism and a resistance to compulsory education became apparent to me at an early age. In my native South Wales, it is not unusual (even for speakers of English) to refer to the fine art of truancy as 'mitching' or 'mooching' (both spellings are assumed; I have only ever come across the terms in conversation). In this, I cannot help hearing an echo of *'mochyn'*, the Welsh word for 'pig'. To 'mitch' or 'mooch', then, is to become an animal, an inhuman thing.
18. Judith Butler, *Gender Trouble: Feminism and the Subversion of Identity* (New York and London: Routledge, 1990), p. vii.
19. Higher education continues the trend. As an undergraduate at the University of California in the early 1990s, I was amazed to see regular television coverage of, and huge crowds at, college football games. While sport is a part of university life in Britain – it is traditional to keep Wednesday afternoons free from teaching in order to allow sporting fixtures to take place – its profile is considerably lower.
20. See Jean-François Lyotard, *The Differend: Phrases in Dispute*, trans. Georges Van Den Abbeele (Manchester: Manchester University Press, 1988). In Lyotard's account, a differend exists when a conflict between two or more parties cannot be settled or even phrased in a language that would do justice to all sides. To bear witness to a differend is, as he puts it, to acknowledge that 'a universal rule of judgment between heterogeneous genres is lacking in general' (p. xi). By the same token, to ignore a differend is to deny justice.
21. Don DeLillo, *End Zone* (Harmondsworth: Penguin, 1986), p. 118. Emphasis added.
22. Similar situations arise in 'Skin and Bones', when Max is unable to save Nasedo, and the later 'Cry Your Name', in which attempts to revive Alex are unsuccessful.
23. In the novelisation, Max's love for Liz is established as early as the scene in which he heals her gunshot wound. See Melinda Metz, *Roswell High: The Outsider* (New York: Pocket Books, 1998), pp. 11–12.
24. The friendship does, of course, falter in the later 'Heatwave', but remains intact at the moment of crisis in 'Blood Brother'. And Alex's subsequent hostility soon disappears when Liz tells him the truth about the aliens.

25. This is particularly evident in 'Heatwave', where the soaring temperature prompts a veritable epidemic of lust.
26. Jacques Derrida, *Writing and Difference*, trans. Alan Bass (London: Routledge and Kegan Paul, 1978), p. 296.
27. My reading is not framed in terms of authorial intent. I have no way of knowing whether or not the creators of *Roswell High* are deliberately putting posthumanist theories into practice. What matters, rather, is the movement of meaning, the undecidability that invades at every turn.
28. Sigmund Freud, 'Remembering, Repeating and Working-Through: (Further Recommendations on the Technique of Psycho-analysis II)', in James Strachey et al. (ed. and trans.), *The Standard Edition of the Complete Psychological Works of Sigmund Freud* (London: Hogarth Press and the Institute of Psycho-analysis, 1953–1974), 24 vols, vol. 12, pp. 145–56.
29. For Derrida's account of *différance* (with an 'a'), see *'Speech and Phenomena' and Other Essays on Husserl's Theory of Signs*, trans. David B. Allison (Evanston, IL: Northwestern University Press, 1973), pp. 129–60.
30. Cary Wolfe, 'In Search of Post-humanist Theory: The Second Order Cybernetics of Maturana and Varela', *Cultural Critique*, no. 30, 1995, p. 33.

# 13

# 'Feels Like Home': *Dawson's Creek*, Nostalgia and the Young Adult Viewer

## Clare Birchall

> 'You think like people twice your age . . . Reclaim your youth.'
> (Principal Green, *Dawson's Creek*, episode 301, 'Like a Virgin')

The culture industries have long been accused of infantilising their audiences, but the marketing of television about teenagers to young adults needs to be considered beyond a discussion of lowest common denominator viewing and 'cultural dopes'. This chapter will examine the appeal of the American teen television drama, *Dawson's Creek*, for the young adult viewer; in particular, it will explore the commercial and political implications of the show's 'nostalgic strategies'.

### *Dawson's Creek* and Other Visual Homes

*Dawson's Creek*, filmed in Wilmington; NC, is set in Capeside, a fictional small town in Massachusetts. Dawson Leery ( James Van Der Beek) is a film-obsessed teenager. Joey Potter (Katie Holmes) is the girl next door with whom he has been friends since the age of seven. The programme's narrative focuses on the love lives and teen problems of Dawson, Joey and other teens who are or become their friends (mainly Jen, Jack, Andie and Pacey).

    *Dawson's Creek* is just one in a long list of American television programmes about and aimed at the much coveted teen and young adult market (12–34-year-olds).[1] A shift in the way the television industry measures success has occurred – one which privileges demographics over ratings. Traditionally, as Dolan states, 'programmers have logically assumed the easy money was in broad-focus programming, with shows that appeal to every member of the family, maybe even at the same time. But Warner Brothers' success is proving teenagers are the real ticket. Advertisers already know older people watch tons of TV; it's the youngsters they're after now.'[2] Niche television means that a programme with low ratings can be a success (if it is aimed at the hard-to-get-to youth and young adult market) and a programme with very high ratings might be deemed a failure (if it is watched by the over-65s). In fact, the search for 'quality demographics' has been going on for decades, though the abundance of increasingly specialist digital and satellite channels have made this process more apparent.[3]

Since the recognition of the teenager as a distinct consumer category after World War II, the culture industries have employed various strategies to attract them.[4] The late 1940s and early 1950s produced teen-exploitation movies by the dozen (such as *Bad Boy* [Kurt Neumann, 1949]), a genre which continued throughout the decade spawning titles such as *The Cool and the Crazy* (William Witney, 1958) and *Dangerous Youth* (Herbert Wilcox, 1958). Deviant youth, the perils of drug abuse and uncontrollable promiscuity were recurrent themes.[5] By 1960, as Thomas Doherty notes, teen-pics had become 'an industry staple, if not the dominant production strategy for Hollywood cinema'.[6]

Given this history of the teen consumer, Bernstein's description of the 1980s as 'the decade when the teen movie [came] into its own'[7] might be an overstatement, but does point towards the changes that occurred in this genre during that decade. *Porky's* (Bob Clark, 1981) and *Fast Times at Ridgemont High* (Amy Heckerling, 1982) continued the tradition of screwball teen-pics, but were perhaps unusual in their sexual explicitness. Jonathan Bernstein cites a number of identifiable teen-pic types in the 1980s: loss of virginity movies; spring-break movies; stupid movies; pioneer slasher movies and other teen horror.[8] Onto this burgeoning teen market, John Hughes (either as director or producer) launched a series of films which were by turns comic and melodramatic, but always took the teen experience seriously – *Sixteen Candles* (1984), *The Breakfast Club* (1985), *Pretty in Pink* (1986), *Ferris Bueller's Day Off* (1986) and *Some Kind of Wonderful* (1987). They came to be known as the 'brat pack' movies because of the inclusion of particular teen actors in their ensemble casts. In these teen-pics, the sexual frivolity of previous films gave way to a prudity influenced, Thomas Doherty thinks, by the rising awareness of AIDS: 'the once-required content of teen-pics – coupling, nudity, voyeurism, and the desperate surrender of virginity – was censored with a Production Code-like ferocity.'[9] It was not only the content of teen-pics which changed, but the technical means of viewing them. The rise of home video (and, in America, the saturation of cable) changed the experience of film consumption. Teen-pics could be viewed again and again in the comfort of the home.

At the end of the millennium, Tom Brooks hailed a teen-pic renaissance: '1999 is only three months old – but already it has been dubbed "the year of the teen movie". Teen power is most definitely lighting up the American box office. Not since the mid-1980s . . . has there been so much Hollywood product aimed at the teen crowd.'[10] This resurgence of teen-pics at the turn of the century – including *Bring It On* (Peyton Reed, 2000), *Cruel Intentions* (Roger Cumble, 1999), *She's All That* (Robert Iscove, 1999), *Ten Things I Hate About You* (Gil Junger, 1999) and *Save the Last Dance* (Thomas Carter, 2001) – is assured and mocked by the recent pastiche, *Not Another Teen Movie* ( Joel Gallen, 2001). These films need to be considered alongside recent and past teen television, some of which is profiled elsewhere in this book, such as *Buffy the Vampire Slayer*, *My So-Called Life*, *Party of Five*, *Freaks and Geeks*, *Roswell High*, *Beverly Hills 90210* and *Popular*. Together, they indicate the market in which *Dawson's Creek* (launched in 1998) continues to air.

*Dawson's Creek* pays homage to other teen television series. For example, Dawson asks, 'Now what did we learn from this *90210* moment?';[11] Joey jokes about not being able to go out because '[she] hear[s] Luke Perry's back on *90210*' (episode 201, 'The

Kiss'); and Pacey warns his friend that they are 'about this far from the Peach Pit' (episode 220, 'Reunited'). Similarly, Brittany Daniel (Eve) who used to appear on *Sweet Valley High*, is allowed a nod towards her TV history: 'I'll get quite the perverse little thrill out of making things profoundly uncomfortable for you and the rest of the *Sweet Valley High* extras you call your friends' (episode 305, 'Indian Summer'). References are also made to the teen movies of the 1980s, especially those of John Hughes, who *Dawson's Creek* creator, Kevin Williamson, has cited as his biggest influence.[12] In recognising this homage, we can begin to see how the show rewards those who understand these references – usually the young adult viewer – acknowledging their previous televisual and filmic experiences.

In this way, *Dawson's Creek* announces its predecessors, recognises its filmic and televisual history. Michael Dunne claims that 'self-referential television can accommodate the pressures generated by an ever-increasing audience awareness',[13] but it is also a way of acknowledging those films and television shows that have made teen television 'possible' – commercially viable and generically recognised. The relationship *Dawson's Creek* has with this history is ambivalent. By the very virtue of citation, its role in a particular tradition is established and yet, *Dawson's Creek* also seems to transcend, claim superiority to, these other teen texts (by commenting on the naiveté of *90210*, for example). The show both utilises and rejects the clichés and mythologies of teen-ness. The ambivalent relationship between *Dawson's Creek* and its predecessors manifests itself as a tension between rejection and repetition. This tension can even occur in the same episode and focus on the same ur-text. For example, in episode 106, 'Detention', respectful repetition of Hughes' *The Breakfast Club* (in terms of the plot) is offset by resistant dialogue:

> DAWSON: This is so *Breakfast Club*.
> JEN: *Breakfast Club*?
> DAWSON: That John Hughes movie where the five kids are stuck in detention all day.
> JOEY: At first they hate each other and then they become really, really good friends.
> JEN: That movie stunk. Whatever happened to those actors?
> DAWSON: Anthony Michael Hall developed some weird thyroid condition, Molly Ringwald lost her gawky appeal, and the rest are languishing somewhere in TV obscurity.

Whether the similarities or differences between *Dawson's Creek* and its precursors are being stressed, the viewer familiar with these texts is rewarded. It's not necessary to have seen the 'original' movies and television programmes that are drawn upon in order to enjoy *Dawson's Creek* – the plot can be read on a primary level – but this televisual capital (knowledge or competence of television) will enable the (often older) audience to be included in a particular kind of address. The series can in this way, as Dunne states, '[exploit] the audience's familiarity rather than being restricted by it'.[14]

In these moments of reference and re-viewing (especially of the John Hughes' films) several things might be taking place for the young adult viewer. First, the simple reward of reference – the 'I understand that joke' feeling. Second, the enjoyment of referentiality itself – the sheer play of texts before us. And third, the invitation to recall the experience(s) of watching the 'original' text possibly at the age of the characters in *Dawson's Creek* (15/16 in the first series). As Fredric Jameson suggests in a different context, this referentiality (what he calls intertextuality) invokes the past in an indirect fashion. The kind of intertextuality we see in *Dawson's Creek* is 'now a constitutive and essential part of the film's [or television show's] structure: we are now, in other words, in "intertextuality" as a deliberate, built-in feature of the aesthetic effect and as the operator of a new connotation of "pastness" and pseudohistorical depth, in which the history of aesthetic styles displaces "real" history'.[15] For the purposes of this essay, we must retain both the idea that a collection of past styles can inhabit the present and that 'pastness' (as a mix of historical styles that becomes read as a general reference to history or a time that is no longer available to us) can be connoted. Whole decades or an amalgam of decades can be signified by a confused combination of visual codes. I want to argue that through such a practice of connotation, nostalgia becomes generalised, rather than specific. As we shall see below, this generalised nostalgia plays a central role in the appeal of teen television for the young adult audience.

## Nostalgia and Intertextuality

The term 'nostalgia' was first coined by the Swiss physician Johannes Hofer in the seventeenth century to designate, as Davis writes, 'a familiar, if not especially frequent, condition of extreme homesickness among Swiss mercenaries fighting far from their native land'.[16] It is a modern compound of two ancient Greek words: *nostos* and *algos*. Nostalgia is commonly used to mean homesickness (even after the pathological connotations were lost) because of the way in which *nostos* refers to the idea of 'return'. This return gets associated with going back home in relation to Odysseus' desire to return to Ithaca after the Trojan war in Homer's epic. Even if we can return home in a geographical sense, it might have ceased to be 'home' with all the emotional resonance and expectations we have attributed to it during our absence. We sometimes say that we miss home, but we mean that we miss home in a particular state or time. As Linda Hutcheon observes, one can sometimes go back 'home', but nostalgia or homesickness can remain.[17] What is longed for might be a 'place', but that place is always caught in and secured by the specificity of time – the fact that it is '*the* past'. This specificity of place caught in or by time ensures the structure of longing, the *algos* – pain – that characterises nostalgia, but we should note that although *algos* initially referred to somatic pain, it has come to be associated with emotion. Nostalgia, then, needs to be thought of in terms of an emotional mediation of space *and* time. The *Oxford English Dictionary* negotiates this by describing nostalgia as both homesickness 'caused by prolonged absence from one's home or country', and 'regret or sorrowful longing for the conditions of a past age; regretful or wistful memory or recall of an earlier time'. We will need to keep these meanings in mind as we turn back to television in general and teen television in particular.

As a recording technology, television seems at first sight to offer us a way out, a respite from the pain of nostalgia. We can record events onto film and video; these media can show us the past in a documentary fashion. But this might only replicate the activity of nostalgic memory. It may not be able to relieve the pain of non-return and may even exacerbate it – drawing one closer yet reiterating the distance or radical irretrievability. 'This is what you had, this is what you will never have again', the images seem to say. The message provided by fictional television and film is of a slightly different order: 'This is what you *never* had' (although, of course, on its own terms, a TV programme or film is 'real', and we can 'have had' them through the experience of consumption; this will have implications for the discussion below).

Period set pieces such as *American Graffiti* (George Lucas, 1973) or *Peggy Sue Got Married* (Francis Ford Coppola, 1986) rely to some extent on the nostalgic identification of an audience with the general context of the pasts they evoke. These renditions of the past are always selective representations, often drawing on easily recognisable filmic histories and iconography (the period *in general*) rather than marginal or obscure specific historical detail from the period.[18] The fictional nostalgic text, then, provokes a longing for something general (which often becomes generic), not personal or specific (although this does not foreclose the possibility of very personal identifications and investments).

Rather than the workings of 'period' film and television, what is relevant to us here is the idea that a fictional text can produce a complex nostalgic reaction, one that is not reliant on any specific memory. As opposed to the period nostalgia text, *Dawson's Creek* more accurately fits a type identified by Jameson which is set in the present, but evokes the past.[19] Jameson's filmic example of this particular kind of nostalgia text is *Body Heat* (Lawrence Kasdan, 1981). A remake of Billy Wilder's *Double Indemnity* (1944), *Body Heat* is set in modern-day Florida but 'from the outset a whole battery of aesthetic signs begin to distance the officially contemporary image from us in time'.[20] Though not nearly as stylistically consistent in terms of connoting the past, *Dawson's Creek* evokes both the traditional America of riverside rural settings, large-porched, weatherboard houses and provincial picket-fence communities (what is commonly described as 'Rockwellian America'[21]) and, through the plots and concerns with teen angst, the 1980s' brat pack films. As we shall see, the fashioning of these visual and tropic references as nostalgic is supported by a series of 'strategies' in *Dawson's Creek*.

To fashion *Dawson's Creek* as nostalgic television, I need to distinguish between the audience's extra-diegetic experience of nostalgia and the diegetic and aesthetic 'strategies' used by the text. Though different in kind they are intricately linked: the first is a response to the latter, the latter assumes its full meaning through the former.[22] A number of different 'nostalgic strategies' are employed by the text, supporting the nostalgia felt by the young adult viewer. First, contextual nostalgia as expressed by the characters within the narrative. Second, conservative and traditional values that hark back to 1950s' America. Third, romanticising and eulogising aesthetic effects and *mise en scène*. Fourth, the references to 1980s' brat pack films and other examples of past popular culture. I want to consider these in closer detail in order to explore how the young adult viewer's relationship with *Dawson's Creek* is informed by a logic of generalised nostalgia.

## Nostalgic Strategies
### 1. Narrative Nostalgia
Nostalgic sentiments are expressed by *Dawson's Creek* characters. In some episodes, flashbacks of Joey and Dawson appear (mostly played by younger actors). Though flash-

backs are not necessarily nostalgic, as representations of the characters' memories, it is clear that they represent the characters' experiences of nostalgia. Dawson and Joey's 'history' is aggrandised and romanticised, not only by them, but by the other characters around them, including the adults.[23] And the characters (especially Joey and Dawson) talk frequently about being 'stuck in the past'. For example, in episode 501 ('The Bostonians'), Joey's new roommate comments on her inability to 'move on':

> AUDREY: If you actually met someone you liked, you might have to let go of the past.
> JOEY: About me being stuck in the past. Here I am a college freshman . . . yet there's a part of me that's still 15 years old. Still stuck back in Capeside. Still in love with this boy from down the Creek who only sees me as a friend.

The dialogue highlights a paradox within *Dawson's Creek*. 'Moving on' is held in high esteem by the show and is a cliché often espoused within American popular cultural texts. The desire to 'move on' is in keeping with the individualism and therapeutic ideal that, as will be explored below, permeates the show. However, although moving on is presented as the most desirable emotional state for the characters, if achieved, it would render the show (so reliant on nostalgia as it is) unrecognisable or unworkable (in thematic and narrative terms). If Joey could leave her 15-year-old Capeside self behind, the main tension in *Dawson's Creek* (around Dawson and Joey's romance) would dissolve.[24]

It is not coincidental that one of Dawson's favourite films is *ET* (Steven Spielberg, 1982): a film about an extraterrestrial who longs to go home. Moreover, Joey refers to Dawson's 'Peter Pan Syndrome', suggesting he is a boy who won't grow up (episode 112 'Decisions'; episode 202 'Crossroads'). Given that the teens are predominantly portrayed as proto-adults, Dawson's love of *ET* and Joey's accusation of Peter Panism are probably included to remind us that they were recently children, but these elements also clearly put nostalgia on the agenda.

In addition to the nostalgic evocation of, and excessive investment in the past (an unsurprising narrative technique given the need to establish a whole history in which the audience should be invested), the idea of 'instant' or even 'proleptic' nostalgia might be helpful to describe the way in which the characters narrate their relationships and the events around them. Instant nostalgia is perhaps best exemplified by the ever-quickening turnaround time for 'retro' fashion (for example, the 1980s' revival in the 1990s), but this still insists on a chronological structure. 'Prolepsis' signifies anticipation: with proleptic grief, for instance, the anticipation and fear of a loved one's death invades or influences the present relationship. There is a deeply sentimental strand in *Dawson's Creek* not only towards the past but also the present which suggests that nostalgia, like grief, can be felt in advance of its occasion. The temporality of nostalgia is not clear cut. Through dialogue, the characters anticipate the nostalgia that they will supposedly feel for the Creek (and later, Boston) and the time which secures their particular experience of it, but this anticipation also shapes their relationship to the present. They are acutely aware of time passing, of their own situations in flux, referring constantly to their next big decision and change. They sentimentalise their own situations, creating pathos for the present which already seems like the past. This might just be an awareness of transience; there may not be anything inherently nostalgic here. By itself, we may not be able to read such sentiment as nostalgia – indeed, many of the other strategies can also be read in alternative ways. Together, however, as aspects of a text, they contribute to the creation of a nostalgic effect.

## 2. Traditional Values

Crystal Kile has produced a comprehensive account of the ways in which *Beverly Hills 90210* refers back to the culture of the 1950s and 1960s and suggests that the show's nostalgic subtext has a conservative function as it neutralises and contains volatile contemporary issues such as the LA riots.[25] Despite its often sexually frank discussions, a contemporary soundtrack and modern wardrobe, *Dawson's Creek* harks back to a Capraesque America. (Dawson says, 'This is Capeside, we don't lock up' (episode 301, 'Like a Virgin').) The smalltown life in Capeside and its picket-fence aesthetic (not to mention the lack of racial and cultural diversity) is caught in a media-collage time-warp. Stephanie Coontz goes some way to debunking myths about the traditional family, claiming that they are merely collages of 1950s' television shows rather than the more complex social reality: '[the 'traditional family'] is an ahistorical amalgam of structures, values, and behaviours that never co-existed in the same time and place.'[26] *Dawson's Creek* utilises a similarly confused reference to an idealised American past.

If *90210* aesthetically evokes the suburban and filmic 1950s, with its retro diner (the Peach Pit), classic cars, idealised nuclear Walsh family and James Dean lookalike (Luke Perry), *Dawson's Creek* aesthetically refers back to a provincial version of the same or even previous era. Deep conformity to ideals around the nuclear family (many of the *Dawson's Creek* teens react against their own broken or dysfunctional families) and the individualist American dream (most evident in Dawson's dream of becoming a film director, Joey's quest for intellectual fulfilment and Pacey's adventures on the open sea) are offset by the references to 1980s' brat pack movies.[27] Contained, white, teen rebellion is invoked as a counterpart to a more conservative framework. Though there is no coherent ideology to be detected in the John Hughes' movies, the rebellion in them concerns class and clique transgression (*Pretty in Pink*, *Some Kind of Wonderful*, *Sixteen Candles*), or disavowal of parental and adult care and values (*The Breakfast Club*, *Ferris Bueller's Day Off*). But, as in *Dawson's Creek*, such rebellion takes the reactionary form of trying to have better, sustainable relationships and a more durable sense of individuality and hope than their parents, rather than creating alternative values altogether. This can be seen less as a rebellion, more as hyper-conformity.

*Dawson's Creek* is populated by teens whose ideal is the nuclear family, safe sex (when ready) and lifelong coupling. Like *90210*, in which conservative family values seek to contain problematic elements of LA life, potentially progressive storylines in *Dawson's Creek*, such as Jack's homosexuality, are neutralised by the post-AIDS (which may as well be pre-1960s') moral code. The teens in *Dawson's Creek* are characterised by their responsible reactions to different situations. They do have sex outside of marriage and parties when their parents are away, but even when they rebel, there is much rationalisation as to why the 'rebellion' is acceptable; it actually supports the ideological order that organises life in Capeside rather than subverts it. We can read such values as political nostalgia – a mix of utopianism and conservatism. While the references to 1980s' brat pack films try to indicate that the *Dawson's Creek* teens are deeply individual and unafraid to go against the majority, these 1980s' films represent that individuality as being more invested in American conservatism, not less.

### 3. Aesthetic Effects

As well as the smalltown setting, *Dawson's Creek* includes various technical effects which promote nostalgia as the programme's dominant register. The title sequence provides us with an interesting case in point (I am thinking primarily of that of the first series, but those of later series show similar traits). This sequence is compiled of specially filmed, extra-narrative scenes rather than actual footage from the series. A montage of generic 'good times' is edited together, producing a document of friendship. Although, of course, this title sequence is read by a media-literate audience as a way of introducing characters and providing a backdrop to the credits, it also serves to heighten the nostalgic effect. Some of the scenes are made to look as if they have been shot by a handheld camera, and the characters acknowledge the camera by looking into and playing to it (in a way that isn't permitted during the episodic narrative). Coupled together, these stylistic choices connote, among other things, a home-video aesthetic. We are encouraged to view the characters as if we are looking at camcorder footage of friends. This effect is increased by the ambiguity of who is recording the footage. Group shots complicate the possibility that one of the friends is filming the sequence. The viewer is therefore put behind the camera. It could, then, be 'our' footage that we are re-viewing.

The nostalgia is underlined by light reflecting on the water; sun-bleached images (as when a camera is overexposed, directly facing the sun); the carefree attitude of the characters locked in eternal summer; the superimposition of golden sprinkles; and the way each scene fades slowly into another. None of these filmic devices and modes of representation are inherently nostalgic (any effect can be made to work in a number of ways), but in this sequence, the cumulative effect is overwhelmingly one of nostalgia.

### 4. Referentiality

References to films and pop culture abound in *Dawson's Creek*. A brief look at the episode titles suggests as much ('The Graduate', 'The Usual Suspects', 'Ch . . . Ch . . . Ch . . . Changes', etc.).[28] The pilot episode is typically liberal with references: in the video shop where Dawson and Pacey work, there is a poster for the latest *Scream* movie (written by Kevin Williamson); and Pacey's forty-something teacher, Tamara, with whom he later has an affair, asks if they stock *The Graduate* (episode 100, 'Emotions in Motion'). But are these quotations put to work in any meaningful way? Clever references may keep the audience awake, but do they provide us with anything?

A text filled with references might bring to light how television images and the experience of watching television are constitutive of our past, as part of our memory. Ninety-eight per cent of the UK population watch TV on average for over twenty-five hours a week, while the average American watches twenty-eight hours a week.[29] The sheer amount of time spent watching television (and videos) suggests that the experience is susceptible to the same laws of memory as other activities.[30] The recent spate and popularity of nostalgia shows on British television compiled of footage of television from the 1970s and 1980s suggests as much. David Marc uses the term 'shadow memory' to describe the experience of growing up and old with television: 'This shadow memory is interactive with individual memory; it provides images that function as personal signifiers (e.g. the music of a TV show that played during a certain sexual experience) and at the same time serves to document and redocument collective experience.'[31]

So 'home' (what is longed for) might become a specific experience or set of experiences of watching TV; or even of watching a particular programme because of the associations it may activate (who you watched it with, what feelings and desires it prompted). For the young adult viewer, the references in *Dawson's Creek* might configure nostalgia as a longing not exactly for our own teenage years, but for the teen-age we didn't have – for our teenage viewing and the identifications it may have prompted back then. The longing evoked by *Dawson's Creek* for the young adult viewer might be for a past longing: wanting to dress, challenge class confines, or find love like Molly Ringwald in *Pretty in Pink*, for example.

*Dawson's Creek*, then, encourages nostalgia, but it is a nostalgia for our past identifications, for the teen identity that we never quite achieved. What does this desire focus on? Before answering this question, it is important to emphasise that what follows is a particular kind of reading, one that subscribes to a psychoanalytic model of the unconscious and the role of language. Having declared my framework, I want to suggest that as well as more superficial aspects (romantic liaisons, rural setting and good looks), the programme exploits our teen desire for mastery over language. Though not achievable, such mastery is desirable because it would keep mental phenomena out of the unconscious (in other words, prevent them from being repressed or suppressed), thus avoiding distortion by unconscious processes. The unconscious, in Freud's model, is where the 'excitations' (outside stimuli) that we cannot consciously process get deposited and later emerge in various forms (as symptom, for example, or disguised in a dream). The unconscious is the repository of suppressed (traumatic) and repressed (socially unacceptable) material. The desire I am describing is for total self-presence – allowing no time-lag to occur between an event and our processing of it – pre-empting any suppression and the manifestation of trauma as symptom (a symptom can be anything from debilitating obsessive compulsive behaviour, to a nervous tick or stutter).[32]

Just as '[Hughes's] teen leads', as Bernstein states, 'were smarter, hipper, more sensitive, more articulate [than] their adult oppressors',[33] the teens in *Dawson's Creek* speak in voices well beyond their years, even reflecting in metaconversations on the fact that they speak in this fashion: Pacey says, 'What's with all the psychobabble insight? How many teenagers do you know that talk like that?' (episode 201, 'The Kiss'). In one interview, James Van Der Beek has stated, 'Of course, we've gotten criticism that our characters sound too smart. And while the show isn't representative of the way every teenager speaks, it's absolutely representative of the way every teenager feels.'[34] The *Dawson's*

*Creek* characters may profess to be crippled by teenage angst, but their ability to articulate such angst, and name, announce, process and reflect upon it on a conscious level (to describe 'the way every teenager feels'), suggests otherwise. In fact, the programme indicates that this articulate facility produces healthy, wholesome teens.

In combining the tribulations of being on the cusp of adulthood with post-teen knowledge and power, the characters in *Dawson's Creek* articulate the pain which renders us inarticulate at that age. As Jack Stenz writes, 'The *Dawson's Creek* characters . . . don't so much talk to each other as deliver running analyses of their own actions and motivations with lines like "I'm trying really hard to hold my rebellious nature in check."'[35] Being a teenager in *Dawson's Creek* is like being able to live our teenage years again after a lifetime of accumulating emotional knowledge and language. In this way, the young adult viewer can occupy the subject position proclaimed by the creator of *Dawson's Creek*: 'It's my childhood come to life', Williamson says, 'but now I get to go back to these places and create these situations where I can change the ending and have it turn out like I wish it would have.'[36] As these characters voice the dialogue of thirtysomething writers, they occupy positions of past identifications, and thus stage and provide 'solutions' to the young adult viewer's past problems.

## Nostalgia, Politics and Subjectivity

If a common-sense notion of nostalgia is guided by the idea that we can't go back in time, *Dawson's Creek* tries to offer a way out, suggesting that, in a sense, we can. The prompting of a viewer's past identifications and teen desires means that the programme can be 'better' than even our nostalgic selectivity would allow: teen problems are not eradicated in *Dawson's Creek* as one would expect with our own nostalgia, but romanticised, processed, kept fully conscious and articulated. We imagine what it would be like to be 'healthy' – free from symptom and repression. The inarticulacy and general discomfort (the 'trauma' even, though not in the strictest sense of the word) of the teen years can be relieved or re-written by *Dawson's Creek* (from non-expressible and suppressed to fully expressible and unsuppressed psychic material).

The success of the 'School Disco' phenomenon in London, a popular club night at which adults dress in school uniforms and listen to 1980s' music, also relies heavily on nostalgia.[37] It provides adults with a controlled environment in which they can safely perform their teen-age. It is a space able to be sexually and socially negotiated in a way that wouldn't have been possible as a teenager. Like 'School Disco', *Dawson's Creek* provides access to a teen-age without putting oneself in 'danger'. The young adult viewer is allowed to miss and feel nostalgia for teen trauma in general without the risk of experiencing the specific ways in which such trauma might be suppressed. Such a 'safe' excursion into a generalised teen-age is a calculated marketing strategy. In the case of *Dawson's Creek*, it welcomes a young adult audience that might otherwise not be interested in watching a programme about teenagers. The network can therefore not be interested space to those wishing to reach the much coveted 12–34-year-old market with one programme. Nostalgia, then, is a calculated marketing tool able to make an American teen show appeal to a young adult, and even a non-American, audience.[38] But

I want to conclude by pointing out that the personal solution (to teen trauma) offered by the nostalgia in *Dawson's Creek* is secured at the expense of the social.

In order to reach this concluding remark, we need to think more about the significance of these 'self-reflexive' (as Matt Hills calls them elsewhere in this volume), hyper-articulate teens beyond the nostalgic desire (for a non-traumatic teen-age) they might prompt. The hyper-articulacy of the teens might indicate a fear of unconscious work, for, as we've already noted, everything gets articulated, everything gets brought into the open, and, equally, nothing is allowed to slip back, perhaps irrevocably, into the underworld of the unconscious. This underworld is where the lack of articulacy, the lack of transparency, the lack of presence to self (a realm where the illusion that we are the master of all our cognitive faculties is lost), indicates not just a realm of ambiguity but the absolute loss of all the life-affirming values (such as health, youth, wealth, freedom from war, the illusion of eternity, etc.) that *Dawson's Creek* upholds.

Any 'work' that gets done by the teens occurs principally at the therapeutic, conscious (rather than unconscious) level.[39] Laplanche and Pontalis explain that this conscious working-through – or 'durcharbeiten', as Freud called it – is:

> the process by means of which analysis implants an interpretation and overcomes the resistances to which it has given rise. Working-through is taken to be a sort of psychical work which allows the subject to accept certain repressed elements and to free himself from the grip of mechanisms of repetition.[40]

The analysand works through their unconscious resistances to achieve mental health; but such working-through would be meaningless without an unconscious to 'work' with. Paradoxically in *Dawson's Creek*, the characters' conscious work relates to an unconscious that has never had the chance to form itself (because they externalise and analyse every experience) – repression itself is repressed, or, if you prefer, *Dawson's Creek* represses repression. One could therefore speak of a 'phantom unconscious' in the way one speaks of a phantom pregnancy. Without this phantom that is the fear of repression, the therapeutic language of *Dawson's Creek* would be entirely redundant – and it justifies all that imperative force to working-through that the show relies upon.

The overwhelming message of such therapeutically charged language and interpersonal relationships is that the self is the most valued element of the social, and that the social (as a political formation) is not important. We therefore need to also describe this fear and avoidance of the unconscious in political terms for, on the assumption that the phantom unconscious harbours all the things that *Dawson's Creek* does not, what gets avoided are questions of real social belonging (and the responsibilities and compromises that accompany this), for example, as opposed to the homogeneous interpersonal community lived in by the characters. Any 'socius' they manage to form is at best the aggregate of the bland values endlessly circulated between the characters, and at worst a determined exclusion of all social elements not pre-approved by their own prejudices (the lack of cultural diversity is the most obvious example of such excluded elements, but a general endorsement of conservative values also forecloses alternative culture and politics).[41] In these very circumscribed terms, the characters may claim 'subjectivity' to the extent that they so programmatically comply with laws of behaviour apparently preordained at some ideal American level – but it is a subjectivity that lacks a political dimension.

While we may be attracted to any personal solution offered to us through a nostalgic desire for trauma that is reflected upon but never repressed – for an unconscious we can lay claim to, but that doesn't have to function as an unconscious – we must recognise that this instant processing or auto-therapy poses a number of problems for any politically informed notion of the social. Before extending our nostalgic desire to these asocial, interpersonal American ideals, we would need to take on board such problems.

## Notes

1. 'We know who our audience is and it allows us to focus all of our developing of programming, marketing and PR specifically to 12 to 34 year olds', explains Warner Bros. marketing vice-president Brad Terell. 'That gives us a tremendous advantage because that group represents 84 million people who watch more TV than any other sector with the exception of 65+, and advertisers aren't interested in them anyway'. Quoted in Deidre Dolan, 'WB Knows Its Teens', *Media Network*, 9 February 1999: http://www.geocities.com/Heartland/Valley/8414/wb.htm (accessed 20 October 2002).
2. Dolan, ibid.
3. See Betsy Williams, 'North to the Future: *Northern Exposure* and Quality Demographics', in Horace Newcomb (ed.), *Television: The Critical View* (New York and Oxford: Oxford University Press, 1994 (5th edn)), pp. 141–54.
4. See Celia Lury, *Consumer Culture* (Cambridge: Polity Press, 1996), pp. 194–5.
5. The fear of teen rebellion evident in teen-exploitation movies, and the stereotypes that appear in them, are mocked by *Dawson's Creek*'s teens. For example, Jen says to her fretting grandmother, 'Well Dawson has a gun, I thought we'd go knock off a liquor store, then go get tattoos' (episode 100, 'Emotions in Motion').
6. Thomas Doherty, *Teenagers and Teenpics: The Juvenilization of American Movies in the 1950s* (Philadelphia, PA: Temple University Press, 2001), p. 189.
7. Jonathan Bernstein, *Pretty in Pink: The Golden Age of Teenage Movies* (New York: St Martin's Griffin, 1997), p. 4.
8. Ibid.
9. Doherty, *Teenagers and Teenpics*, p. 201.
10. Tom Brooks, 'Teen Power Storms US Box Office', *BBC Online*, 5 March 1999: http://news.bbc.co.uk/1/hi/special_report/1999/03/99/tom_brook/290955.stm (accessed 20 October 2002).
11. Quoted in Jack Stenz, 'Kevin Williamson Turns Teen Sex into Teen Shtick in Muddy *Dawson's Creek*', *Metro*, California, 5–11 February 1998: http://www.metroactive.com/papers/metro/02.05.98/ tv-9805.html (accessed 12 October 2002): episode not referenced.
12. See Stenz, ibid.
13. Michael Dunne, *MetaPop: Self-Referentiality in Contemporary Popular Culture* (Jackson and London: Mississippi University Press, 1992), p. 38.
14. Ibid.

15. Fredric Jameson, *Postmodernism, or the Cultural Logic of Late Capitalism* (Durham, NC: Duke University Press, 1991), p. 20.
16. Fred Davis, *Yearning for Yesterday: A Sociology of Nostalgia* (London and New York: The Free Press, 1979), p. 1.
17. Linda Hutcheon, 'Irony, Nostalgia and the Postmodern', 1998: http://library.utoronto.ca/www.utel/criticism/HutchINP.html (accessed 10 October 2002), p. 3.
18. See Jameson, *Postmodernism*, p. 19, and Jean Baudrillard, 'The Evil Demon of Images and the Precession of Simulacra', in Thomas Doherty (ed.), *Postmodernism: A Reader* (New York: Columbia University Press, 1993), p. 195.
19. Jameson, *Postmodernism*, p. 20.
20. Ibid.
21. In fact, Dawson himself claims, 'We live in like this Norman Rockwell picture postcard town with whitewash fences, and beachfront houses' (episode 103, 'Discovery').
22. Such a claim inevitably invokes debates around reader-reception theory that cannot be dealt with here. See Wolfgang Iser, *The Act of Reading: A Theory of Aesthetic Response* (Baltimore, MD: Johns Hopkins University Press, 1978) and Hans Robert Jauss, *Towards an Aesthetics of Reception* (Minneapolis: University of Minnesota Press, 1982).
23. A typical sentiment is expressed by Jack when he says to Joey regarding her and Dawson, 'It's okay. I understand. You guys have a history' (episode 208, 'The Reluctant Hero').
24. The narrative centrality of this romance is detailed by Matt Hills elsewhere in this volume.
25. Crystal Kile, 'Recombinant Realism/Caliutopian Re-Dreaming *Beverly Hills 90210* as Nostalgia Television', in *Bad Subjects: Political Education for Everyday Life*, issue 8, October 1993: http://eserver.org/bs/08/Kile.html (accessed 10 December 2002).
26. Stephanie Coontz, *The Way We Never Were: American Families and the Nostalgia Trap* (New York: Basic Books, 1992), p. 9.
27. Other examples of episodes which cite Hughes' films, as well as 'Detention', include episode 202, 'Crossroads' (in which Pacey has a 'bad case of the Molly Ringwalds' – i.e. his sixteenth birthday is forgotten), and episode 508, 'Text, Lies and Videotape', in which Audrey refers to *Sixteen Candles*.
28. See also Matt Hills' list of intertextual references to horror films elsewhere in this volume.
29. See Paul Willis, *Common Culture* (Milton Keynes: Open University Press, 1990), p. ix, and the A. C. Nielsen Co. website at http://www.nielsen.com.
30. Our memory of the experience of watching television is different from, but bound up with, the way in which, at the time of watching, we had to remember what had happened within the narrative of the programme, but also take on board the memory of the characters, so that we understood the meaning of certain comments or events.
31. David Marc, *Demographic Vistas: Television in American Culture* (Philadelphia: University of Pennsylvania Press, 1984), p. 135.
32. Laplanche and Pontalis define trauma as '[a]n event in the subject's life defined by its intensity, by the subject's incapacity to respond adequately to it, and by the upheaval and long-lasting effects that it brings about in the psychical organisation. In economic terms, the trauma is characterised by an influx of excitations that is excessive by the standard of the subject's tolerance and capacity to master such excitations and work them out psychically'

(Jean Laplanche and Jean-Bertrand Pontalis, *The Language of Psycho-analysis*, trans. Donald Nicholson-Smith [London: Karnac, 1988 (3rd edn)], p. 465).
33. Bernstein, *Pretty in Pink*, p. 53.
34. James Van Der Beek, quoted in Kinney Littlefield, '*Dawson's Creek*'s Van Der Beek Has Buzzing in His Ears', *Jacksonville*, Tuesday, 20 January 1998: http://www.jacksonville.com/tu-online/stories/012098/0120TV_r.html (accessed 12 October 2002).
35. Stenz, 'Kevin Williamson'.
36. Kevin Williamson, quoted in ibid.
37. See www.schooldisco.com.
38. The British viewer is not excluded from the nostalgic address. *Dawson's Creek*, as one by-line says, 'feels like home'. This is because 'home' is what we miss, what is longed for. We do not have to have 'had' what we feel nostalgia for; indeed, capital has taught us to 'miss' – to want and desire – 'many things that we have never lost' (Hutcheon, 'Irony, Nostalgia and the Postmodern', p. 8). This is why *Dawson's Creek* can feel like home – it's not home, but we can configure it as a lost object of desire – even for the British viewer whose televisual, textual home might well be America, given the exposure to American visual culture we had as children and teens. The fantasy element involved for the British viewer with, perhaps, no actual experience of rural East Coast America might only exaggerate the experience of many viewers, including Americans, whose experiences of 'America' might be wholly different from the upper-middle-class fantasy portrayed in *Dawson's Creek*. Beyond this discussion of geography, the non-American young adult is able to desire a non-traumatic teen-age as much as anyone else.
39. Condensation and displacement are two modes which process psychic material in the unconscious. Condensation involves the way in which one idea represents several associated chains (so I might dream of a bucket, but the bucket can be representative of my father and my unborn child, etc., if the chain of connection can be ascertained) (see Laplanche and Pontalis, *The Language of Psycho-analysis*, pp. 82–3). Displacement is when the importance we attach to one idea or object gets transferred onto another idea or object that would be related to the first through a chain of association (I might have a phobia of spiders, but this might really be fear of my brother who liked spiders) (ibid., pp. 121–3).
40. Ibid., p. 488.
41. A successful 'socius' would provide a platform for a community which steps beyond individual and immediate needs. Individual compromises (such as taxes) are made in such a 'socius' for the sake of the whole.

# Index

Page numbers in **bold** type indicate detailed analysis. *n* = endnote.

Abrams, J.J. 92
Abrams, Mark 78
Adams, Bryan 106
adults
   appeal of teen programmes to
     5, 11–12, 27*n*7, 59–60, 107
     (*see also* nostalgia)
   as programme makers 3, 185
*The Adventures of Ozzie and*
   *Harriet* 74
advertising 52*n*18
   teen-oriented 79, 187*n*1
   *see also* merchandising
Aguilera, Christina 121
Alcott, Louisa May, *Little Women*
   42, 44–5
*Alien Resurrection* (1997) 92
aliens (as characters)
   on American TV 17–18, 19–20,
     **22–7, 166–73**
   on Australian TV 30, 31–2,
     38–9, 39*n*6
   linked to teenage condition
     167–9, 181
   use/implications of superpowers
     24–5, 169–71, 174*n*22
*All My Children* 139*n*15
Allen, Dennis 129, 130, 135
*Ally McBeal* 144
Althusser, Louis 168
*American Bandstand* 73, 113, 117,
   120
*American Beauty* (1999) 92
*American Graffiti* (1973) 180
*American Idol* 113
Andrews, Scott 56
*Angel* 136
'(Anglo-)American Girl', as
   heroine **41–50**

'(Anglo-)American Girl' *Cont.*
   historical development 42,
     44–6
   represented by Buffy 41–2, 43,
     46–50
*anime,* influence on UK/US TV
   33
Applegate, Eddie 76
Aquilia, Pieter 153, 159
Arden, Jann 106–7
*Armageddon* (1998) 92
Armstrong, Louis 105
*As If* 135
Australia
   social/educational conditions
     160, 164*n*28, 164*n*33, 164*n*44
   television 11, **29–39, 151–61**
   vocabulary 162*n*6, 164*n*31,
     164*n*41
Avalon, Frankie 75

Backstreet Boys 120
*Bad Boy* (1949) 177
Badmington, Neil 7
Baez, Joan 106
Baldwin, Hugh 156
Banks, Miranda J. 6–7, 136
Barenaked Ladies 109
Barker, Bob 114
*Basement Tapes* 113
*Basic Instinct* (1991) 134
Bavidge, Jenny 7
Bazlen, Brigid 74
Beanbag 105
*Beavis and Butthead* 113
Behr, Jason 23–4, 28*n*17, 140*n*31
Ben Folds Five 104
Benshoff, Harry 135
Bernard, Edwin J. 127

Bernard, Jessie 77
Bernstein, Jonathan 177, 184
Berry, Heidi 104
*Beverly Hills 90210* 30, 83, 158,
   177–8
   characterisation 21–2, 26
   critical literature 4, 129
Birchall, Clare 6, 11, 58, 107
Bisley, Steve 34
*Blade Runner* (1982) 33, 37
*Blair Witch II* (2000) 92
*The Blair Witch Project* (1999) 94
Blake, Karen 109
Blundell, Jake 163*n*25
Blyton, Enid 42, 45
*Body Heat* (1981) 180
*Bonanza* 21
Boone, Pat 91
Bordwell, David 117
Boreanaz, David 136
Bowlby, Rachel 52*n*22
Brando, Marlon 24
Brandy (performer) 91–2
Branson, Richard 108
Brazil, Angela 42
*Breakers* 139*n*15
*The Breakfast Club* (1985) 94–5,
   97*n*15, 177, 178, 182
*Bring It On* (2000) 177
Brooker, Will 59
Brooks, Tom 177
*Brookside* 139*n*15
Brunsdon, Charlotte 20
*Buffy the Vampire Slayer* 1, 5, 30,
   **41–50,** 83, 91, 92, 158, 177
   adult appeal 5
   characterisation 46–9, 53*n*30
   critical literature 4, 41, 84*n*6
   fan base/sites 63, 65

*Buffy the Vampire Slayer Cont.*
  feminist content/readings 7, 71
  intertextual referencing 41, 94–5
  merchandising 90–1
  storylines 48–9
  treatment of sexuality 135, 136, 140*n25*
  *see also* 'Anglo-American Girl'
*Bunty* (comic) 45
Burawoy, Michael 120
Burnett, Frances Hodgson 42, 44–5
  *A Little Princess* 45, 51*n13*
Butler, Judith 169

*Cagney and Lacey* 142
Caldwell, John 62–3, 95
Capra, Frank 182
Carrey, Jim 113, 115, 117
Carson, Johnny 114
Carter, Angela 48
Carter, Chris 54
Carter, Thomas 177
*Celebrity Deathmatch* 113
character transformations 28*n16*
The Chemical Brothers 105
Chickenpox 103
Children's Television Standards (Australia) 29
Chomsky, Noam 120
Christianity, and (soundtrack) music 105–6, 107
cinema, relationship with (teen) TV 6, 7–8, **87–96**, 97*n12*, 177
  *see also* intertextuality
Clark, Bob 177
Clark, Dick 114
class
  of protagonists/presenters 77–8, 81–2
  in UK/US society 78–9, 81–2
Clause 28 139*n21*
Clift, Montgomery 23
Cloud, Dana 118

Coco, Salvatore 153
Cogan, Frances B. 42
Cohn, Nick 80–1
Cole, Paula 106–7, 109
Collins, Jim 93
Colvin, Shawn 104
consumerism, role in teen culture 3–4, 8–9, 10
Conway, J. 118
*The Cool and the Crazy* (1958) 177
Coolidge, Susan, *What Katy Did* 42, 44–5
Coontz, Stephanie 182
Coppola, Francis Ford 180
Corrigan, Timothy 97*n12*
The Corrs 106
Crofts, Stephen 155
Crosdale, Darren 56
crossover, definitions/examples 90, 91–3, 96*n3*, 97*n8*, 98*n22*
*Crossroads* 139*n15*
*Cruel Intentions* (1999) 177
'cult' TV, characteristics/examples 54–5, 62–5, 65–6*n3*
Cumble, Roger 177

D'Acci, Julie 142
Dale, David 163*n26*
*Dallas* 20
Daly, Carson 114, 122
  dress sense 115, 120–1
  presentation style 115–17, 118–19
Danes, Claire 137*n2*
Daniel, Brittany 178
*A Date with Judy* 74, 75–6, 77
Davis, Fred 179
Davis, Glyn 10–11
Davis, John 81
*Dawson's Creek* 5, **54–65**, 91, 156, 158, **176–87**
  authorship 54–5, 59, 60–2
  characterisation 21, 26, 182–3, 184–5, 186–7
  cinematography 183

*Dawson's Creek Cont.*
  critical literature 58, 63
  'cult' status 54–5, 62–5, 65*n2*
  dialogue 1, 111*n12*, 178, 181, 184–5, 186
  flashbacks 180–2
  intertextual referencing 87, 90, 92–3, 94, 177–9, 183–5, 187*n5*, 188*n27*
  'quality' status 8, 11, 13*n14*, 54, 64, 65
  scheduling 59–60
  setting 180, 182, 188*n21*, 189*n38*
  soundtrack 100, 101, **102–7**, 109, 110, 111*n10*, 111*n12*
  target audience 59–61, 107
  treatment of relationships 56–7, 65
  treatment of sexuality 111*n15*, 130, 133–4, 138*n6*, 140*n30*, 182
  web sites/discussions 62–4, 66*n13*, 102, 111*n10*
De Palma, Brian 166
Dean, James 21, 23, 27*n9*, 182
Dean, Jodi 166
Dee, Sandra 75
Deetz, Stanley 120
*Degrassi (Junior) High* 152
DeLillo, Don, *End Zone* 170
Derrida, Jacques 173, 175*n29*
Desser, David 39–40*n13*
Dickinson, Kay 9
Dido (singer) 19, 104
Dimitriades, Alex 152, 153, 159
Dingo, Ernie 153
Doherty, Shannon 83
Doherty, Thomas 73, 89, 177
Dolan, Deirdre 176
*The Donna Reed Show* 74
Donohoe, Amanda 129
*Don't Forget Your Toothbrush* 3
Doty, Alexander 89
*Double Indemnity* (1944) 180
Douglas, Jo 79

# INDEX

Douglas, Kate 5, 6, 11
*Dracula* (1931/sequels/remakes) 94–5
Dreyfuss, Richard 76–7
Driscoll, Catherine 42, 43, 49–50, 51*n*4
*Drive Me Crazy* (1999) 87, 90
Duke, Patty 74–5, 96*n*3
Dunne, Michael 178
Dylan, Bob 109
Dymhouse, Carol 42
*Dynasty* 20

Early, Frances 41
*East of Eden* (1955) 19
Eco, Umberto 94
*The Ed Sullivan Show* 100, 105
Eden's Crush 87–8
education(al settings) **151–61, 166–73**
Edwards, Gavin 114
Eels 104
*Ellen* 129, 137
The Elms 105
Eminem 118
*Emmerdale* 139*n*15
*Escape from Jupiter* 29, **33–5,** 37, 38
*E.T. the Extra-Terrestrial* (Spielberg, 1982) 30, 181
evan and jaron 104

Fabian, Lisa 104
*The Facts of Life* 82
*Fair Exchange* 74
Faith, Adam 79
family life
  screen depictions 25–6, 74, 182–3
  and viewing culture 10
fan sites/activities 62–3
*see also under programme titles*
*Fast Times at Ridgemont High* (1982) 177
*Father Knows Best* 74
*Felicity* 92

treatment of race/relationships **141–9**
feminism 5, 7, 71
Fernback, Jan 122
*Ferris Bueller's Day Off* (1986) 177, 182
Field, Sally 71
film *see* cinema
Fitzgerald, Ella 105
Five for Fighting 104
Foley, Scott 87
folk, use on soundtracks 106–7
Fordyce, Keith 80
Foster, David 88
Foucault, Michel 120
*Freaks and Geeks* 177
Freud, Sigmund 173, 186
Friedan, Betty 82
*The Feminine Mystique* 75
*Friends* 129
Frith, Simon 99
Fudge, Rachel 41
The Fugees 105
Funicello, Annette 91, 96*n*3
Fuqua, Joy V. 137*n*3

Gallen, Joel 177
Gannon, Ben 162*n*11
Gauntlett, D. 2
gay themes, treatments of 10–11, **127–37,** 138–9*nn*13–15, 156, 163*nn*23–6
  appeal to gay viewers 28*n*13, 136–7
  characterisation 134–6
  'coming-out' scenes 128–9, 131–2, 137, 138–9*n*13
  critical approaches 129–31, 134
  timeslots 163*n*26
Geffen, David 108
Gellar, Sarah Michelle 52*n*18, 91
gender
  of protagonists 19–20, 26–7, **72–83**
  of target audience/consumers 79, 141, 149

'generation gap'; depictions of 33
genre fluidity/hybridity 20–1, 27*n*5
*see also* intertextuality
Gibson, Mark 152, 156
Giddens, Anthony 54, 55–7
*Gidget* (and cinema sequels, 1959-63) 75
*Gidget* (TV) 71–2, 76–7, 81–2
Gilbert, Eugene 73–4
*The Gilmore Girls* 144
*The Girl from Tomorrow* 29, **30–3,** 34, 35–6, 37–8, 39, 39*n*6
Giroux, Henry A. 8, 131
globalisation, cultural 95–6, 98*n*20, 98*n*22
Good, Jack 79
Goodwin, Andrew 118
Gordon, Deni 153
Gove, Ben 131, 135
*The Graduate* (1967) 183
*Grange Hill* 4–5, 152
Gross, Larry 129–30
Grossberg, Lawrence 107–8
Grundy, Bill 100

Hallam, Julia 130, 131
*Hang Time* 7
Hanson, Ellis 134
*Happy Days* 28*n*16
Hardy, Valerie 159
Hart, Melissa Joan 87, 91
Harvey-Beavis, Adrian 160
Hay, James 6
*Head Start* 156, 160, 165*n*45
*Heartbreak High* **151–61,** 162*n*4
  scheduling 152, 158–9, 162*n*11
  social/ethnic composition 152–3, 156–8, 159
  storylines 153–6, 164*n*40
  treatment of sexuality 155–6
*The Heartbreak Kid* (1993) 152
Heckerling, Amy 177
Hewitt, Jennifer Love 91–2
higher education, characters' moves to 4–5, 158, 159–61

Hill, A. 2
Hills, Matt 7–8, 11, 107, 186
*Hit Parade* 79
Hofer, Johannes 179
Hoffs, Susanna 109
Holland, Patricia 35
Hollinger, Karen 142
*Hollyoaks* 4–5, 139n15
Holmes, Katie 176
Holzman, Winnie 138n12
*Home and Away* 151, 152, 155–6, 159–60
Hornby, Lesley 81
*House of Style* 113
Howard, Sue 159
Hudson, Barbara 58
Hughes, John 94, 177, 178, 182, 184, 188n27
Hutcheon, Linda 179

idiot savant, figure of 30, 31–2
intertextuality (as characteristic of genre) 1, 93–5, 97n6, 177–9, 183–5
Isaak, Chris 106
Iscove, Robert 177

*Jackass* 113
*Jackie* (magazine) 46
Jackson, Janet 117
Jackson, Joshua 87, 91
Jacobs, David 79–80
*James at 15* 21
Jameson, Frederic 39–40n13, 179, 180
*Jaws* (1977) 94–5
The Jayhawks 104
Jenkins, Henry 45, 63
Jewel 104, 110
Johnson, Ryan 156
Joyrich, Lynne 141
Juhlin, Dag 109
*Juke Box Jury* 79–80
Junger, Gil 177
*Junior High School Quiz* 73
*Just Seventeen* (magazine) 46, 71

*Karen* 75
Kasdan, Lawrence 180
Kasem, Casey 114
Kaveney, Roz 4
Kazan, Elia 19
Kearney, Mary Celeste 74, 76
Kennedy, John F. 25
Kennedy, Rosanne 129, 130, 135
Kile, Cristal 182
Kimmel, Jimmy 114
Kinder, Marsha 4, 9
Knowles, Beyonce 105
Kohner, Frederick/Kathy 75
Korn 119
Kuhn, Annette 30, 149

*LA Law* 129
Laplanche, Jean 186, 188–9n32
Laurie, Peter 79
Lavery, David 4
*Leave It to Beaver* 74
Ledger, Heath 163n24
*Letter from an Unknown Woman* (1948) 19
Levin, Jordan 92
Lewis, Jon 131, 157
Light, Alan 121–2
Littrell, Brian 120
London, 'Little' Laurie 79
Lopez, Elizabeth 152, 158
Lucas, George 180
Luckett, Moya 76, 77
Lury, Karen 2, 3, 11, 99, 100, 101, 130–1
Lyotard, Jean-François 168, 174n13, 174n20

Mack, John E. 166
Madonna 117
*Making the Band* 99
*Malibu* 7
Manson, Marilyn 105
Marc, David 184
Marshall, Amanda 109

Marshment, Margaret 130, 131
Masen, Sarah 105
Maziarz, Mary Beth 104
Mazzarella, Sharon 42
McCabe, Janet 59
McCarthy, Anna 129, 130, 135, 137
McCormack, Patty 74
McCullough, Mary 148–9
McGowan, Cathy 80–1
McIntosh, Tammy 163n25
McKee, Alan 152
McKinley, E. Graham 4
McLaren, Spencer 163n25
McLean, A.J. 120
McRobbie, Angela 29, 45–6, 71–2, 81, 82, 84n7
McWilliam, Kelly 5, 6, 11
media conglomeration **87–96,** 96–7n4, 97n6, 98n22
*Meet Corliss Archer* 74, 75, 76, 77
melodrama
  history of genre 18, 19
  impact on modern TV genres 6–7, 19–20, 26–7, 136, 141, 142–9
*Melrose Place* 129, 138n6, 168
merchandising 8, 64–5, 90–1, 166
Metz, Melinda 17
Michal 104
Mines, Stephen 76, 77
*The Miracle Worker* (1962) 74
*Mission to Mars* (2000) 166
Mitchell, Joni 106
Mitchell, Sally 42
Mizejewski, Linda 35
Moby 105
Modlewski, Tania 145
*Moesha* 83, 144
*The Monkees* 87
Montgomery, L.M., *Anne of Green Gables* 42, 44–5
Moore, Abra 109
*More!* (magazine) 71
Moritz, Neal 91

Moseley, Rachel 2, 7, 136
Mr Peepers 74
*Mrs Miniver* (1942) 19
*MTV Unplugged* 113
Mundy, John 99
Murdoch, Rupert 89
Murray, Janet H. 63
Murray, Pete 79
music
  discussion/play programmes 79–81, 85*n*40, **112–22**
  narratives based around 87–8, 108–9, 110–11*n*9
  role in TV drama 1, 9, 18–19, 27*n*3, 47, 52*n*23, **99–110**
  youth tastes in 79, 99
*My So-Called Life* 1, 138*n*12, 177
  axed by network 4, 8, 137*n*2
  critical success 8, 13*n*18, 127
  soundtrack 100, **101–3,** 106–7, **108–10**
  treatment of sexuality 127–9, 132, 135, 137, 138–9*n*13

Nabokov, Vladimir, *Lolita* 46–7, 52*n*22
Nas 105
*Neighbours* 151, 152, 155–6, 159–60, 163*n*21
Nelson, Claudia 44, 49
Neumann, Kurt 177
The Newsboys 105
niche marketing 20, 73, 141–2, 176, 185, 187*n*1
Nicholls, Janice 80, 81
Nine Days 104
1950s, social developments 2, 12*n*3, 77, 177
nostalgia **179–87**
  derivation/definition 179
  evoked among audiences 179–80, 182–3, 185–6, 188*n*30, 189*n*38
  experienced by characters 181–2
*Not Another Teen Movie* (2001) 177

*Now, Voyager* (1942) 19

*Ocean Girl* 29, 38, 40*n*15
*Off the Record* 79
*Official Watcher's Guide* 98*n*18
*Oh Boy!* 79
O'Keefe, Paul 76
Olsen, Richard K. 9
*One Life to Live* 139*n*15
Ophuls, Max 19
*Oranges Are Not the Only Fruit* 130
Orton, Beth 104
Osgerby, Bill 2, 8–9
*Our Miss Brooks* 74

Palladino, Grace 77
*The Pallbearer* (1996) 92
Parker, Ian 58
Parker, Penney 74
*The Parkers* 144
*Party of Five* 140*n*29, 177
  characterization 21–2, 26, 27*n*10, 28*n*16
  treatment of sexuality 132–3, 138–9*nn*13–14
*The Patty Duke Show* 74–5, 76, 77–8, 81–2, 83
*Paul Whiteman's Teen TV Club* 73
Pazanti, Aaron 92
*Peck's Bad Girl* 74, 76, 77
Pecora, N.O. 42
*Peggy Sue Got Married* (1986) 180
Pepper, Cynthia 74
Peranio, Vince 92
*The Perfect Storm* (2000) 94
Perrault, Charles 52*n*26
Perry, Luke 21, 177, 182
*A Place in the Sun* (1951) 19
*Planet Pop* 99, 110*n*6
Pontalis, Jean-Bertrand 186, 188–9*n*32
*Pop Stars* (talent show) 99
*Popstars* (reality serial) 87–8, 90, 151

*Popular* 177
*Porky's* (1981) 177
'posthumanism' 169, 172–3, 174*n*17, 175*n*27
postmodernism 93–5
  *see also* intertextuality
pre-teen viewers 13*n*22
Presley, Elvis 91, 96*n*3, 100
*Press Gang* 165*n*45
*Pretty in Pink* (1986) 177, 182, 184, 188*n*27
Priestley, Jason 83
Pullen, Kirsten 63

'quality' programming 7–8, 13*n*14, 54, 64, 162*nn*3–4
Quant, Mary 81
*Queer as Folk* 130, 139*n*15, 140*n*31
Quirk, Justin 137*n*2

race/racial issues 10–11, **141–9,** 156
  of protagonists 77–8, 83, 152–3
  and (soundtrack) music 105
  in US society 77, 85*n*27
  radio 79, 85*n*38
The Ramones 106, 107
*Rapido* 101
Rapper, Irving 19
*Raw FM* 160, 162*n*3
Ray, Nicholas 21
Reader, Eddi 104
*Ready, Steady, Go!* 80–1
*Real World* 113
*Rebel Without a Cause* (1955) 21
Red Riding Hood, story of 48, 52–3*nn*26–7
Reed, Peyton 177
Reeves, Matt 92
*Regarding Henry* (1991) 92
Reith, Lord 134, 139*n*18
relationships, theory/treatment of 55–7, 141, 155–6, 171–3
  *see also under programme titles*

Reynolds, Debbie 75
Rice, Damian 163*n25*
Rich, B. Ruby 134
Richardson, Kevin 120
*The Rifleman* 21
Ringwald, Molly 184
*Rites of Passage* 140*n31*
*Road Rules* 113
Robinson, Lyn 160
Rockwell, Norman 180, 188*n21*
Roddenberry, Gene 30
*Roseanne* 129
Rosenbaum, Michael 140*n33*
Ross, Diana 104
Ross, Sharon 6, 10–11
*Roswell (High)* 1, 6, **17–27,** 27*n4,*
  28*n17,* 30, 140*n31,* **166–73,**
  174*n22,* 177
 characterisation 22–7, 27*n11,*
  28*n16,* 42, 169
 generic qualities 17–18, 19–20
 pseudo-scientific background
  17, 167
 treatment of relationships
  171–3, 174–5*nn23–5*
Rubin, A. 118
Rutherford, Leonie 7

*Sabrina the Teenage Witch* 13*n14,*
  87, 88, 90, 91, 93
Sasaki, Kazuo 33
*Save the Last Dance* (2001) 177
*Saved by the Bell* 4–5, 140*n31*
Saxton, Ruth 44
Say-So 105
Scanlon, Toni 163*n25*
Schatz, Thomas 89–90
Schiff, Jonathan 29, 40*n15*
Schneider, John 26
Schneider, Steven Jay 60, 61
'School Disco' 185
Schwarzenegger, Arnold 35
science fiction 7, 19–20, **29–39**
 sub-genres 40*n15*
 *see also* aliens
Scott, Ridley 33, 37

*Scream 1/2/3* (1996-2000) 61–2,
  87, 90, 92–3, 94, 183
*Search for a Supermodel* 151
self-referencing *see* intertextuality
*Seventeen* (magazine) 73, 77
The Sex Pistols 100
sex(uality), treatments of *see* gay
 themes; relationships *and*
 *under programme titles*
Shakira 121
Shapiro, Helen 81
Shary, Timothy 20
*She's All That* (1999) 177
*Shindig!* 75
Shrimpton, Jean 81
Simpson, Jessica 104, 105
*The Simpsons* 63
Sirulnick, Dave 116–17
*Sister, Sister* 83
situation comedy 7, 74, 81–2,
  144
*Six Feet Under* 130
*Six-Five Special* 79
Sixpence None the Richer 105
*Sixteen Candles* (1984) 177, 182,
  188*n27*
*Smallville* 1, 6, **17–27,**
  28*nn18–20,* 43, 136, 140*n33*
 characterisation 22–7, 27*n11,*
  28*n15,* 42
 generic qualities 17–18, 19–20
Smith, Jeff 89
Smith, Kerr 134, 135, 138*n6*
*Snub TV* 3
soap opera 20–1, 139*n15,* 155–6,
  159–60
social conditions, impact on
 viewing/programming 72
social issues, TV treatment of 3,
  10–11, 22, 153–4
'socius,' concept of 186–7,
  189*n41*
*Some Kind of Wonderful* (1987)
  177, 182
Spears, Britney 87, 90, 93, 121
*Speed* (1994) 92

Spielberg, Steven 30, 103, 108,
  181
sport, role in US education/
 culture 169–70, 174*n19*
Springsteen, Bruce 106
Stafford, Freya 156
Staiger, Janet 35, 36, 39–40*n13*
*Star Trek: First Contact* (1996) 94
*Star Trek* (TV) 30
*Star Wars* (1977) 65–6*n3*
Steele, Tommy 79
Stenz, Jack 185
Stevens, George 19
Stigers, Curtis 106
Stranks, Susan 80
Stupin, Paul 61
Sullivan, Ed 100, 105
*Sweat* 160, 163*n24*
Sweeney, Gael 23
*Sweet Valley High* 178
Switchfoot 105

Tait 105
*Taken* 166
talent shows 73–4, 113
*Tales of the City* 130
*Tammy and the Bachelor* (and
 cinema sequels, 1957-63) 75
*Tammy* (TV) 75, 78
target audiences *see* gender; niche
 marketing; 'teenagers'
Tasker, Yvonne 145
*Teen Canteen* 73
*Teen Club Party* 73
'teen idol,' figure of 21, 23
*Teen Time Tunes* 73
'teen TV,' generic characteristics
  1, 5–8, 20, 50, 93, 177–8
*Teen Twirl* 73
*Teenage Book Club* 73
'teenager(s)'
 adult attitudes/stereotyping 5,
  169–70, 177, 187*n5*
 conformism 3, 182–3
 as cultural phenomenon 2–4,
  8–9, 11, 72, 78–9, 177

'teenager(s)' *Cont.*
  population/earnings 72, 78, 83
  as target audience 5, 20, 73, 83, 152, 176–7, 187*n1*
  viewing habits 2, 4, 10
television, social role of 10, 13*n12*
Temple, Shirley 45
The Temptations 105
*Ten Things I Hate About You* (1999) 177
Terrell, Brad 187*n1*
*Thank Your Lucky Stars* 80
Thatcher, Margaret 139*n21*
Thurber, James 52–3*n7*
Timberlake, Justin 117
*Tinsel Town* 139*n15*
*Titanic* (1997) 65–6*n3*
*Today's Teens* 73
'Toddlers' truce' 79
Tomlinson, John 96
*Tomorrow's End* 29, 33, **35–7**
*Too Young to Go Steady* 74, 77
*Top of the Pops* 99, 110*n6*
*Total Request Live* **112–22**
  presentation style 115–19
  'shout-outs' 118, 119–20, 121
*Toy Story* (1995) 92
*Tracey* (comic) 45
Train 104
Tredinnick, David 163*n25*
Tushingham, Rita 81
*TV Music Shop* 79
Twiggy 81

Uhlman, Chris 156
unconscious, workings of 186, 189*n39*
United Kingdom
  reception of US culture 189*n38*
  social conditions/developments 78–9
university *see* higher education
Unks, Gerald 134
*The Usual Suspects* (1995) 94

Valli, Frankie 96*n3*
Vallone, Lynne 44, 45, 49
Van Damme, Jean-Claude 35
Van Der Beek, James 176, 184
Vinton, Bobby 75
Violent Femmes 101

Waldman, Diane 134
Walkerdine, Valerie 45–6
Walley, Deborah 75
Walters, David 163*n25*
*The Waltons* 21
*Water Rats* 163*n25*
Waters, John 92
Watson, Debbie 75
The Weathergirls 105
Wee, Valerie 7, 8–9, 61
Weezer 104
Welling, Tom 23–4, 28*n13*, 136, 140*n33*
Whatling, Clare 134
Wheatus 104
Whedon, Joss 42, 45, 54, 92

White, Mike 62
*The White Shadow* 21
Wilcox, Herbert 177
Wilcox, Rhonda 4, 50
Wilder, Billy 180
*Will and Grace* 140*n29*
Williams, Raymond 168
Williams, Sue 152, 159
Williamson, Kevin 54–5, 59, 60–2, 87, 90, 92, 138*n6*, 178, 183, 185
Winter, Lynette 76
Winterson, Jeanette 130
Witney, William 177
Wolcott, James 136
Wolfe, Cary 173
Wolfe, Tom 166–7
'women's picture,' genre of 14, 15, 136
*The Word* 3, 101
Wyatt, Justin 91
Wyler, William 19

*The X-Files* 63, 65, 94–5

Yorn, Peter 104
Younane, Doris 153
*Young Americans* 92

Zero, Remy 19
Zipes, Jack 48